Lateness and Modernism

In the aftermath of World War I, a sense of impasse and thwarted promise shaped the political and cultural spheres in Britain. Writers such as D. H. Lawrence, Hilda Doolittle, T. S. Eliot and Wyndham Lewis were among the literary figures who responded by pursuing vividness, autonomy and impersonality in their work. Yet the extent to which these practices were reflected in ideas about music from within the same milieu has remained unrecognized. Uncovering the work of composer-critics who worked alongside these figures – including Philip Heseltine (Peter Warlock), Cecil Gray and Kaikhosru Sorabji – Sarah Collins traces the shared tendencies of literary and musical modernisms in interwar Britain. Collins explores the political investments underpinning these tendencies, as well as the influence of English Nietzscheanism and related intellectual currents, arguing that a particular conception of the self, history and the public characterized an ethos of 'lateness' within this milieu.

SARAH COLLINS is a senior lecturer in musicology at the University of Western Australia. She is the author of *The Aesthetic Life of Cyril Scott* (2013) and editor of *Music and Victorian Liberalism* (Cambridge, 2019). Her work has appeared in journals including the *Journal of the Royal Musical Association, Twentieth-Century Music, Music & Letters* and the *Musical Quarterly.*

MUSIC SINCE 1900

General editor Arnold Whittall

This series – formerly *Music in the Twentieth Century* – offers a wide perspective on music and musical life since the end of the nineteenth century. Books included range from historical and biographical studies concentrating particularly on the context and circumstances in which composers were writing, to analytical and critical studies concerned with the nature of musical language and questions of compositional process. The importance given to context will also be reflected in studies dealing with, for example, the patronage, publishing and promotion of new music, and in accounts of the musical life of particular countries.

Titles in the series

Jonathan Cross *The Stravinsky Legacy*

Michael Nyman *Experimental Music: Cage and Beyond*

Jennifer Doctor *The BBC and Ultra-Modern Music, 1922–1936*

Robert Adlington *The Music of Harrison Birtwistle*

Keith Potter *Four Musical Minimalists: La Monte Young, Terry Riley, Steve Reich, Philip Glass*

Carlo Caballero *Fauré and French Musical Aesthetics*

Peter Burt *The Music of Toru Takemitsu*

David Clarke *The Music and Thought of Michael Tippett: Modern Times and Metaphysics*

M. J. Grant *Serial Music, Serial Aesthetics: Compositional Theory in Post-War Europe*

Philip Rupprecht *Britten's Musical Language*

Mark Carroll *Music and Ideology in Cold War Europe*

Adrian Thomas *Polish Music Since Szymanowski*

J. P. E. Harper-Scott *Edward Elgar, Modernist*

Yayoi Uno Everett *The Music of Louis Andriessen*

Ethan Haimo *Schoenberg's Transformation of Musical Language*

Rachel Beckles Willson *Ligeti, Kurtág, and Hungarian Music during the Cold War*

Michael Cherlin *Schoenberg's Musical Imagination*

Joseph N. Straus *Twelve-Tone Music in America*

David Metzer *Musical Modernism at the Turn of the Twenty-First Century*

Edward Campbell *Boulez, Music and Philosophy*

Jonathan Goldman *The Musical Language of Pierre Boulez: Writings and Compositions*

Pieter C. van den Toorn and John McGinness *Stravinsky and the Russian Period: Sound and Legacy of a Musical Idiom*

(continued after index)

Lateness and Modernism

Untimely Ideas about Music, Literature and Politics in Interwar Britain

SARAH COLLINS

University of Western Australia

CAMBRIDGE
UNIVERSITY PRESS

University Printing House, Cambridge CB2 8BS, United Kingdom

One Liberty Plaza, 20th Floor, New York, NY 10006, USA

477 Williamstown Road, Port Melbourne, VIC 3207, Australia

314-321, 3rd Floor, Plot 3, Splendor Forum, Jasola District Centre, New Delhi - 110025, India

103 Penang Road, #05-06/07, Visioncrest Commercial, Singapore 238467

Cambridge University Press is part of the University of Cambridge.

It furthers the University's mission by disseminating knowledge in the pursuit of
education, learning and research at the highest international levels of excellence.

www.cambridge.org
Information on this title: www.cambridge.org/9781108722667
DOI: 10.1017/9781108673747

© Sarah Collins 2019

First published 2019
First paperback edition 2022

A catalogue record for this publication is available from the British Library

Library of Congress Cataloging in Publication data
Names: Collins, Sarah, 1984– author.
Title: Lateness and modernism : untimely ideas about music, literature and
politics in interwar Britain / Sarah Collins.
Description: New York : Cambridge University Press, 2019. |
Series: Music since 1900 | Includes bibliographical references and index.
Identifiers: LCCN 2019019443 | ISBN 9781108481496 (hardback) |
ISBN 9781108722667 (pbk.)
Subjects: LCSH: Modernism (Music)–Great Britain. |
Music–Great Britain–20th century–History and criticism. |
Modernism (Literature)–Great Britain. |
English literature–20th century–History and criticism.
Classification: LCC ML285.5 .C6 2019 | DDC 941.083–dc23
LC record available at https://lccn.loc.gov/2019019443

ISBN 978-1-108-48149-6 Hardback
ISBN 978-1-108-72266-7 Paperback

We are not only the 'last men of an epoch' [...] we are more than that, or we are that in a different way to what is most often asserted. *We are the first men of a Future that has not materialized.* We belong to a 'great age' that has not 'come off'. [...] all that is 'advanced' moves backwards, now, towards that impossible goal, of the pre-war dawn.[1]

[1] Wyndham Lewis, *Blasting and Bombardiering* (1937; London: John Calder, 1982), 256. Original emphasis. Thank you to the Wyndham Lewis Memorial Trust for permission to use this quotation as an epigraph.

Contents

Illustrations

Simon McVeigh, Eric Saylor, J. P. E. Harper-Scott, Michael Spitzer, David Larkin, Rachel Campbell and Laura Tunbridge, all of whom unwittingly had a hand in shaping the project through various informal means over the past few years. I had the opportunity of being a visiting fellow at Harvard University in 2017, and my work there on this project received particular encouragement and input from Carolyn Abbate, Anne and John Shreffler and Suzannah Clark. Significant thanks are also due to Daniel Grimley, Roger Parker and Arnold Whittall, for their sustained intellectual generosity, critique and encouragement throughout the development of this project. Thank you also to Laura Macy, who cast her keen editorial eye over the final manuscript.

The research for this book would not have been possible without the unfailing assistance of staff at the British Library; the King's College Archive Centre, Cambridge University; the Grainger Museum, University of Melbourne; the Houghton Library, Harvard University; and the Beineke Rare Book & Manuscript Library, Yale University; as well as the document delivery skills of the librarians at the University of New South Wales and Durham University. I am also grateful to those who contributed to the creation of The Modernist Journals Project (supported by Brown University and the University of Tulsa), which enables open access to digitized periodicals that were crucial forums for the discussion of the aesthetics and politics of cultural modernism in Britain in the early twentieth century. This has been an invaluable repository. In addition to the fellowships mentioned above, this book has been supported by a publication subvention from the Manfred Bukofzer Endowment, awarded by the American Musicological Society.

Finally, to family both far and near who have supported the project in innumerable ways – the Collinses, Gillespies, Everitts and Maynes – I am forever indebted. And to Trent, Lucia and Charlie in particular, who have tolerated with such grace being relocated around the world for all these various adventures over the past few years, your companionship means everything to me.

Acknowledgements

Just as the writers and composers described in what follows partook of a particular milieu, this book bears the mark of certain people, places and ideas. The early stages of the project were nurtured by discussions among an interdisciplinary group of North American, British, French and Australian scholars associated with the Centre for Modernism Studies in Australia at the University of New South Wales, and its stimulating reading sessions on the works of Friedrich Nietzsche and Walter Benjamin. In this sense the book takes part in the ongoing institutional response to the legacy of cultural modernism. In particular, it issues from a sense of frustration that the field of literary studies known as 'modernist studies' on the one hand, and the vibrant debates about musical modernism within musicology on the other, rarely interact. Special thanks are due to Sean Pryor, who read and provided insightful comments particularly on Chapter 3, and also to Helen Groth, Julian Murphet, Chris Danta, Mark Steven, Michael Hooper and John Attridge for many fruitful discussions about all things modernism, and for their outstanding collegiality.

The project extended beyond my research fellowship in Sydney to a fellowship appointment at Durham University, which was co-funded by the European Commission under the Marie Skłodowska Curie scheme. In Durham, I had the benefit and pleasure of input on this project from my colleagues Katherine Hambridge, Julian Horton and Jeremy Dibble. During this period I also benefitted from the useful feedback of audiences at several presentations I had the opportunity to give at the University of Glasgow and the University of Birmingham – with special thanks due to Björn Heile, Matthew Riley and Benjamin Earle in these contexts – as well as at the following conferences: 'Modernist Musics and Political Aesthetics' (University of Nottingham, 2015), 'The State We're In: Directions in Researching Post-1900 British Music' (University of Surrey, 2015), 'Music and the Middlebrow' (University of Notre Dame, London, 2017), and the annual meetings of the British Association for Modernist Studies and the Royal Musical Association, respectively. At these events and others, special thanks are due to Peter Franklin, Kate Guthrie, Christopher Chowrimootoo, Christopher Mark, Christopher Norris, Jennifer Doctor,

Figure 1.1 William Orpen, 'The Café Royal, London 1912', courtesy of Bridgeman Images.

1 | The Afterlife of a 'Beaten Ghost'

> Now that the famous haunt has been overshadowed by the added eating accommodation, the uneasy ghost of pre-war days that ventures within its doors must turn away, affrighted, before an endless vista of glittering napery, and resort in despair to the doubtful consolations of club or pub, or merely retreat to bed – a beaten ghost.[1]

In this remark, the Welsh painter Augustus John cast the changing format and clientele of London's Café Royal in terms of a broader sense of receding hope and cultural failure. John recalled nostalgically the 'Byzantine splendour' of the bar and the 'fly-blown rococo of the famous saloon', and noted how it was one of the few continental-style public houses in England. He sketched the disparate groups who gathered within – the sporting fraternity, 'loud raucous-voiced men seeking to intimidate each other into bets'; a 'colony of our future allies *d'outre-manche*'; a group of 'unusually bulky and grave persons, collected from the vicinity of the British Museum' who 'conversed in voices pitched like the speaking of bats so high as to be inaudible except to the trained ear' and whose female members '*portaient barbe*'; a '*schemozzle* of Cubist painters'; the 'leader of the Avorticist [sic] movement', who kept a 'vigilant eye on the balance of power as indicated by the number and consuming capacity of the different parties'; a 'well-dressed gang of blackmailers, pimps, con-men, *agents provocateurs* and bullies'; a 'cluster of intoxicated social reformers'; a 'body of exquisite Old Boys of the nineties, recognizable by their bright chestnut wigs and raddled faces' who 'exchanged unctuous *facetiae* in the sub-dialect of the period'; and finally 'within easy reach of the exit a mixed company of poets, prostitutes and portrait painters drank shoulder to shoulder', together with a 'sprinkling of the less reputable nobility'.[2]

John's image of the Café emphasizes the heterogeneity of the cultural milieu that the famed late-Victorian institution supported during the

---

[1] Augustus John, foreword to *Peter Warlock: A Memoir of Philip Heseltine*, by Cecil Gray (London: Jonathan Cape, 1934; second impression, 1935), 11.
[2] John, foreword to *Peter Warlock*, 11–12.

years before World War I – he evokes representatives of the old and new, near and far, and the high and low all occupying the same space within its walls. French and French-inspired artists are prominent in his description, as are a number of canonical modernist literary figures associated with Vorticism and Bloomsbury. Wyndham Lewis – who, together with Ezra Pound, established the vorticist agenda through the short-lived but influential journal *BLAST* – is present in this picture, and among the Bloomsbury writers, John perhaps alludes to Virginia Woolf, with a reference to her appearance as a bearded Abyssinian Royal in the 'Dreadnought Hoax' of 1910.

In this account of cultural recession and others like it written between the wars[3] there is a sense in which the avant-garde had been 'beaten' in part by their own success. Their art had come to serve a market desire for newness and novelty, and their commitment to lifestyle experimentation was ideal fodder for gossip columns and fashion magazines.[4] Indeed Daniel Bell's description of the late-twentieth-century avant-garde as 'modernism mummified' might equally be applied to the interwar generation: 'Contemporary bourgeois society, seeing its inflated, decorative, culture collapse under the onslaught of cultural modernism, had in an astonishing *tour de force* taken over cultural modernism and flaunted it as its own culture.'[5] The popularization of forms of cultural modernism was not simply viewed as a symptom of decadence. Characterizations of the conditions of culture in the 1920s and 30s more often emphasized the feeling of coming *after* an ending, yet without the promise of new possibilities. One of the most evocative characterizations appeared in George Orwell's 1935 review of Henry Miller's *Tropic of Cancer* (1934), where he offered a powerful image of 'modern man' as being 'like a bisected wasp which goes on sucking jam and pretends that the loss of its abdomen does not matter.'[6] In the context of the original review Orwell was referring to humankind's anxious sense of purposelessness in the wake of the decline of religion, yet the image also encapsulated a collection of concerns that have

---

[3] In George Orwell's noted essay 'Inside the Whale' (1940), for example, he gives a similar account of the parallel cultural shift experienced in Paris: 'the cosmopolitan mob of artists vanished, and the huge Montparnasse cafes which only ten years ago were filled till the small hours by hordes of shrieking poseurs have turned into darkened tombs in which there are not even any ghosts' (George Orwell, *Inside the Whale and Other Essays* (London: Victor Gollancz, 1940), 132).

[4] For more on the relationship between musical modernism and fashion see Mary E. Davis, *Classic Chic: Music, Fashion and Modernism* (Berkeley: University of California Press, 2006).

[5] Daniel Bell, 'Modernism Mummified' *American Quarterly* 39.1 (1987): 122–32, 124.

[6] George Orwell, 'Some Recent Novels' *New English Weekly* (14 Nov. 1935): 96–7, 96.

since become associated with the aging of modernism.[7] Orwell's bisected wasp pursued a mechanical adherence to its task and displayed all the outward signs of vitality and urgency despite having lost any genuine imperative for its actions. The wasp had a blind need for continuation in the wake of a catastrophic event, linking a cultural sense of 'lateness' to the trauma of the War.[8]

Even as early as 1915, writers such as T. E. Hulme were using similar imagery to decry the middle-class pretensions of 'Liberal socialism' as a 'pathetic spectacle of an apparently exuberantly active being which is all the time an automaton without knowing it'.[9] After the War's end, the Scottish music critic Cecil Gray similarly warned against the spectre of lifeless replication in the cultural sphere, describing 'our moderns' as lacking any genuine vitality, and merely 'drinking the spilt wine from the overturned and broken glasses and licking the plates' of the previous generation of artists.[10]

Still, the disillusionment of Augustus John, Cecil Gray and others in the early decades of the twentieth century was of a particular type – a type specifically shaped by a self-conscious desire to define themselves in relation to the 'institution of the new'.[11] In the musical sphere, a similar disillusionment has been ascribed to composers who pursued forms of experimentation that did not accord with the popularized association between musical modernism and the departure from tonality. For example, James Hepokoski has described how

a mid-career decision was [...] forced upon each composer of the 1855–65 generation to confront in some way the innovations of Schoenberg and Stravinsky, many choosing to decline to endorse – much less to embrace – the musical revolutions,

[7] Orwell's image of the bisected wasp is cited to this end by Tyrus Miller in *Late Modernism: Politics, Fiction, and the Arts Between the Wars* (Berkeley: University of California Press, 1999), 7–8.

[8] Like Miller, Robert Spencer has cast Adorno's conception of lateness as a product of 'shellshock' and 'guilt' – as a 'sense of coming after something of which one is a survivor' (Robert Spencer, 'Lateness and Modernity in Theodor Adorno', in *Late Style and its Discontents: Essays in Art, Literature, and Music*, ed. by Gordon McMullan and Sam Smiles (Oxford and New York: Oxford University Press, 2016), 22–34, 229). Elizabeth Bowen gave a similar description of what she called the 'extinct scene' after World War II, referring to the strange ordinariness of everyday life amidst the large-scale violent events of history in a way that emphasized the disconcerting combination of rupture and continuation (Elizabeth Bowen, *The Demon Lover and Other Stories* (London: Jonathan Cape, 1945), xii, cited in Thomas S. Davis, *The Extinct Scene: Late Modernism and Everyday Life* (New York: Columbia University Press, 2016), 1–2).

[9] T. E. Hulme, 'Translator's Preface to Sorel's *Reflections on Violence*' *The New Age* 17.24 (14 Oct. 1915): 569–70, 569.

[10] Cecil Gray, 'Modern Tendencies Again' *The Sackbut* 1.5 (1920): 214–20, 214.

[11] See Rod Rosenquist, *Modernism, the Market, and the Institution of the New* (Cambridge: Cambridge University Press, 2009).

even though each [...] perceived them as watershed events that brought the competitive phase of [their] own modernist projects to an end.[12]

As Hepokoski points out, this withdrawal from modernist competition was not a conservative regression, nor a backward turning – a concession to the progressive authority of the next generation of composers – nor was it akin to neoclassical tendencies of the interwar period. Rather, Hepokoski suggests that this type of response might be viewed in terms of the adoption of a particular attitude, or what he terms a 'compositional persona'. With this in mind he adjures us to 'listen to the post-1910 Sibelius, Strauss, Elgar, and so on, by realizing that these composers are deeply aware of using a language that does not bring to its acoustic surface the "state of the musical material"', and to understand how their decision in this respect placed them at odds with what the 'liberal-bourgeois institution of concert music' consecrated as legitimate musical progress and innovation.[13] Tomi Mäkelä has made a similar point, noting that Sibelius was well aware of Schoenberg's musical experimentation ('very few knew that [Sibelius] was buying and reading Schoenberg's scores')[14] and also well aware that this form of experimentation was quickly being construed as the 'voice of the future', such that his classicizing tendencies after his Fourth Symphony represent a conscious statement about the possibility of alternative forms of modern experimentation informed by a different conception of history and time.

It is my contention that there is a link between the sense of disillusionment described by Augustus John among his artistic associates at the Café Royal and that observed by Hepokoski in the mid-career compositional personae of Sibelius, Strauss and Elgar, in that both were the result of an underlying concern about the codification of modernism – the idea that modernism had hardened into one particular form of stylistic experimentation. I will also contend that this underlying concern provoked a reasonably coherent cultural response, with identifiable characteristics. For figures such as Augustus John, Wyndham Lewis and their disparate associates

---

[12] James Hepokoski, *Sibelius: Symphony No. 5* (Cambridge: Cambridge University Press, 1993), 8.

[13] Hepokoski, *Sibelius*, 8. This generational disposition has also been ascribed to Ravel (see Barbara L. Kelly, 'Ravel's Timeliness and his Many Late Styles', in *Late Style and its Discontents: Essays in Art, Literature, and Music*, ed. by Gordon McMullan and Sam Smiles (Oxford and New York: Oxford University Press, 2016), 158–73, drawing from Emile Vuillermoz, *Musiques d'aujourd'hui* (Paris: Crès, 1923), 93–4). See also Kelly's *Music and Ultra-Modernism* (Woodbridge: Boydell & Brewer, 2013).

[14] Tomi Mäkelä, 'The Wings of a Butterfly: Sibelius and the Problems of Musical Modernity in 1957', in *Jean Sibelius and His World*, ed. by Daniel M. Grimley (Princeton and Oxford: Princeton University Press, 2011), 89–124, 93.

and sympathizers who have recently been collected together under the rubric of 'late modernism', the rejection of 'high' or pre-war modernism was expressed through the embrace of a type of classicism embodied in the writings of T. E. Hulme, and a pragmatic assertion of autonomy and impersonality in literature and art criticism. Likewise, Sibelius and his second-generation Anglophone sympathizers such as Cecil Gray were openly sceptical of the mainstream modernist composers, and they shaped their own brand of 'modern classicism' in response, advocating approaches to music composition and criticism that resisted processes of generalization and abstraction.

Lateness and Modernism

To describe this type of generational disposition as either 'lateness' or 'late modernism' presents a range of possibilities and difficulties. Quite apart from the ambiguities involved in using the term 'modernism', let alone claiming that there was such a moment as its 'late stage' or 'end-time', the term 'late modernism' comes with further complications in that it has been used to refer to different periods in the history of music, literature, architecture and fine art, respectively. For example, 'late modernism' in literature has typically referred to the post-World War I period, from the late-1920s up until the 1940s, including the work of writers such as Wyndham Lewis, Djuna Barnes, Samuel Beckett, Virginia Woolf, George Orwell and Christopher Isherwood.[15] With respect to the work of these literary figures, 'late modernism' has referred to a self-conscious response to the aging of modernism, both institutionally and ideologically – a response which involved a disillusionment with the failure or hardening of modernism's

---

[15] See for example Jed Esty, *A Shrinking Island: Modernism and National Culture in England* (Princeton: Princeton University Press, 2004); Miller, *Late Modernism*; and Alan Wilde, *Horizons of Assent: Modernism, Postmodernism, and the Ironic Imagination* (Baltimore: Johns Hopkins University Press, 1981). By contrast, Fredric Jameson, Raymond Williams, Brian McHale and, in architecture, Charles Jencks all saw late modernism as running parallel with postmodernism in the later part of the twentieth century (Fredric Jameson, *A Singular Modernity: Essay on the Ontology of the Present* (London: Verso, 2002); Raymond Williams, 'When Was Modernism?' *New Left Review* 175 (1989): 48–52; Brian McHale, *Postmodernist Fiction* (New York: Metheun, 1987); and Charles Jencks, 'Postmodern and Late Modern: The Essential Definitions' *Chicago Review* 35.4 (1987): 31–58). These accounts differ both in periodization and also in the extent to which they seek to revive or critique the works they describe. Nevertheless, they often share a view of late modernist work as involving a response to codification, either in terms of the popularity of high modernist art works after World War I, or in terms of the institutionalization of modernism after World War II.

revolutionary mandate, *combined with* a bleak sense of faith in the possibilities of its continuation. Crucially for us, it indicated a combination of pessimism and faith.

By contrast, in music, 'late modernism' usually refers to the post-World War II period, perhaps intensifying in the 1970s and 80s, applying to composers such as Milton Babbitt, Stockhausen, Boulez, Nono, Berio, Ferneyhough and Ligeti, and more broadly to spectralism and new complexity.[16] In this context the term refers loosely to a continuation or revitalization of some aspects of modernism in a modified, late-century form, though perhaps without the same sense of disillusionment with the effects of modernism's institutionalization that is commonly ascribed to the mid-century literary version.

A category of lateness that has perhaps received greater purchase within discussions of music is the idea of 'late style'. The idea of a specifically musical expression of 'late style' was articulated most famously of course by Theodor Adorno with respect to Beethoven's late works, but it has since become a more widely applied category in music, with more recent studies claiming that the category found expression in the late works of other composers such as Schubert, Debussy and Brahms, among others.[17] Despite the application of the concept of 'late style' chronologically – or biographically, as it were – to understanding the late works of these composers, it bears mentioning that the concept should not be understood as necessarily related to aging, nor with imminent death. As Daniel Grimley has suggested in relation to Sibelius, 'late style' 'is not concerned with a purely chronological sense of time, but rather [...] with an *attitude* or *tone of voice*: a mode of musical utterance that both *engages with a rich critical legacy* and also *unfolds new creative space*'.[18] Once again this conceptualization renders

---

[16] See for example Arnold Whittall, '1909 and After: High Modernism and "New Music"' *Musical Times* 150 (2009): 5–18; and David Metzer, *Musical Modernism at the Turn of the Twenty-First Century* (Cambridge: Cambridge University Press, 2009), who draws from Claus-Steffen Mahnkopf's notion of a 'second modernism' and Alastair Williams's idea of a 'transformed modernism' around the period of 1980.

[17] On Schubert's late style see Lorraine Byrne Bodley and Julian Horton, eds, *Schubert's Late Music* (Cambridge: Cambridge University Press, 2016); Laura Tunbridge, 'Saving Schubert: The Evasions of Late Style', in *Late Style and its Discontents*, 120–30; and Susan Youens, *Schubert's Late Lieder: Beyond the Song Cycles* (Cambridge: Cambridge University Press, 2002). On Debussy see Marianne Wheeldon, *Debussy's Late Style* (Indianapolis: Indiana University Press, 2009). On Brahms see Margaret Notley, *Lateness and Brahms: Music and Culture in the Twilight of Viennese Liberalism* (New York and Oxford: Oxford University Press, 2007). Also see Laura Tunbridge, *Schumann's Late Style* (Cambridge: Cambridge University Press, 2007).

[18] Daniel M. Grimley, 'Storms, Symphonies, Silence: Sibelius's *Tempest* Music and the Invention of Late Style', in *Jean Sibelius and His World*, 186–226, 187. Emphasis added.

lateness both backward- and forward-looking – both disillusioned and hopeful – an attribute that Edward Said attributed to its 'allusive silence', or music's embodiment of 'that precarious exilic realm' where we 'first truly grasp the difficulty of what cannot be grasped and then go forth to try anyway'.[19] It suggests a heightened self-consciousness about being in a state of transition – an unwillingness to engage with the youthful charge towards disintegration, on the one hand, but also an unwillingness to consolidate or synthesize, on the other. Stylistically, the late modernist work 'turns to the reader a more reserved and diplomatic face than the fractious modernist monster'.[20] This new sobriety was surely prompted by the War and the need to re-evaluate modernism's 'violence-inciting' rhetoric in the face of wartime realities, yet it also represented a polemical phase within modernism itself as artists sought to distinguish their work from popularized (or 'vulgarized') forms of modernist expression.[21]

Crucially though, late style offers a language to *a form of 'going against' without pre-determining the form of that withdrawal*, as the conventional conception of musical modernism seems to do. As Said points out

this lateness is a thing in its own right, not a premonition or obliteration of something else. Lateness is being at the end, fully conscious, full of memory, and also very (even preternaturally) aware of the present.[22]

---

[19] Edward Said, *Humanism and Democratic Criticism* (New York: Columbia University Press, 2004), 144. This 'tension between what is represented and what isn't represented' was thematized by Julian Johnson in his recent discussion of lateness, in terms of Orpheus's tragic backward glance. See Julian Johnson, *Out of Time: Music and the Making of Modernity* (New York and Oxford: Oxford University Press, 2015), 13–46.

[20] Miller, *Late Modernism*, 11.

[21] Michael H. Levenson, *A Genealogy of Modernism: A Study of English Literary Doctrine, 1908–1922* (Cambridge: Cambridge University Press, 1984), 140–54. An exemplary case of this factionalism can be seen in the argument between Pound and Amy Lowell about the application of the term 'imagist'. Pound became concerned that Lowell was attempting to extend Imagism too far, to apply to any form of *vers libre*, and her refusal to adhere to his more narrow application of the term led Pound to withdraw from the group and pursue the project of Vorticism.

[22] It is in this way that Beethoven and Adorno were able to be 'untimely and scandalous, even catastrophic commentator[s] on the present' (Edward Said, 'Thoughts on Late Style' *London Review of Books* 26.15 (2004): 3–7). For more on the concept of lateness see Ben Hutchinson, *Lateness and Modern European Literature* (New York and Oxford: Oxford University Press, 2016); Michael Bell, 'Perceptions of Lateness: Goethe, Nietzsche, Thomas Mann, and D. H. Lawrence', in *Late Style and its Discontents: Essays in Art, Literature, and Music*, ed. by Gordon McMullan and Sam Smiles (Oxford and New York: Oxford University Press, 2016), 131–46; Whittall, '1909 and After'; J. M. Bernstein, *Against Voluptuous Bodies: Late Modernism and the Meaning of Painting* (Stanford: Stanford University Press, 2006); Notley, *Lateness and Brahms*; and Reinhold Brinkmann, *Late Idyll: The Second Symphony of Johannes Brahms*, trans. Peter Palmer (Cambridge, MA: Harvard University Press, 1995). J. M. Bernstein

Late style can in this sense be associated with a range of artistic outcomes, and need not be specific to a particular historical period.[23] On the other hand, 'late style' undoubtedly receives expression in response to particular cultural and historical circumstances, and therefore can be more broadly generalized in the context of a particular milieu. For example, while certain composers faced having to make a conscious decision about whether or not to align themselves with Schoenbergian experimentation, writers of the same generation found themselves having to contend with the 'shadow of *Ulysses* and *The Waste Land*'.[24]

Recognizing this link between late modernism, late style and lateness is crucial to understanding the cultural milieu of interwar Britain. 'Late modernism' does not merely represent a proliferation of terms to describe modernism. Rather, it describes a particular form of relation – to history, subjectivity and the public – which bears the hallmarks of lateness. Lateness can be understood as a response to codification, or projected codification; it is characterized by a sense of passionate impasse, or tempered utopianism; a fear of transience and fashion; of theory and over-intellectualism; and a rejection of prevailing terms of judgement or competition. Understanding lateness as a style of being, or a 'form of relation' in this way, is important for comprehending interwar concerns about impersonality, autonomy and classicism.

Extending upon this sense of lateness as an ethos, disposition and style – features that can find expression in any historical context – I would like to suggest that the attributes of lateness associated with literary 'late modernism' in the interwar period in Britain did have a counterpart in musical discourses, and that these can be seen in the writings of musical figures who were a part of a common and closely-knit milieu. The historical position occupied by the artists I am implicating in this cultural response has become a subject of significant interest in recent scholarship in literary and musical modernism respectively, leading to highly influential theorizations of 'late modernism' in literary studies, and to revaluations of the music of William Walton, Frank Bridge, Vaughan Williams and Sibelius, among

---

described modernism in fine art in terms of a 'perpetual lateness' – a 'waning and remaining' – conceiving lateness as something that was inherent to modernist aesthetics itself (p. 1). Ben Hutchinson made a similar argument with respect to what he claimed was the 'constituent' lateness of modern European literature.

[23]   It is worth noting, for example, that aspects of this form of relation (namely, autonomy) were exhibited as a part of the 'high' modernism aesthetic as well, though not perhaps so readily combined with pragmatism and classicism, as it was in late modernism.

[24]   Miller, *Late Modernism*, 28.

others. In other words, untimely ideas have been rendered prescient, as studies of modernism increasingly turn towards exploring the disparate anxieties of a generation of artists whose mid-career phase was cut short by the War – a war in which many of them did not actively participate. So while lateness is by no means *necessarily* a matter of timing, the particular form of lateness described in this book was shaped by the alignment of historical events with the career trajectories of a certain generation of artists.

Jed Esty has described a 'generational fatigue' evident in interwar literary culture in Britain in a way that echoes Hepokoski's invocation of a 'generational crisis' affecting certain composers. Tracing changes in literary form to the realities of imperial decline in interwar Britain, Esty attributes 'many of the generic and stylistic changes that characterize late modernism' to a sense of fatigue and contraction, 'especially since the canonical group of Anglophone modernists seemed to enter into dogmatic middle age (Eliot, Pound, Lewis) or to expire (Yeats, Joyce, Woolf) with remarkable consistency sometime around 1940'.[25] Even more significantly, Esty suggests a causal explanation for the same combination of pessimism and faith that we saw above in the words of Augustus John and others:

the end of British hegemony was a fait accompli to the Auden-Greene generation and therefore not the occasion for searching attempts to manage the transition between imperial universalism and national particularism. That generation's minor-chord lament stems in part from not having come of age artistically during the days of imperial centrality; they inherited the cultural detritus and political guilt of empire without the corresponding advantages of metropolitan perception.[26]

Unlike the Auden-Greene generation, the late modernists had experienced part of that older world, and they bore the mark of lateness as an expression of that experience. For example, many of the writers and composer-critics discussed in this book outwardly rejected the impressionist criticism of Walter Pater and the cosmopolitan ethos of the Bloomsbury group, yet their derision was nostalgic and idealizing, betraying a continuing sympathy for the cause. Equally, they tended to advocate collective forms of social organization and expression as a way of resisting the type of individualism they associated with late-Victorian and Edwardian thinkers. Yet they were also staunch advocates of individuality and autonomy, and they sought to secure a sense of universal beauty and artistic permanence to counter the sensationalism of the market and the waywardness of popular opinion. They

[25] Esty, *A Shrinking Island*, 4.
[26] Esty, *A Shrinking Island*, 8.

wanted to regain autonomy from market forces by pursuing an individual view of 'tradition' – a process that involved the cultivation of untimeliness.

The preceding generation of the musico-critical lineage described in this book included musical figures born in the 1860s and 70s such as Ralph Vaughan Williams (1872–1958) and Edward J. Dent (1876–1957), as well as Frederick Delius (1862–1934), Jean Sibelius (1865–1957) and Ferruccio Busoni (1866–1924), the latter three of whom became idealized by the British late modernist critics under consideration here.[27] Norman Douglas (1868–1952) and W. B. Yeats (1865–1939) were also figures from this generation who are relevant to our discussion not only intellectually and artistically but also by close personal association (particularly Douglas) with the milieu described. The second generation, born in the 1880s and 90s – who were personally associated with their direct literary contemporaries such as Robert Nichols (1893–1944), T. S. Eliot (1888–1965), Ezra Pound (1885–1972), Wyndham Lewis (1882–1975), D. H. Lawrence (1885–1930), Edith Sitwell (1887–1964), Hilda Doolittle (H. D.) (1886–1961), John Middleton Murry (1889–1957), Katherine Mansfield (1888–1923) and Richard Aldington (1892–1962), and with whose 'lateness' I am concerned here – included Cecil Gray (1895–1951), Bernard van Dieren (1887–1936), Philip Heseltine (also known by his pseudonym Peter Warlock) (1894–1930) and Kaikhosru Sorabji (1892–1988). And the third generation, whose agenda coincided for a time with this stream of thinking in the interwar period, and who were personally acquainted with the group just identified, included Constant Lambert (1905–1951) and William Walton (1902–1983) (who were contemporary to the Auden (1907–1973)/Greene (1904–1991) generation in Esty's formulation).

The artists of these three generations did not represent any kind of intellectual consensus, and indeed were often in direct opposition, yet they did occupy a discernible lineage of critical ideas in the early twentieth century across music and literature, and their intellectual interaction was reinforced by the fact that they were often in close association, partaking of the same milieu, writing for the same journals, drinking at the same London haunts, studying at the same educational institutions, living together and sharing intimacies. I will argue that the three generations of musical figures

---

[27] We might also include as affiliates in this milieu the first generation of British Sibelians: Granville Bantock (1868–1946), Ernest Newman (1868–1959), Henry Wood (1869–1944) and Rosa Newmarch (1857–1940). For more on Sibelius's British supporters see Byron Adams, '"Thor's Hammer": Sibelius and British Music Critics, 1905–1957', in *Jean Sibelius and His World*, 125–57; and Peter Franklin, 'Sibelius in Britain', in *The Cambridge Companion to Sibelius*, ed. by Daniel M. Grimley (Cambridge: Cambridge University Press, 2004), 182–95.

mentioned above were closely embedded in the world of literary late modernism – they were positioned at its very heart, and partook of its intellectual, emotional and libidinal alliances.

Musical and Literary Modernisms

Given the recent interest in the collection of concerns and practices described as 'late modernism', it is curious that the alliances between composer-critics and authors within this milieu have not received more attention. There are several issues at play in this omission. On a disciplinary level, and for all its interdisciplinary potential, 'modernist studies' is still predominantly a sub-discipline of literary studies.[28] In this context, music's significance is predominantly for the role of musical aesthetics in shaping ideas about autonomy in literary and poetic modernism. Equally, when music *is* taken on its own terms in literary studies, the focus tends to favour the canon of musical modernism that Sibelius and his sympathizers positioned themselves against. It is interesting to note, for example, that Michael Levenson's chronology of modernism in the *Cambridge Companion to Modernism* includes works by Puccini, Strauss, Mahler, Schoenberg, Stravinsky and Bartók alongside texts by figures such as Joseph Conrad, Oscar Wilde, Gertrude Stein, E. M. Forster, Marcel Proust and Bertrand Russell from 1904 to 1913, and then no other musical work until Shostakovich's Symphony No. 1 in 1935. The intervening years see the publication of seminal modernist literary texts such as James Joyce's *Dubliners* (1914), *A Portrait of the Artist as a Young Man* (1916) and *Ulysses* (1922), T. S. Eliot's *Prufrock* (1917) and *The Waste Land* (1922) and Virginia Woolf's *To the Lighthouse* (1927) and *A Room of One's Own* (1929) – representing artistic developments that, in this admittedly schematic example, are presented as having no musical counterpart. Further, there has been some interest in the enduring influence of nineteenth-century Austro-German composers and music critics on modernist literary figures such as Ezra Pound, T. S. Eliot, D. H. Lawrence and Wyndham Lewis, yet there have been few studies of the activities of musical thinkers who themselves occupied the same milieu, many of whom rejected

---

[28] The disciplinary particularly of modernist studies is reflected most explicitly in the literary focus of survey texts such as the *Oxford Handbook of Modernisms* and the *Cambridge Companion to Modernism*; of the field's flagship journals such as *Modernism/Modernity* and *Modernist Cultures*; and of the major professional bodies such as the *British Association for Modernist Studies* and the *Modernist Studies Association*.

the Schoenberg–Stravinsky axis of modernism in preference for a scheme occupied primarily by Sibelius, Delius, Busoni and Van Dieren.

In what follows, I will sketch the contours of an intellectual and cultural milieu involving both literary and musical figures that these disciplinary peculiarities have hitherto obscured, and thereby suggest a new model for understanding the ethos of modernism during the interwar period. My argument in this book has two parts, which are developed concurrently. The first is the claim that there was a shared set of concerns and responses among certain literary and musical figures that can be fruitfully described using the rubric of lateness. This is *not* a claim about periodization, in the sense of claiming that a 'late' modernism might be thought of as indicating a chronologically later phase of modernism to counter an 'earlier' phase. Indeed, some of the figures within the milieu described here came to represent the *earliest* expressions of what has been construed as a distinctively British musical modernism, particularly Walton. As we have seen, lateness is not a chronological demarcation, but instead involves a particular type of approach to questions about art's relation to its past, its context and its audience. As an abstract claim that sets out to characterize a collection of intellectual tendencies as part of a common thread of thinking, its reach may be extended across the arts, or indeed across historical periods.

The second claim situates the first by showing that these conceptual similarities were supported by personal relationships between the figures involved, and that they bear the mark of shared spaces, such as the Café Royal, Garsington and Cornwall; shared publication forums, such as *The New Age*, *The Athenaeum* and *The Sackbut*; and shared projects. What is being described is thus the manifestation of the intersection of a particular set of personalities and agendas.

There are two further points to note about the approach adopted in this book. First, it bears mentioning that my approach here contrasts from Esty's and Miller's in the sense that I am not primarily concerned here with reading lateness into aspects of musical or literary style. Rather, the cultural response that I am attempting to map was expressed in the form of a *critical tradition* – that is, in ideas *about* music or ways of evaluating music, rather than as a compositional development. It was a historiographical development, and in this sense it forms a part of the story of our 'discipline', such as it was in the early twentieth century when the differences between serious scholarship, music criticism and the tradition of essayism were less distinct. Thus, I focus on the critical writings of my central musical protagonists – Philip Heseltine, Cecil Gray and Kaikhosru Sorabji, who are selected here for their personal association with literary late modernists – rather than on their compositions. Equally, it is with an expanded conception of *style* – one encompassing attitude, disposition and ethos – that I address the particular generational conditions of related composers such as Sibelius, Delius and Van Dieren. The *style* in question in this case was an attitude or form of relation towards history, subjectivity and the public.[29]

Second, the literary figures involved in this milieu – including Lewis, Pound, Lawrence, Eliot, the Sitwells, Murry, Aldington, Mansfield and H. D. – already occupy acknowledged positions in the pantheon of literary modernism, and in descriptions of late modernism in particular. With this in mind, and given that I am arguing for the recognition of the manifestation of late modernism through certain ideas about music and literature, this book seeks to extrapolate the degree and manner of its expression in writings about music. I therefore examine at some length the work of generally lesser-known writers on music to whom I attribute a central role in this milieu, focusing on the musical thinkers who worked shoulder-to-shoulder with the canonical literary modernists involved. This approach is designed to counteract the disciplinary tendency to relegate music criticism and historiography to the status of supplementary material, and also to highlight the potential of exploring characterizations of musical modernism that are not based on stylistic factors in the narrow sense. It also serves as a means to introduce certain works of music literature into the sphere of modernism studies, and to suggest why they merit further attention from scholars seeking a more multifaceted view of the intellectual tendencies of the time.

With these points in mind, the next chapter offers a contextual sketch that outlines the types of writers, artists, relationships, activities and ideas that constitute the milieu to which I am ascribing a sense of lateness. Taken on its own this sketch may appear rather like a process of 'name-dropping', though it is intended to provide a basic map of co-ordinates, as it were, that can serve as a limiting background to the more substantive discussions that take place in the chapters that follow. It may be significant to note, for example, that this map of co-ordinates does not include such musical contemporaries as Arthur Bliss, Arnold Bax or Frank Bridge, and neither

---

[29] Some of these themes of lateness and 'late modernism' have already begun to be explored in relation to the music of Sibelius (see for example Grimley, 'Storms, Symphonies, Silence') and Walton (see J. P. E. Harper-Scott, '"Our True North": Walton's First Symphony, Sibelianism, and the Nationalization of Modernism in England' *Music & Letters* 89.4 (2008): 562–89); and of the same generation but not the same milieu, Ravel (see Kelly, 'Ravel's Timeliness and his Many Late Styles').

does it include significant mention of iconic writers and critics of British cultural modernism such as Virginia Woolf, Roger Fry and Clive Bell. In other words, this sketch lays the foundation for demonstrating that a sense of lateness received expression within a defined cultural formation, and that it was not simply a catch-all term for the cultural malaise produced by imperial contraction or by World War I. This chapter's final sections 'Untimeliness, Impasse and Lateness', and 'Men of 1914', summarize the characteristics of lateness that were manifest within this milieu.

Each of Chapters 3, 4 and 5 examines a particular constellation of themes that illuminate the forms of relation that are of interest here as markers of 'lateness' – namely a relation to the self (Chapter 3); to the public (Chapter 4); and to history (Chapter 5). These chapters take as their focus a specific association between a musical and literary figure within the milieu of late modernism. Chapter 3 focuses on temporal conceptions of the self, viewed through the lens of the relationship between Philip Heseltine and D. H. Lawrence, with Delius serving as the mediating figure in Heseltine's thinking. I will suggest that Heseltine's valorization of Delius's music as being an apotheosis on the very crest of a decline offers a musical corollary to Lawrence's conception of the ideal artist as a poppy whose seed is only released at its moment of death. This temporalization of subjectivity can also be seen in personal terms in that Lawrence viewed Heseltine as 'unborn' or not yet created – namely, too early – and Heseltine himself suffered intensely from his own internalized sense of untimeliness.

Chapter 4 outlines the 'fear of abstraction' that informed anti-democratic and anti-liberal discourse in interwar Britain, and its implications for music discourse. It uncovers the temporal component of pursuing 'reactionary' views in response to the progressively oriented pre-war cultural and political sphere, and explores how this was manifest across a range of matters of public debate including women's rights, eugenics, public education, social reform and literary realism, in addition to music. The discussion then focuses on Sorabji's interaction with the politics of the literary circle of figures who wrote for *The New Age* – one of the most significant forums for the propagation of 'radical conservatism' in Britain during and immediately after World War I. Sorabji's writings describe a convenient vision of the degradation of public taste and the obscuring of aesthetic beauty being driven by the philistinism of daily musical journalese, yet his self-inscribed leadership in the combat of these symptoms of consumerism betrayed his active commitment to the interests of the public that he denounced, and his polemical stance of autonomy was undercut by his sincere participation in the dialogical make-up of the journal itself. The chapter argues that Sorabji and his fellow members of the 'anti-democratic intelligentsia', who argued against state education and other egalitarian measures aimed at increasing access, were not simply disgruntled about consumer culture and mass opinion (as were the 'high' modernists), but rather with what they saw as the bureaucratization of authority and the ruling power of a reformist elite. It traces these ideas to the work of T. E. Hulme and explores the political and aesthetic influence of Hulme's notion of the 'classical temperament' on this milieu, as an expression of lateness.

The final chapter draws a speculative link between a cyclic conception of music history and a contemporaneous spatialized theory of poetry. It proceeds from the relationship between Cecil Gray and the modernist poet and novelist Hilda Doolittle (H. D.). Gray was perhaps the foremost spokesperson for the musical aspect of the discourse of lateness within the milieu described throughout the book (with Lambert occupying that position in the next generation). Sibelius serves as a mediating figure (or more accurately, a mediating idea) between Gray and his exposure to Imagism. Underlying all chapters is an ongoing concern with the intellectual impact of anti-democratic (and particularly anti-parliamentarian) discourses and English Nietzscheanism during and immediately after the War.

Finally, a note on sources. Exploring the manifestation of the ethos of lateness involves drawing from textual sources that range from the private realm of letters, diaries and sketches to the very differently oriented public-facing genres such as autobiography, memoir, biography, fiction, criticism, essays and lectures. Needless to say, texts can be illuminating for different reasons, and while many of the published texts from the 1920s and 30s that I draw upon must be viewed in light of the entangled interests of the authors and subjects involved, they are approached here as documents that reveal certain shared preoccupations that are of central interest to the topic at hand. These sources exhibit varying degrees of attention to accuracy, or even consistency, and they should not be treated as equally illuminating. Throughout this book they will be presented as forming a part of a broader dialogue of texts, lifestyles and agendas that together contributed to the constellation of ideas that I am aiming to map. It need hardly be emphasized that extrapolating the views of the thinkers involved in this milieu does not imply any claim regarding their legitimacy or truth-content. Rather, my concern here is with revealing a type of sensibility or attitude that may be productively construed as an expression of interwar lateness.

2 | Sketch of a Milieu: Impasse and Lateness

The artists and ideas collected together here under the rubric of 'lateness' can be usefully described as a 'milieu'. This term is used advisedly, to encompass both of the meanings attributed to it in the *OED* – first, in the sense of an 'environment' or 'surrounding'; and second, in the sense of a 'group of people with a shared (cultural) outlook'. The first definition can encompass a set of intellectual tendencies that arose in response to contemporary circumstances and were shaped by a complex web of discursive practices and institutional structures. The second definition gestures towards the possibility of a specific historical grouping – in this case the three-generation critical lineage identified in Chapter 1.

In its ability to carry this dual meaning, 'milieu' shares some features in common with Raymond Williams's notion of a 'cultural formation' that likewise encompasses both a set of discourses or cultural products, on the one hand, and their social location, on the other. The idea of a 'cultural formation' has proved particularly useful for the study of 'little magazines' in the early twentieth century. These were short-lived periodicals that represented fleeting but influential alliances between artists within the field of literary modernism.[1] In the musical field, one such moment of crystallization can be seen in the first issues of *The Sackbut*, edited by Philip Heseltine, with the help of Cecil Gray, from May 1920 to June 1921. During this time, contributors to the journal included composers Béla Bartók, Ferruccio Busoni, Frederick Delius and Kaikhosru Sorabji; writers and poets Arthur Symons and Robert Nichols (and a translation of an article by Hermann Bahr that was first published in the *Neues Wiener Journal*); music historians and critics Adam Carse and Barbara C. Larent; and occultist photographer and Pictorialist Alvin Langdon Coburn, and others. The journal was established with an explicitly radical agenda, which I have outlined elsewhere.[2] It would be incorrect to suggest that these disparate artists constituted a grouping or

---

[1] See the three-volume collection edited by Peter Brooker and Andrew Thacker, *The Oxford Critical and Cultural History of Modernist Magazines* (Oxford and New York: Oxford University Press, 2009). See also David Peters Corbett and Andrew Thacker, 'Raymond Williams and Cultural Formations: Movements and Magazines' *Prose Studies* 16.2 (1993): 84–106.

[2] Sarah Collins, 'A Critical Succession: Aesthetic Democracy and Radical Music Criticism between the Wars' *Music & Letters* 95.3 (2014): 404–28.

'cultural formation' in any formal sense, though their common association with the radical project of the journal during this defined period offers a moment of intersection that can be usefully mapped in order to uncover certain shared habits of mind. The term 'milieu' can feasibly capture both these habits of mind and the informal grouping of artists who exhibited them at a particular moment.

Other figures involved in the milieu of late modernism have been retrospectively grouped in various ways, each designed to reinforce a different argument or position – such as the 'Men of 1914' (Eliot, Pound, Joyce and Lewis);[3] 'The Reactionaries' (Yeats, Lewis, Pound, Eliot and Lawrence);[4] the 'Isolationists' and 'Doomed Generation' (Heseltine, Gray and Sorabji);[5] and the 'Romantic Moderns' (including the Sitwells, Evelyn Waugh, E. M. Forster, Virginia Woolf and John Piper).[6] Of our associated figures at least two were involved in the 'Poets' Club' who met at the Café Tour d'Eiffel in London in 1909–10 (Hulme and Pound); and several identified – at least temporarily – as Post-Georgians (the Sitwells and Huxley), or with the projects of Imagism (Pound, H. D., Aldington) or Vorticism (Pound, Lewis, Aldington, Epstein, Coburn). Many of these temporary affiliations were also reflected in these writers' contemporaneous contributions to periodicals such as *The New Age*, *The Athenaeum* and *BLAST*, as well of course as *The Sackbut*.

It is not my aim in this book to offer an empirical study of the interactions and activities of all of the figures within this milieu. Rather, my primary concern is with extrapolating how a particular sense of lateness shaped some of their ideas about music and literature, and to show how these expressions of lateness were reinforced by specific personal and intellectual exchanges. While the relevant exchanges will be treated in depth in later chapters, it is important here to provide an introductory sketch of the associations that form the background to what will be described.

The Café Royal and Wartime London

To begin we must return for a moment to Augustus John's seething image of the Café Royal, described at the opening of the previous chapter. After

---

[3] Coined by Wyndham Lewis, *Blasting and Bombardiering* (London: Eyre & Spottiswoode, 1937).

[4] Coined by John R. Harrison, *The Reactionaries* (London: Victor Gollancz, 1966). Harrison added the more explicit subtitle 'A Study of the Anti-Democratic Intelligentsia' for the American market when the book was reprinted in 1967 with Schocken in New York.

[5] Coined by Arnold Whittall, 'The Isolationists' *Music Review* 27 (1966): 122–9.

[6] Coined by Alexandra Harris, *Romantic Moderns: English Writers, Artists and the Imagination from Virginia Woolf to John Piper* (London: Thames & Hudson, 2010).

sketching the '*schemozzle*' of pre-war modernists who frequented the establishment, John introduces the composer and critic Philip Heseltine. Heseltine appeared on the scene in the Café 'with a strange derisive smile for ever about his pale handsome features', and 'always accompanied by three or four young females carrying portfolios and scrolls of paper' giving the impression that he was engaged in 'some urgent and evidently important literary work', which John later learned was the editing of *The Sackbut*.[7] John goes on to recount an incident from his friendship with Heseltine, involving folk-singing, debauchery, a 'somewhat defective motor-cycle' and a curious display of Heseltine's 'Baudelairian devotion to cats'. He notes Heseltine's invectives against socialism and over-population, as well as his desire to acquire a penny-farthing bicycle in order to see over hedges as he rode through the countryside.[8]

John's attempt to position Heseltine within the milieu of Bohemian London was undoubtedly well founded. Heseltine did reportedly frequent the Café Royal, and his personal associations and oppositional character seemed well suited to the revolutionary ethos of the pre-war literary avant-garde. Heseltine was introduced to the Café Royal around 1915 or 1916, shortly after settling in London and during the time of his initial acquaintance with D. H. Lawrence, when the young composer was in his early twenties and Lawrence a decade older.[9] At the Café, Heseltine held

---

[7] Augustus John, foreword to *Peter Warlock: A Memoir of Philip Heseltine*, by Cecil Gray (London: Jonathan Cape, 1934; second impression, 1935), 12. John's chronology is slightly askew here, because Heseltine began to frequent the Café Royal in the early years of the War, and yet he edited *The Sackbut* from 1920–21.

[8] John, foreword to *Peter Warlock: A Memoir of Philip Heseltine*, 14–15. For a detailed and well-written account of Heseltine's activities and outlook, see Barry Smith, *Peter Warlock: the Life of Philip Heseltine* (Oxford: Oxford University Press, 1996). Other key texts for tracing the fascinating web of relationships within this milieu from the perspective of the lives of the central musical figures include Stephen Lloyd's biographies of William Walton and Constant Lambert (*William Walton: Muse of Fire* (Woodbridge: Boydell & Brewer, 2001) and *Constant Lambert: Beyond the Rio Grande* (Woodbridge: Boydell & Brewer, 2014), and, although more idiosyncratic, Cecil Gray's autobiography *Musical Chairs: or Between Two Stools* (London: Home & Van Thal, 1948; reprt. London: Hogarth Press, 1985).

[9] Heseltine had moved to London in October 1914, after having quit his course at Oxford and convincing his mother that he would need a lesser allowance to live in London, now that war had been declared. His first place of residence in London was in Cartwright Gardens, Bloomsbury. He described the area excitedly in a letter to Frederick Delius as 'thoroughly alive […] and unrespectable' (qtd. in Smith, *Peter Warlock*, 60–64). Heseltine's initial residence in Bloomsbury and his acquaintance with the social hostess Lady Cunard as early as 1914 may have put him into contact with relevant figures from the Café somewhat earlier than his initial appearance at the establishment (70). Heseltine met D. H. Lawrence at a dinner party in November 1915.

the closest company with the American-born (though naturalized British) sculptor Jacob Epstein, as well as the Dutch composer Bernard van Dieren, and Augustus John himself. Only a few years earlier, Epstein had created the striking stone sculpture atop the tomb of Oscar Wilde (1911–12) and the uncompromisingly modernist work *Rock Drill* (1913). Epstein was also one of the contributors to the vorticist credo in the first issue of *BLAST*, edited by Wyndham Lewis with input from Ezra Pound. In 1915 Cecil Gray joined the group, having just moved to London, and within a year he and Heseltine were living together and working jointly on a range of fantastical projects, including a radical music journal, a concert series presenting old and new works side-by-side, a company to publish pianola roles of contemporary music, an opera season at a West End theatre involving minimal staging and symbolist techniques, and an independent training school of composition (many of which, as Gray fondly remembered, ended 'in the same invariable fiasco').[10] Van Dieren and Gray served as models for the head and hands, respectively, of Epstein's famous anti-war sculpture 'The Risen Christ' (1917–19), depicted on the cover of this book.[11]

The presence of this 'triumvirate of Heseltine, van Dieren and Gray'[12] at the Café Royal was noted in a range of sources, usually via retellings of two instances of physical confrontation. The first was Gray's brawl – in defence of Epstein – with Horace Cole, who was the infamous prankster behind the 'Dreadnought Hoax', and who later suffered the vitriol of Lewis's satire when depicted as the character Horace Zagreus in the *Apes of God* (1930). The second incident was Heseltine's fight with Edwin Evans, who had written disparagingly of Heseltine and Gray's plans to organize a concert of Bartók's music during the War. Evans was at the time the music critic for the *Daily Mail* (a publication to which Heseltine had also contributed, from February to June 1915) and later played a significant role

---

[10] Cecil Gray, *Peter Warlock: A Memoir of Philip Heseltine* (London: Jonathan Cape, 1934), 129.

[11] There is an alternative claim that the hands of the sculpture were in fact modelled on the artist Jacob Kramer. Epstein also made busts of Vaughan Williams, Joseph Holbrooke, Augustus John, Van Dieren and Gray; and Van Dieren wrote a book about Epstein in 1920, published by John Lane, The Bodley Head. Such was the friendship between Heseltine and Van Dieren that Heseltine bequeathed all of his material possessions (being a piano and two suits) to the Dutch composer. According to Heseltine's son Nigel, because Heseltine also stood to inherit some property from his mother, and his mother was concerned about the ongoing welfare of Nigel (for whom she was primary carer), she paid Van Dieren 6,000 GBP to relinquish his rights in Philip's inheritance (Nigel Heseltine, *Capriol for Mother: a Memoir of Philip Heseltine* (London: Thames, 1992), 31).

[12] Guy Deghy and Keith Waterhouse, *Café Royal: Ninety Years of Bohemia* (London: Hutchinson, 1955), 141.

in the establishment of the International Society for Contemporary Music, lending a certain irony to his supposedly xenophobic opposition to the planned concert, by Gray's account.[13] When Evans came to be honoured in 1923 for his services to 'British and other contemporary music', Heseltine and Gray were conspicuously absent from the celebratory dinner – a dinner at which Eugene Goossens presented Evans with his portrait painted by Wyndham Lewis, and at which a number of otherwise like-minded figures were in attendance, including Augustus John, Edward J. Dent, Arthur Bliss, Frank Bridge and others.[14]

By the time Heseltine arrived on the scene in London at the outbreak of the War, he had been corresponding with a young Parsi composer Kaikhosru Sorabji for three years, and Sorabji had become acquainted with several modernist literary figures whom Heseltine also knew. In 1918 Sorabji lived in the same building as T. S. Eliot in Clarence Gate Gardens, in Marylebone, London,[15] and he also visited Lady Ottoline Morrell's house at Garsington, together with Heseltine and D. H. Lawrence.[16] Sorabji was acquainted with the ultra-modern Sitwells, who also played an important role in the lives of the next generation of British Sibelians – including William Walton and Constant Lambert – and who had been acquainted with Edward J. Dent

---

[13] This irony was noted by Gray in his own description of this event in his memoir, *Musical Chairs*, 112–13.

[14] Other guests included Arnold Bax, Lord Berners, Adrian Boult, Alfredo Casella, Edward Clark, Louis Durey, Manuel de Falla, Gustav Holst, Herbert Howells, John Ireland, Cyril Scott, Percy Pitt, Maurice Ravel, Florent Schmitt, Ethel Smyth, Igor Stravinsky, Percy Scholes and Adolf Weismann. This guest list was reported in Evans's obituary notice that appeared in the *Musical Times* 86 (1945): 105–8, 106–7 (thank you to Kate Bowan for drawing my attention to this article). In an additional irony, the event was held at Pagani's – an establishment with which Gray had a special relationship: 'one of the favourite lunchtime gathering places during the war for Cecil and his companions was a couple of small and shabby rooms above a pub in Great Portland Street. When the nearby premises of Pagani's were bombed during the blitz, the proprietors rescued the cellar-full of wines which had escaped being damaged, and opened up a small restaurant above the pub. Cecil was one of the privileged few who knew about this, and he and others of his circle worked their way systematically through the wine list until nothing was left. Walter Legge, William Walton, Constant Lambert and Michael Ayrton were among those often to be found there, talking and drinking, drinking and talking, well into the afternoon' (Pauline Gray, Afterword to *Musical Chairs*, n. p.).

[15] Sacheverell Sitwell, 'Kaikhosru Sorabji', programme notes for the concert by Yonty Solomon on 7 December 1976 in Wigmore Hall, 7, qtd. in Kenneth Derus, 'Sorabji's Letters to Heseltine', in *Sorabji: A Critical Celebration*, ed. by Paul Rapoport (Aldershot: Scolar Press, 1992), 195–255, 239.

[16] The hostess at Garsington, Lady Ottoline Morrell, wrote that '[D. H.] Lawrence and Frieda have been here again, and they brought with them […] an Indian, called Sarawadi [sic], who is at Oxford, and who is a friend of Heseltine' (Ottoline Morrell, *Ottoline at Garsington: Memoirs of Lady Ottoline Morrell, 1915–18* (New York: Knopf, 1975), 77, qtd. in Derus, 'Sorabji's Letters to Heseltine', 219).

Figure 2.1 Percy Wyndham Lewis, 'Portrait of Edwin Evans' (1922–23), National Galleries Scotland, GMA 1079, © Estate of Percy Wyndham Lewis. All Rights Reserved 2018/ Bridgeman Images.

from the previous generation of this critical lineage. Osbert Sitwell wrote in his autobiography *Laughter in the Next Room* (1949), that instead of

sending William [Walton] to Kensington or Bloomsbury, we were able to keep him in touch with the vital works of the age, with the music, for example, of Stravinsky, and to obtain for him, through the kindness of our old family friend E. J. Dent, an introduction to Busoni, a modern master of counterpoint, who looked at some of William's compositions and wrote him a kindly polite letter about them.[17]

The Sitwells become important for Walton in financial terms, as did the poet Siegfried Sassoon, who was also an old friend of Dent, and to whom

[17] Qtd. in Lloyd, *William Walton: Muse of Fire*, 14.

Walton's *Portsmouth Point* is dedicated. Stephen Lloyd has pointed out that it was Sassoon who suggested that Walton send the piece to Oxford University Press, where the music department (established in 1923) was headed up by Hubert Foss (1899–1953), who subsequently supported the work of Vaughan Williams, Walton, Lambert, Van Dieren and Moeran. In addition to being committed to these figures as part of an agenda to promote 'modern' British music, Foss was also personally acquainted with Heseltine, allowing Heseltine and Moeran to rent his house at Eynsford, which became the scene of both debauchery and creativity. Foss wrote the introduction to the revised edition of Heseltine's book on Delius.[18]

Both Heseltine and Gray had been declared unfit for war service – Heseltine due to a 'nervous stricture' and Gray because of a heart condition. Joyce and Eliot also did not participate in the War as combatants. Gray had planned to travel to study with Vincent d'Indy, though war conditions saw him stay in England, entering the Midland Institute at Birmingham in the Autumn of 1914. Gray found his studies at Birmingham quite chaotic, and he complained of there having been too much freedom and not enough discernment between the relative merits of modern trends. Heseltine was similarly disillusioned at Oxford, though his time there was not without consequence. At Oxford, Heseltine met the poet Robert Nichols, with whom he shared a kindred sensibility – both young men were 'sensitive to the beauties of nature' and committed to 'earthy words for their own sake'.[19] Together they discussed their reading of Joyce, who over the next three years would produce *Dubliners* and *A Portrait of the Artist as a Young Man*. They also discussed the work of the sexologist Havelock Ellis (whom Sorabji was to meet in person in 1924), the social reformer Edward Carpenter, and the American poet Walt Whitman, whose work had attained a striking vogue among British composers in the previous decade, including in the work of Heseltine's musical idol, Delius. Nichols wrote in his reminiscence of Heseltine in Gray's biography that 'sex, literature (particularly Elizabethan literature) and music were our great subjects'.[20]

---

[18] Hubert Foss, 'Introduction', *Frederick Delius*, by Peter Warlock (London: Bodley Head, 1923; rev. ed. 1952), 9–26. Foss described Heseltine's book as in itself a 'work of art' and that 'for itself alone, as a piece of English prose, it is worth reading and re-reading' (10). For more on Foss's activities in music publishing see Duncan Hinnells, *An Extraordinary Performance: Hubert Foss, Music Publishing, and the Oxford University Press* (Oxford: Oxford University Press, 1998) and Kirstie Asmussen, 'Hubert Foss and the Politics of Musical Progress: Modernism and British Music Publishing', PhD diss., University of Queensland, 2016.

[19] Smith, *Peter Warlock: the Life of Philip Heseltine*, 57.

[20] See Gray, *Peter Warlock: A Memoir of Philip Heseltine*, 69.

Cornwall and Garsington; *The Athenaeum* and *The New Age*

Nichols introduced Heseltine to the work of D. H. Lawrence, who had published *Sons and Lovers* the year of their introduction at Oxford in 1913. Two years later, the twenty-one-year-old Heseltine contrived to meet D. H. Lawrence in person at a dinner party. The details of this meeting and the subsequent interactions between Heseltine and Lawrence will be explored in depth in the next chapter. Both men were at the time angered by the war effort, and their meeting occurred just after the suppression of Lawrence's *The Rainbow*. Together they planned a colony of escape in Florida, and Heseltine hoped to persuade his mentor Delius that the colony could be set up in his disused orange plantation. Gray was invited to join them, and so was Aldous Huxley, who notionally accepted the invitation. Heseltine's negotiations with Delius proved unsuccessful, and by 1917 the plan for the colony was relocated to the Andes, at which point Gray withdrew his participation: 'the idea of spending the rest of my life in the Andes in the company of Lawrence and Frieda, filled me with horror – the combination of mountain heights and the psychological depths was more than I could sanely contemplate'.[21]

Only a few months after their initial meeting, Heseltine travelled to Cornwall and stayed for a time in the home of Lawrence and his wife Frieda. It was early 1916, and Heseltine contrived a scheme to reprint the suppressed *The Rainbow* and other neglected works. John Middleton Murry and Katherine Mansfield had previously been involved in a venture with Lawrence called *The Signature*, and Murry wrote that 'Katherine and I were rather nettled by this sudden intrusion of Heseltine, whom we did not know, and of whom (perhaps jealously) we boded no good'.[22] Like Mansfield, Murry was a central figure in the circulation of literary modernism – he was the opponent of T. S. Eliot in a famous literary debate in the 1920s on the topic of 'impersonality', and was for a time the editor of the important literary magazine *The Athenaeum*. Murry and Mansfield were close friends of D. H. Lawrence during the same period in which Heseltine was living with the Lawrences in Cornwall.

D. H. Lawrence wrote for *The Athenaeum* at the time that it was edited by Murry, and Dent contributed essays on German music culture to the magazine during the same period. Lawrence attended the salon of Lady Ottoline Morrell at her Tudor manor house at Garsington, near Oxford,

---

[21] Gray, *Musical Chairs*, 132.
[22] Qtd. in Gray, *Musical Chairs*, 112. No original source given.

which was also frequented by Dent's Cambridge friends Strachey, E. M. Forster, Bertrand Russell and Siegfried Sassoon, as well as Virginia Woolf (also associated with Cambridge of course, and whose cousin was married to Vaughan Williams), the poet Robert Nichols (with whom Heseltine became friends during his brief time at Oxford), Augustus John (whom Heseltine knew through his drinking sessions at the Café Royal), and the Sitwells (who also associated with Dent, Gray and Lambert, supported and collaborated with Walton, and admired Sibelius). It was Lawrence who invited Heseltine to Lady Ottoline's house. At this time Lawrence was seeking assistance from the hostess to set up his utopian community. Nichols and William Walton also frequented this salon, and it is clear that Woolf was familiar with Gray's writing at least, as she quoted from his *Survey of Contemporary Music* in *A Room of One's Own*, as evidence of misogyny in the musical sphere.

In the summer of 1917, exemptions from military service were withdrawn, and Heseltine was summoned for further medical examination. At the time, Heseltine was in Cornwall with Lawrence, but decided to flee to Ireland, where he stayed for a year and became embroiled in occult investigations. Also in the summer of 1917, Gray moved to Land's End, renting a house at Bosigran Castle near to D. H. Lawrence, with whom Gray had become acquainted through his friendship with Heseltine.

During Gray's period in this cottage, he pursued a relationship with the American imagist poet Hilda Doolittle ('H. D.'), who was at the time married to Richard Aldington and romantically attached to Lawrence. Aldington was then the editor of the modernist literary journal *The Egoist*, which published contributions by Wyndham Lewis, Ford Madox Ford, Ezra Pound, Eliot, Lawrence and others. Imagist anthologies also included work by T. E. Hulme, whose classicist leanings will become important in our investigation of Gray's conception of music history, as well as for the anti-liberal tendencies of 'reactionary modernism' with which Sorabji was associated, as we shall see. The relationship between H. D. and Gray resulted in the birth of a child, but by that time H. D. was estranged from both Gray and Aldington, and her personal difficulties during this period were compounded by the loss of her brother in the War.

Historically, H. D.'s poetry is associated with Imagism, which was an interwar movement involving a number of the same figures who were involved with Vorticism. Imagism advocated simplicity, clarity and economy of language, which would no doubt have appealed to Gray's burgeoning classicism. H. D.'s change in signature to 'imagiste' was suggested to her by her one-time fiancé Ezra Pound, who wrote music criticism for *The*

New Age, a journal in which the music writings of Sorabji, Gray, Heseltine and Van Dieren also appeared. In the years before the War, Pound had collaborated with Wyndham Lewis on the avant-garde journal *BLAST*, and Sorabji, Heseltine and Gray had each read the explosive first issue of this magazine.[23] Indeed Hubert Foss described *The Sackbut* as the musical equivalent of the type of castigating critique offered by *BLAST*, and as inaugurating a 'much needed' 'new attitude towards the history of music'.[24] Heseltine, Sorabji, Gray and their associates were clearly enmeshed within the milieu of literary modernism during and directly after World War I, and they utilized the same kinds of weaponry to forward their agenda as their literary counterparts, including revisionist history, 'little magazines', manifestos and staged intellectual debates.[25]

Heseltine, Gray and Sorabji formed a central part of the musical contingent of literary 'late modernism', and through their essays they provided the clearest articulation of how lateness shaped ideas about music within this milieu. The names of these figures may not be widely known today – or may be known for reasons other than their contribution to this critical tradition – but they should in no way be considered parasitic or marginal to the milieu. Even from the brief sketch above we get a sense of how closely they were embedded within it, and this is further attested to by letters, anecdotes,

---

[23] Gray later became personally acquainted with Lewis (see Gray, *Musical Chairs*, 270–71; and the letters from Lewis to Gray held in Cecil Gray Papers, *GB-Lbl*, Add MS 57785). In the Cecil Gray Papers there are also letters to Gray from other figures within this milieu, including John Middleton Murry, Sacheverell Sitwell, Arthur Symons, H. D., Michael Ayrton, Roy Campbell, Jacob Epstein, Ralph Vaughan Williams and William Walton.

[24] Hubert Foss, 'Cecil Gray, 1895–1951' *The Musical Times* 92 (1951): 496–8, 496.

[25] From the perspective of cultural materialism, 'little magazines' have been recognized as serving a constitutive role in the development of modernism, as noted above. The culture of little magazines in modernism, for example, often served as the central point around which coteries and communities would gather, or against which they could position themselves. Closely associated with the manifesto genre, little magazines acted as points of coalescence whereby a momentary affiliation between artists, a robust discussion that began at the Café Royal, or a mutual agenda that was agreed upon in the salon of a society hostess between artists of disparate backgrounds could suddenly be given a public face. As Brooker and Thacker have noted, these magazines actualized: 'the struggle to establish and maintain criteria of aesthetic and cultural value as a force in society from an embattled and combative position. [...] At every point a study of the magazines renders a seemingly homogenous and linear history back in to the miscellaneous initiatives, fluid mergers, contentious factions, and strongly alternative *partis pris* which have composed it, revealing a loosely assembled cultural tradition of critical thinking: fragile, and transitory, but, by that very token, testimony to an attitude of dissent and artistic innovation which is of lasting value' (Peter Brooker and Andrew Thacker, eds, *The Oxford Critical and Cultural History of Modernist Magazines: Vol I: Britain and Ireland, 1880–1955* (Oxford and New York: Oxford University Press, 2009), 25–6). The interaction between Heseltine, Gray, Sorabji and their literary associates is certainly of the nature suggested here.

cross-promotional efforts and biographical detail, as well as their regular appearance – in often none-too-flattering caricatures – as characters in several novels from the period.[26]

Untimeliness, Impasse and Lateness

Modern art is beginning to lose its powers of negation. For some years now its rejections have been ritual repetitions: rebellion has turned into procedure, criticism into rhetoric, transgression into ceremony. Negation is no longer creative. I am not saying that we are living at the end of art: we are living the end of the *idea of modern art*.[27]

For Augustus John, Heseltine's death in 1930 – 'that fatal hour [...] when he put the cat out, locked the door, and turned on the gas'[28] – seemed to be bound up with the same cultural shift represented by the addition of dining facilities to the Café Royal. Not only did the redevelopment of the Café and Heseltine's death seemed to signal for John the end of an era, but also the end of the possibility of a particular type of artistic persona. There is a narrative of lost sincerity here that John clearly believes a personality like Heseltine's had the power to overcome – moving beyond the concession to the 'glittering napery' of a consumer culture that had come to expect and prize the radical expressions of modernism.

Although these artists cultivated an attitude of opposition and withdrawal, their positions were characterized by dogmatic declarations of untimeliness rather than by isolationism. Their untimeliness was not only a protest against prevailing hierarchies and conventions (as with other modernisms), nor simply a claim for the revival of pre-Romantic values and styles in response (as with other interwar classicisms). Rather, their

---

[26] Characters that have been attributed – with varying degrees of reliability – to Heseltine include Julius Halliday in D. H. Lawrence's *Women in Love* (1920); Coleman in Aldous Huxley's *Antic Hay* (1923); Roy Hartle in Osbert Sitwell's *Those Were the Days* (1938); Giles Revelstoke in Robertson Davies's *A Mixture of Frailties* (1958); Maclintick (alongside Constant Lambert as Hugh Moreland) in Anthony Powell, *Casanova's Chinese Restaurant* (1960); and Peter Warlock in David Pownall's play *Music to Murder By* (1976). Characters that have been attributed to Cecil Gray include James Sharpe in D. H. Lawrence's *Kangaroo* (1923); Mr. Mercaptan in Aldous Huxley's *Antic Hay* (1923); Duncan Forbes in D. H. Lawrence's *Lady Chatterley's Lover* (1928); and Vane in Hilda Doolittle's *Bid Me to Live* (1960).

[27] Octavio Paz, *Children of the Mire: Modern Poetry from Romanticism to the Avant-Garde* (Cambridge, Mass: Harvard University Press, 1974), 148–9, qtd. in Daniel Bell, 'Modernism Mummified' *American Quarterly* 39.1 (1987): 122–32, 128.

[28] John, foreword to *Peter Warlock: A Memoir of Philip Heseltine*, 15.

untimeliness combined these positions with an acute awareness that neither would result in the type of change they desired. Their outlook was to a
large extent an aesthetic expression of the political impasse of the immediate
post-World War I years in Britain, particularly in light of the government's
contentious handling of demobilization and reconstruction.[29] In this context, calls for art to remain autonomous from politics were in fact explicitly
political gestures that reflected the prevailing frustration with the absence
of viable social, political and aesthetic alternatives:

The lack of credible options, however, left them all the more aware of their naked-
ness before the social facts. Reflecting on their own practice, they discerned in the
evolution of modern writing disturbing changes in the ways in which literature
was produced and read. Yet unable to formulate any radical alternative to the modernist legacy within which they continued to work, they labored to tunnel through
it undermining and leaving it behind in a painstaking pursuit of literary 'failure' –
isolated, furtive, and uncertain of allies.[30]

In a sense, this response was peculiar to the context of Britain, where
processes of industrialization and constitutional reform began earlier and
moved more steadily than elsewhere in Europe, making the rupture of social
modernity less pronounced, and diluting the forces required for the crystallization of a revolutionary mandate.[31] In the absence of this kind of consolidation, the self-conscious *ennui* of middle-class modernists appeared
increasingly inauthentic, hence the vitriol of late modernists against the
bourgeois modernism of Bloomsbury and the Sitwells.[32]

    For figures like Wyndham Lewis, the final damning of modernist ideals
had coincided with the General Strike of 1926, which saw the manifest
failure of revolutionary action to offer a viable alternative to entrenched
social hierarchies, and which resulted in a severe undermining of liberal
politics in Britain. This sense of failed ideals, compounded by economic

[29] For a discussion of how literary culture responded to this sense of disenchantment, see David
Goldie, *A Critical Difference: T. S. Eliot and John Middleton Murry in English Literary Criticism,
1919–1928* (Oxford: Clarendon, 1998).

[30] Tyrus Miller, *Late Modernism: Politics, Fiction, and the Arts Between the Wars*
(Berkeley: University of California Press, 1999), 32.

[31] See Matthew Riley, 'Introduction', in *British Music and Modernism*, ed. by Matthew Riley
(Farnham: Ashgate, 2010), 6–7; and Stefan Collini, *Public Moralists: Intellectual Life in Britain,
1850–1930* (Oxford: Clarendon Press, 1993), 345.

[32] See also Stefan Collini, 'British Exceptionalism Reconsidered: Annan, Anderson and other
Accounts', in *Anglo-French Attitudes: Comparisons and Transfers between English and French
Intellectuals since the Eighteenth Century*, ed. by Christophe Charle, Julien Vincent and Jay
Winter (Manchester: Manchester University Press, 2007), 45–60.

recession, provided the context for the burgeoning support for socialist and fascist tendencies in British politics in the 1930s. Lewis actively took part in these debates, as did Cecil Gray (who briefly praised the virtues of Mussolini's regime, and once boasted that he was the first to wear a 'black shirt' in London) and Sorabji (who became, following Ezra Pound, the music critic for *The New Age*, which was a mouthpiece for Guild Socialism).

There was also, however, an important transition in the liberal ethos itself, which Amanda Anderson has termed 'bleak liberalism'. For Anderson, the 'bleak' turn in liberalism involved a new sense of pragmatism or taking stock – a reordering of liberal values so as to acknowledge the 'tension between moral aspiration and sober apprehension of those historical, sociological, or psychological tendencies that threaten its ambition'.[33] Anderson noted how the 1930s and 1940s witnessed the collapse of the notion of human perfectibility that had characterized Victorian Liberalism, and a reduced pre-eminence of optimism and rationalism. This shift occasioned a change in the liberal ethos between the wars, after World War II and into the Cold War era that is conventionally perceived as neo-conservative in nature, and which prepared the way for the strident critique of liberalism that came with the rise of Theory. Anderson re-imagines this shift as 'bleakness' rather than conservatism, describing how political aspiration combined with a pessimistic awareness of the 'tragic limitation and negative forces' of the historical situation, leading to a sense of restraint and pessimism among liberals. This 'bleakness' shaped a newly pragmatic[34] approach to liberal reform, including 'endorsement of democratic process, piecemeal reform, and limited or ad hoc political measures',[35] while maintaining an outwardly optimistic political vision.

The combination of pessimism and faith that led to a new pragmatism or restraint in liberal reform could also be seen in the musical sphere, especially among composers who retained a commitment to tonal music well into the twentieth century. For example Ben Earle has described how the

---

[33] Amanda Anderson, 'Character and Ideology: the Case of Cold War Liberalism' *New Literary History* 42.2 (2011): 209–29, 215.

[34] Pragmatism here is used in its colloquial sense rather than as referring to Pragmatic philosophy, although Anderson raised pragmatism's influence more directly elsewhere. Also, there does exist a school of thought that links pragmatic philosophy to major modernist figures such as Gertrude Stein, Henry James and even Marcel Proust, arguing for their adherence to an idea of habit over shock, as part of a trend in recasting the rupture of modernism as continuity (see Lisi Schoenbach, *Pragmatic Modernism* (New York: Oxford University Press, 2011).

[35] Anderson, 'Character and Ideology', 219.

ambivalent character of [Frank Bridge's] later music bears within it a kind of 'know-ledge'. The 'progressive' confidence of the late bourgeois past is gone; but it is far from clear what should replace it. In a manner that might be compared to the work of Berg in terms of 'tone', Bridge's later music accepts separation from the bourgeois, but holds out no 'false hopes' of a better state to come.[36]

Constant Lambert's book *Music Ho!: A Study of Music in Decline* (1934) offers a similar set of observations. Lambert depicts 'post-war' musical stag-nation in terms of the aging of modernism. In a manner so redolent of the interwar critiques of New Liberalism and the compromises of Fabian Socialism, Lambert describes for example how many post-war composers in the 1920s were 'lacking in the genuine spirit of revolt [...] or the genuine spirit of conservatism [...] for [them] revolution has become merely a mechanical reaction and classicism merely a receptacle, a roll-top desk into which he can thrust incongruous scraps of paper'.[37]

For artists who still identified with the modernist legacy, yet found themselves disillusioned by its increasing marketization, there emerged a renewed appreciation for clarity, economy and objectivity – values that shaped a range of interwar classicisms. Underpinning these aesthetic preferences were also a range of powerful propositions regarding the nature of art criticism, history and autonomy. The kinds of claims that are of interest here, put schematically, include: the belief that the revolutionary period of pre-war artistic experimentation had been nothing more than a continuation of romantic tendencies; that this kind of art, which was deemed to be 'modern' in the sense of reflecting the spirit of the time, was doomed to transience because it was idiosyncratic and tied to the course of history (just as national art was marred by its attachment to a particular place); and that the only way to be truly new was to stand above history by being 'untimely', or out of sync with the spirit of the time.

Artists who subscribed to these types of view tended to be wary of over-intellectualization in art, and they detested theory and pre-compositional processes. They spoke out – often violently – against institutional elitism and the professionalization of criticism, yet at the same time they derided the tastes of the consumer masses. Their political commitments – including their views of equality, self-determination, liberty, autonomy and democra-tization – exhibited these same paradoxes.

---

[36] Ben Earle, 'Modernism and Reification in the Music of Frank Bridge' *Journal of the Royal Musical Association* 141.2 (2016): 335–402, 402.

[37] Constant Lambert, *Music Ho!: A Study of Music in Decline* (1934; 3rd ed. London: Penguin, 1948), 201.

'Men of 1914'

Intuiting this constellation of positions among his own generation, Wyndham Lewis coined the collective attribution 'Men of 1914' to describe T. S. Eliot, Ezra Pound, James Joyce and himself in his autobiography of 1937, *Blasting and Bombardiering*:

What I think history will say about the 'Men of 1914' is that they represent an attempt to get away from romantic art into classical art, away from political propaganda back into the detachment of true literature: just as in painting Picasso has represented a desire to terminate the Nineteenth Century alliance of painting and natural science. And what has happened – slowly – as a result of the War, is that artistic expression has slipped back again into political propaganda and romance, which go together. When you get one you get the other. The attempt at objectivity has failed. The subjectivity of the majority is back again, as a result of that great defeat, the Great War, and all that has ensued upon it.[38]

Gray, Heseltine and Sorabji were a decade younger than Lewis and his associates, though undoubtedly of the same generation. They came of age just as the Great War was beginning, and bore heavily the mark of thwarted promise, which conditioned their ingrained and life-long sense of belatedness. Like Pound, Joyce, Eliot and Lewis, they were all outsiders to the London scene – Gray was Scottish, Heseltine significantly identified with his Welsh heritage and Sorabji trumpeted his Parsi and Sicilian ancestry – though they were also, like their literary counterparts, profoundly concerned with notions of Englishness, and with ensuring the health of English culture. The onset of the War coincided with formative transition points in their lives – Heseltine had recently left Oxford and was for the first time making his way in the world, and Gray had recently discovered Marjory Kennedy-Fraser's collection of *Songs of the Hebrides*, which, as he described it, 'banished for ever [...] the Teutonic Wagnerian fogs and the seductive exoticism of the Slavonic world'. Gray wrote of his turn to classicism that he 'reverted to the national polarity – that of the Celt and the Latin, and have never since deserted it.'[39]

The overtly gendered nature of the 'Men of 1914' has since been tempered by the scholarly recognition of the work of female literary modernists such as Virginia Woolf, Katherine Mansfield, Rebecca West, Dora Marsden,

---

[38] Wyndham Lewis, *Blasting and Bombardiering* (1937; Berkeley: University of California Press, 2nd rev. ed., 1967), 250.

[39] Gray, *Musical Chairs*, 98–9.

H. D., and Beatrice Hastings. Yet Lewis's description remains highly intuitive, and could equally apply to some of his musical counterparts. In their
ideas about music, Heseltine, Gray and Sorabji valued what they called
'objectivity', and raged against 'philosophical music', or what they saw as
the artificial connection of music with ideas. In terms of compositional
persona, they valued sincerity and spontaneity, individuality (but not
individual*ism*) – 'sobriety and restraint of idiom [… and] impersonality of
style'.[40] And in the critic they valued objectivity, rigor and intuition. Or as
a young Heseltine described Delius's music at the height of his admiration
for the older composer:

Simplicity, directness, avoidance of anything remotely suggestive of the bombastic,
the pretentious or the over-intellectualized – these are qualities that have always
been conspicuous alike in his life and in his art. His lack of interest in the technical
problems of music, except in so far as they concern himself, is paralleled by his
complete indifference to the music of his contemporaries.[41]

These classical values have little to do with the music or literature of the
eighteenth century, in the sense of being able to be described as Classical
'style'. Rather, the classicism of 'late modernism' was an expression of isolation and self-creation, an absence of history and a cultivated attitude of
untimeliness.

Similarly, untimeliness for Heseltine meant that there was no absolute
standard of beauty in the same way that there was no absolute standard
of morality. He drew explicitly from Nietzsche to develop this link, basing
upon it his whole approach to music criticism:

the necessary antecedent to the possibility of such a condemnation would be a fixed
standard of objective beauty, which, as a matter of plain fact, simply does not exist.
'No one yet knoweth what is good and bad', said Zarathustra […]

Neither a good nor a bad taste, but my taste, of which I have no longer either shame
or secrecy. 'This is now my way, where is yours?' Thus did I answer those who asked
me 'the way'. For the way – it doth not exist! Thus spake Zarathustra.[42]

In rejecting a fixed standard of beauty as well as a convention-based standard,
Heseltine was advocating an individualist approach based on sincerity and

---

[40] Gray describing Sibelius in Cecil Gray, *Sibelius* (1931; 2nd ed. London: Oxford University
    Press, 1945), 200.
[41] Philip Heseltine, 'Delius: Composer and Interpreter of Nature' *Radio Times* 25 (4 Oct.
    1929): 7–18, reprt. in *The Occasional Writings of Philip Heseltine (Peter Warlock)*, ed. by Barry
    Smith, Vol. 3 (London: Thames, 1998), 29.
[42] Philip Heseltine, 'Some Reflections on Modern Musical Criticism' *Musical Times* 54 (1 Oct.
    1913), 652–4, reprt. in *The Occasional Writings of Philip Heseltine*, Vol. 3, 58.

an avowed indifference towards the tastes of the public. Indeed, among the writers in this milieu there was a prevailing notion that an artist should create work that pleases himself only (and artists are resolutely male in this type of rhetoric) in order to achieve lasting beauty – 'the distinction between mere eccentricity and true originality lies solely in the sincerity of purpose with which the music is written'.[43] This 'Personal Equation', as Sorabji described it – whereby 'the expression of my own emotions and individuality' is sought 'with all the force, sincerity and conviction at my command'[44] – is contingent with the desire to regain the autonomy lost to the market and to political ideology, as described by Lewis. This mandate is therefore both an *epistemology* (shaping how an artist comes to his artistic creation), a *critical method* (determining the standards by which a work may be judged), and an *ethos* (involving the cultivation of character). Its tripartite nature differentiates it from the modernist mandate of rupture, giving the artist the freedom to pursue a *sui generis* relationship with convention.

[43] Heseltine, 'Some Reflections of Modern Musical Criticism', reprt. in Smith, *Occasional Writings*, Vol. 3, 59.
[44] Kaikhosru Sorabji, letter to Philip Heseltine, June 1917, reprt. in Derus, 'Sorabji's Letters to Heseltine', 233.

Figure 3.1 Photograph of Philip Heseltine (Peter Warlock),
Phyl Crocker and one other, © The British Library Board,
Cecil Gray Papers, MS 57803, pencil mark 90.

3 | Impersonality and Vividness: *'Le Gai Savaire'*, Philip Heseltine and D. H. Lawrence

Lateness was not only an attitude towards history and time; it was also an attitude towards subjectivity. It encompassed what Heseltine described as the ability to *'be* before attempting to *do'*.[1] This ability was thematized in temporal terms, so that an artist might be considered either timely or untimely according to his ability to be 'vivid' or fully himself. Likewise, within this milieu art was not to be judged by its newness or innovation, but by its degree of 'vitality' – its 'vividness and power for new life and vigour', in the words of Ferruccio Busoni.[2] As a measure of both artist and art, the idea of vividness was neither progressive nor conservative.

In what follows, I will first offer a fuller description of the tendency to thematize the self in temporal terms, before examining the aesthetic and critical implications of this tendency using the relationship between D. H. Lawrence and Philip Heseltine as a lens. Heseltine, who from 1916 adopted the pseudonym Peter Warlock, is of course the lesser-known of the two, but to the extent that his name is familiar today it is primarily as the composer of songs, vocal chamber works such as *The Curlew* (after Yeats) (1920–22), and works for string orchestra such as *Capriol Suite* (1926). He was also known for his highly idiosyncratic personality, and for his polemical writing style across an extensive list of critical and occasional writings.[3] Heseltine's reputation was as an avant-garde figure in early-twentieth-century Britain, yet he was also interested in Elizabethan music, literature and art. When he moved to London as a young man in 1913, after leaving his studies at Oxford, he spent much of this time in the British Museum editing early music manuscripts. He was also involved in a number of book projects in this area, including on the English Ayre and

---

[1] Philip Heseltine, 'Predicaments Concerning Music' *The New Age* 21.2 (10 May 1917): 46, reprt. in *The Occasional Writings of Philip Heseltine (Peter Warlock)*, ed. by Barry Smith, Vol. 3 (London: Thames, 1998), 125–7, 126. Original emphasis.
[2] Ferruccio Busoni, 'The Oneness of Music and the Possibilities of Opera' (1921), in *The Essence of Music and Other Papers*, trans. Rosamond Ley (New York: Dover, 1957), 4.
[3] A selection of his writings has been reprinted in four thematically organized volumes under the title *The Occasional Writings of Philip Heseltine (Peter Warlock)*, ed. by Barry Smith (London: Thames, 1997–99).

the Italian Renaissance composer Carlo Gesualdo, and a collaboration with Jack Lindsay reproducing sixteenth- and seventeenth-century texts, images and music.[4] Heseltine's attraction to this music was to some extent a reflection of his view that a work's newness was to be determined by its degree of vitality rather than its contemporaneousness, writing of these early works that 'they are not "antiques" in need of restoration and adjustment to 19th century standards, but living music, as perfect (the best of them) in technique as in vital expression'.[5] Indeed Gesualdo held an ongoing fascination for both Heseltine and Cecil Gray, with the pair co-authoring a book about the composer in 1925–26, and Gray collaborating with William Walton on a proposed opera on the subject.[6]

Lawrence's activities and intellectual development have received wider consideration, though it is worth noting at the outset that his relationship to modernism, and specifically with 'lateness', is ambiguous. Distinguishing 'late style' from a more general 'perception' of lateness,

---

[4] Heseltine's book projects include Philip Heseltine, *Frederick Delius* (London: John Lane, 1923); Peter Warlock [Philip Heseltine], *Thomas Whythorne: an Unknown Elizabethan Composer* (London: Oxford University Press, 1925); *The English Ayre* (London: Oxford University Press, 1926); Philip Heseltine and Cecil Gray, *Carlo Gesualdo: Prince of Venosa: Musician and Murderer* (London: Kegan Paul, 1926); John Harington, *The Metamorphosis of Aiax: a New Discourse of a Stale Subject by Sir John Harrington and the Anatomie of the Metamorphosed Aiax*, ed. by Peter Warlock and Jack Lindsay (London: Fanfrolico, 1927); Jack Lindsay, Robert Graves and Peter Warlock, eds, *Loving Mad Tom: Bedlamite Verses of the XVI and XVII Centuries* (London: Fanfrolico, 1927); Rab Noolas [Philip Heseltine], *Merry-go-down: a Gallery of Gorgeous Drunkards through the Ages: Collected for the Use Interest Illumination and Delectation of Serious Topers* (London: Mandrake, 1929); and the posthumously-published Peter Warlock [Philip Heseltine], *English Ayres: Elizabethan and Jacobean: a Discourse by Peter Warlock* (London: Oxford University Press, 1932).

[5] Philip Heseltine, letter to Colin Taylor, 25 Oct. 1922, *GB-Lbl*, Add MS 54197, qtd. in Barry Smith, 'Introduction', in *The Occasional Writings of Philip Heseltine (Peter Warlock)*, Vol. 2 (London: Thames, 1998), 14. Many of Heseltine's writings on early music convey this sense; in a letter to Robert Nichols in 1923, for example, Heseltine wrote that 'I'm going hammer and tongs now at Elizabethan songs which I am determined to rescue from the besmirching paws of antiquarians and present to the public clear and intact as living music' (qtd. in Smith, 'Introduction', 15). And in another article, on the songs of John Dowland and his contemporaries, Heseltine wrote that 'these songs – and the madrigals too, for that matter – are as fresh and lovely now as they were at the time they were written. They are living music, not antiques. Their composers, besides being inspired singers, were some of the most perfect craftsmen that ever used music as a means of expression [...]. Much of their work seems astonishingly "advanced" and modern (the "New Music" of Caccini and the other Italians, which appeared about the same time, sounds very much older to the historical ear), yet it is never experimental. They knew exactly what they wanted to do and did it; their every "effect" comes off, easily and without effort' (Philip Heseltine, 'Review of *The English School of Lutenist Song Writers* and *English Madrigal Verse*' *The Sackbut* 1.9 (March 1921): 424–6, reprt. in *Occasional Writings*, 2, 46–7).

[6] See Cecil Gray Papers, Vol. 21, *GB-Lbl*, Add MS 57787.

Michael Bell has observed Lawrence's 'moment-by-moment refusal of late style' while at once viewing his writing as being 'always under the sign of lateness' due to his life-long struggle with weak lungs.[7] Lawrence was certainly preoccupied with ends, as is self-evident from his apocalyptic imagery, yet he maintained a belief in the possibility of renewal and regeneration. Lawrence's mature-aged bleakness was prompted by a number of factors, including the suppression of his novel *The Rainbow*, his personal and financial hardships and transient lifestyle during the War, the threat of conscription and repeated medical checks, his general state of ill health, and the gradual slipping away of the possibility of establishing his utopian community – to be called 'Rananim' – to actualize his vision for a 'new world'.[8]

Lawrence's acquaintance with Heseltine was intimately bound up in the experience of these events, marking a period bounded by the publication of Lawrence's novel *The Rainbow* (1915), and the publication of its sequel *Women in Love* (1920). These two works have come to represent, in the history of the novel, the turn from a historical conception of time to a spatialized conception of time, the latter more typical of the modernist novel (and imagist poetic form). This narrative shift has been seen to mirror a shift in Lawrence's sense of 'faith' or hope:

Where Lawrence's fourth novel ends with a rainbow, assuring us of a world containing possibility and even strong promise, his fifth novel ends with a hanging question. No comparable promise is evident, though the possibility has not disappeared.[9]

Lawrence's ideas with respect to this sense of 'possibility' were also embodied in other works that he was drafting during the period of his close relationship with Heseltine. Indeed Lawrence's encounter with Heseltine coincided with the consolidation of his views on vitality as both a life policy, a social desirability and a critical yardstick, which together inform what some have called his 'metaphysic' – articulated variously in his

---

[7] Michael Bell, 'Perceptions of Lateness: Goethe, Nietzsche, Thomas Mann, and D. H. Lawrence', in *Late Style and its Discontents: Essays in Art, Literature, and Music*, ed. by Gordon McMullan and Sam Smiles (Oxford and New York: Oxford University Press, 2016), 131–46, 144 and 142.

[8] Rananim (the title from Koteliansky's Hebrew chants) was to have FIER as its motto, and the emblem of 'an eagle or phoenix agent, rising from a flaming nest of scarlet, on a black background' (D. H. Lawrence, letter to Koteliansky, 3 Jan. 1915, qtd. in Emile Delavenay, *D. H. Lawrence: the Man and his Work: the Formative Years, 1885–1919* (London: Heinemann, 1972), 256).

[9] Stephen J. Miko, *Toward Women in Love: the Emergence of a Lawrentian Aesthetic* (New Haven and London: Yale University Press, 1971), 186.

'Study of Thomas Hardy' (first drafted in late 1914), the multi-part essays 'The Crown' (1915) and 'The Reality of Peace' (1917), as well as 'Goats and Compasses' (begun and abandoned in 1916) and 'At the Gates' (begun in 1917). Indeed, the subsequent disappearance – and possible destruction – of the manuscripts of both 'Goats and Compasses' and 'At the Gates' has been attributed to Heseltine, after he and Lawrence parted ways in acrimonious circumstances, as we shall see.[10]

In Tyrus Miller's account of 'late modernism', Lawrence is grouped together with Joyce and Conrad as a canonical modernist who sought discursive mastery, and against whom the properly 'late' modernist writers such as Wyndham Lewis were reacting.[11] Lawrence is regularly grouped together with the likes of Proust, Joyce, Eliot and Yeats, as in Lionel Trilling's influential text *The Liberal Imagination*, where Lawrence appears alongside these names as one of the 'monumental figures of our time'.[12] However, the extent to which Lawrence's historical position in this respect was itself a result of the active work of contemporary powerbrokers such as Ezra Pound must also be taken into account. For example, Litz notes how

in March 1914, writing to Amy Lowell, Pound could group Joyce with Hueffer, Lawrence, F. S. Flint, and himself as potential staff for a new avant-garde magazine, but four months later in his review of *Dubliners* (*Egoist*, 15 July 1914) he relegated Lawrence to a minor position [...] clearly Pound thought Joyce was more 'rigorous' than Lawrence, who was drawn too much toward the weaker impressionism.[13]

Indeed, Litz reads the ultimate divergence between Pound and Lawrence (for both personal and stylistic reasons) as representing 'a series of either/or choices' with respect to the shape of literary modernism: 'either openness or closure, either the temporal sequence or the spatial image, either expressive

---

[10] Mark Kinkead-Weekes speculated that the latter manuscript was 'possibly destroyed by the young man who had partly inspired it' (Mark Kinkead-Weekes, *D. H. Lawrence: Triumph to Exile, 1912–1922* (Cambridge and New York: Cambridge University Press, 1996), 303).

[11] See Tyrus Miller, *Late Modernism: Politics, Fiction, and the Arts Between the Wars* (Berkeley: University of California Press, 1999).

[12] Lionel Trilling, *The Liberal Imagination: Essays on Literature and Society* (1950; New York: New York Review Books, 2012), 98.

[13] A. Walton Litz, 'Lawrence, Pound, and Early Modernism', in *D. H. Lawrence: A Centenary Consideration*, ed. by Peter Balbert and Phillip L. Marcus (Ithaca, NY: Cornell University Press, 1985), 15–28, 26. Litz noted that 'by late 1915, the divergence between the two writers was radical and permanent, ready to be processed into the history of modernism', with Lawrence moving towards the lyrical and ecstatic, while Pound and Eliot valorized objectivity and discursive economy (27).

form or the rational imagination, either the confessional mode or a poetry of "impersonality".[14]

These binaries may be useful for explanation, but they tend to obscure the ways in which an artist's thinking changes over the course of a lifetime – a truism that undermines the extent to which certain artists may be taken to be representative of particular attitudinal tendencies. It will be especially relevant in what follows to acknowledge that Lawrence's attitude towards the doctrine of 'impersonality' is not clear-cut. Equally, the question of Lawrence's timeliness or his relationship with other literary modernists must be extricated from the active process of his canonization that was undertaken by the Leavisites (the followers of the influential Cambridge critic F. R. Leavis) through the journal *Scrutiny*, and others. By focusing on Lawrence's loathing of mechanization, his critique of industrial capitalism, and his emancipatory evocation of 'spontaneous-creative life', *Scrutiny* was able to position him squarely within a 'great tradition' of liberal humanism in English fiction; yet Lawrence was resolutely authoritarian, anti-humanist, and against democracy and egalitarianism.[15] Terry Eagleton has noted how Lawrence's response to his sense of alienation from English culture was crucially different from 'archetypal modern exile', in that rather than merely feeling external to 'common experience', Lawrence was made to 'fight his way free from a repressive society by a route which, in his best work, involved no loss of inwardness with that determining social reality'.[16] Lawrence's working-class background (or, in the case of

[14] Litz, 'Lawrence, Pound, and Early Modernism', 27–8. Sydney Janet Kaplan made a similar point about a crossroads in the direction of literary modernism based on personal relationships – in her case between Eliot and John Middleton Murry (see Sydney Janet Kaplan, *Circulating Genius: John Middleton Murry, Katherine Mansfield and D. H. Lawrence* (Edinburgh: Edinburgh University Press, 2010).

[15] On this point, Terry Eagleton observed that what began as a movement against middle-class greed and self-interestedness at the expense of working-class rights became a lamentation about the demise of the 'English gentleman': 'The lower middle-class origins of the architects of English are perhaps relevant here. Nonconformist, provincial, hardworking and morally conscientious, the Scrutineers had no difficulty in identifying for what it was the frivolous amateurism of the upper-class English gentlemen who filled the early Chairs of Literature at the ancient Universities [...] *Scrutiny* arose out of this social ambivalence: radical in respect of the literary academic Establishment, coterie-minded with regard to the mass of the people [...] The gain was a resolute singleness of purpose, uncontaminated by wine-tasting triviality on the one hand and "mass" banality on the other. The loss was a profoundly ingrown isolationism' (Terry Eagleton, *Literary Theory: an Introduction* (Oxford: Basil Blackwell, 1983), 43, and 35–6). John R. Harrison made a similar point in his chapter on Lawrence in *The Reactionaries* (London: Victor Gollancz, 1966), 163–92.

[16] Terry Eagleton, 'The Novels of D. H. Lawrence', in *The Eagleton Reader*, ed. by Stephen Regan (Oxford: Blackwell, 1998), 10. This was different from the sense of exile of other literary modernists, according to Eagleton, such as those who felt external to their native culture

his mother, lower-middle class), and his later entry into literary circles in London, shaped a tension between a desire for inclusion and at once a deep suspicion of cliques that resembled the 'intellectual aristocracy' of a previous age, conditioning his outward rejection of the Bloomsbury ethos and his simultaneous idealization of and disdain for his roots in Eastwood.[17]

In a similar recognition that Lawrence's response to his time does not easily map onto conventional discussions of modernism, Bell has attributed to Lawrence a 'parallel modernism', and Sandra M. Gilbert an 'alternative modernism', the latter highlighting that while others were pursuing irony, parody and myth, Lawrence was earnest, and – as we shall see in his relationship with Heseltine – he was urged towards synthesis rather than disintegration and atomization, which seemed to run counter to other modernist tendencies.[18] Baldick also highlighted Lawrence's distance from the likes of Joyce and Proust and I. A. Richardson, on the basis that he sought to be less self-conscious – less concerned with character and more interested in the 'nameless flame behind them all'.[19] Indeed, more in line with Heseltine, Gray and Sorabji, Delavenay attributed to Lawrence 'frustration, his impotent anger, [and] his undirected revolutionary tendencies'.[20] These

---

(Orwell and Greene), or to quotidian life, or the 'impotent passivity of the man trapped as a social exile within a culture which could not be escaped, a form of life too oppressively familiar to be surmounted' (10).

[17]   Emile Delavenay painted a particularly vivid picture of Lawrence's divided relationship with his origins in *D. H. Lawrence: the Man and his Work*, 75–6. While Delavenay highlighted the extent to which Lawrence had achieved a modicum of financial independence by 1906, by working as an uncertificated teacher, which together with his entrance into university secured his route into the middle-class, Raymond Williams emphasized the inescapable effect of Lawrence's childhood context on his later thinking: 'the real importance of Lawrence's origins [...] [is] that his first social responses were those, not of a man observing the processes of industrialism [like his otherwise close contemporary Carlyle], but of one caught in them at an exposed point, and destined in the normal course to be enlisted in their regiments. That he escaped enlistment is now so well known to us that it is difficult to realize the thing as it happened, in its living sequence. It is only by hard fighting, and further by the fortune of fighting on a favorable front, that anyone born into the industrial working class escapes his function of replacement. Lawrence could not be certain, at the time when his fundamental social responses were forming, that he could so escape' (Raymond Williams, 'The Social Thinking of D. H. Lawrence', in *A D. H. Lawrence Miscellany*, ed. by Harry T. Moore (Carbondale: Southern Illinois University Press, 1959), 295–311, 299).

[18]   Michael Bell, 'Lawrence and Modernism', and Sandra M. Gilbert, 'Apocalypse Now (and then)., or, D. H. Lawrence and the Swan in the Electron', in *The Cambridge Companion to D. H. Lawrence*, ed. by Anne Fernihough (Cambridge: Cambridge University Press, 2001), 179–96 and 235–52, 238.

[19]   Chris Baldick, *Criticism and Literary Theory 1890 to the Present* (London: Longman, 1996), 102, quoting D. H. Lawrence, from *A Selection from Phoenix*, ed. by A. A. H. Inglis (Harmondsworth, 1971), 165.

[20]   Delavenay, *D. H. Lawrence: the Man and his Work*, 255.

frustrations – based as they were on unacted political passions – seemed in fact to align quite readily with George Orwell's imagery of the bisected wasp, described earlier, that Tyrus Miller used to symbolize the condition of literature in the 'late modernism' of the 1930s.[21] In other words, once we turn our focus away from an idea of modernism and 'late modernism' as being defined by the pursuance or rejection of discursive mastery, towards questions of ethos and attitude, a different picture begins to emerge that reveals hidden alignments within the cultural field. Even though Lawrence may not unequivocally exemplify the ethos of lateness, his work and his personal interactions with our figures of interest during the War help to illuminate the process of intellectual development out of which their sense of lateness developed. Specifically, the following will show how many of the views on music propagated so vehemently by Gray and Heseltine after the War, particularly in relation to Sibelius, Delius and Van Dieren, might be traced to their temporary enthusiasm for – and ultimate disillusionment with – Lawrence and what he called his 'metaphysic'.

While there has been some degree of focused interest in the circumstances surrounding the relationship between Lawrence and Heseltine,[22] there has been very little commentary on the impact of the relationship on the work of either, or indeed its importance as a paradigmatic instance of the inter-section of a musical and literary milieu that did not have an intermedial outcome of some kind (such as the related collaboration between William Walton and Edith Sitwell). Through letters and accounts it is not difficult to gain a summary vision of the course of the relationship: Heseltine met Lawrence in the winter of 1915, at a pivotal moment in both their lives. Heseltine lived with Lawrence and his wife Frieda for seven weeks during

---

[21] Responding to Orwell's description of 'modern man [as] rather like a bisected wasp which goes on sucking jam and pretends that the loss of its abdomen does not matter', Miller viewed this analysis as identifying 'the endgame of modern individualistic culture, with the late modernist torso gyrating mechanically while the head no longer serves to guide it and no limb propels it on' (Miller, *Late Modernism*, 7–9, quoting Orwell's 'Some Recent Novels' *New English Weekly* 14 Nov. 1935, 96–7.

[22] See for example Ian A. Copley, *A Turbulent Friendship: A Study of the Relationship between D. H. Lawrence and Philip Heseltine (Peter Warlock)* (London: Thames, 1983); Paul Delany, *D. H. Lawrence's Nightmare: The Writer and His Circle in the Years of the Great War* (Hassocks, Sussex: Harvester, 1979), and 'Halliday's Progress: Letters of Philip Heseltine' *D. H. Lawrence Review* 13 (1980): 119–33; Charles L. Ross and George J. Zytaruk, 'Goats and Compasses and/or Women in Love: An Exchange' *D. H. Lawrence Review* 6 (1973): 33–46; and George J. Zytaruk, 'What Happened to D. H. Lawrence's Goats and Compasses?' *D. H. Lawrence Review* 4 (1971), 280–86. In addition, most biographies of Lawrence do make brief reference to the writer's acquaintance with Heseltine.

1916 in Cornwall and became a part of Lawrence's vision for the utopian community of Rananim, for which Heseltine tried to persuade Delius to offer his orange plantation in Florida as a venue. Lawrence's novel *The Rainbow* had just recently been suppressed for obscenity, with over a thousand copies seized and destroyed, and the young and enthusiastic Heseltine attempted to organize a private printing to keep the novel in circulation, and to begin a broader publishing venture to allow for the printing of texts which did not court public popularity. Lawrence loaned Heseltine the manuscript of his philosophical essay titled 'Goats and Compasses', though because of a falling out between them over Lawrence's caricature of Heseltine in his novel *Women in Love* (1920), Heseltine was thought to have destroyed the manuscript. Heseltine threatened legal action for what he claimed was a libellous caricature, but was eventually appeased by the modification of the physical description of the character in question, as well as the withdrawal of the first edition of the book from distribution, and a monetary settlement.

Lawrence and Heseltine's acquaintance can be viewed within a broader network of interactions between certain poets, writers, editors and critics who were associated in some way with the project of Imagism and related ideas during the years surrounding World War I, and who were all born in the late 1880s or early 1890s. We have already noted the role of Cecil Gray in this circle; Gray collaborated with Heseltine and knew the Lawrences well from their time living in close proximity in Cornwall. It is also worth recalling that the group included the imagist poet H. D., who was professionally connected with Pound and romantically connected with Lawrence, Gray and Richard Aldington. During Lawrence's acquaintance with Heseltine, his close circle of collaborators also included Murry and Mansfield, and two other figures who were closely involved in both Lawrence's and Heseltine's lives at this time were the writers Dikran Kouyoumdjian (Michael Arlen, 1895–1956), and Aldous Huxley (1894–1963). These figures met together at venues such as the Café Royal in London, the home of the society hostess Lady Ottoline Morrell at Garsington, and around the area of the Lawrences' various residences in Cornwall.

The presence of the composer Frederick Delius (1862–1934) in Heseltine's young life was also crucial to preparing the way for his encounter with Lawrence. Heseltine idealized Delius at the time he met Lawrence, and many of Delius's own views were coterminous with Lawrence's, including his ambivalence towards the idea of transcendence and towards the Church more generally, and his views on life-affirmation and what Grainger called Delius's 'sex-worshipping'. Delius also shared with Lawrence a cruel individualism arguably gleaned from Nietzsche.[23] Discussions about vividness were in one sense then a part of a wider dialogue on issues like these, and related specifically to the peculiar reception of the works of Nietzsche in Britain.[24] Linking Delius's and Heseltine's Nietzscheanism with Lawrence's heroic vitalism (gleaned from Nietzsche and Whitman, among others), signals a point of intersection between related streams of modernism that shared a temporal conception of the self.

Impersonality and the Process of Becoming Late

Before considering more directly the relationship between Heseltine and Lawrence, it will be useful to map the contours of impersonality as a process of attaining what might be called a 'late' subjectivity. One of the seminal essays in debates about impersonality in the early twentieth century was T. S. Eliot's 'Tradition and the Individual Talent', published over two issues of *The Egoist* in 1919. The article was in many ways a response to the same kind of frustration voiced by Gray and his musical colleagues with the difficulties in critically assessing new works that engage in a high degree of stylistic or formal experimentation, and the sense that the appetite of audiences for novelty and controversy had skewed the basis on which the very possibility of new art rested. Eliot certainly believed, like Gray, that any work that was not vivid and new was not a work of art at all. Yet at the same time new art must proceed from a consciousness of an 'ideal' that is embodied and constituted by the great works of the past – a concept for which he uses the term 'tradition':

The necessity that [the poet] shall conform, that he shall cohere, is not one-sided; what happens when a new work of art is created is something that happens

---

[23] See Colin Milton, *Lawrence and Nietzsche: a Study in Influence* (Aberdeen: University of Aberdeen Press, 1987), who argued that the convergence between Lawrence and Nietzsche's systems of thought is too close to be the result merely of an overarching intellectual climate. It is worth noting though that elements of Lawrence's thought (as well as Heseltine's) have also been attributed to the influence of Otto Weininger (see Emile Delavenay, 'Lawrence, Otto Weininger and "Rather Raw Philosophy"', in *D. H. Lawrence: New Studies*, ed. by Christopher Heywood (London: Macmillan, 1987), 137–57). Delavenay sees particular hallmarks of Weininger in Lawrence's 1914 'Study of Thomas Hardy', in which Lawrence develops his striking imagery of the poppy, as we shall see below.

[24] For more on the reception of Nietzsche in Britain see David Thatcher, *Nietzsche in England 1890–1914: the Growth of a Reputation* (Toronto and Buffalo: University of Toronto Press, 1970); and Patrick Bridgwater, *Nietzsche in Anglosaxony: A Study of Nietzsche's Impact on English and American Literature* (Leicester: Leicester University Press, 1972).

simultaneously to all the works of art which preceded it. The existing monuments form an ideal order among themselves, which is modified by the introduction of the new (the really new) work of art among them.[25]

The shaping influence that new works have on the 'ideal' of art – an ideal that has no past or future but is eternally present, in this account – means that the artist of today bears a great deal of responsibility. Accordingly, Eliot gives a list of directives appropriate to the artist's weighty task: artists must cultivate their 'historical consciousness'; be aware of the 'main current'; be alive to the fact that 'art never improves, but that the material of art is never quite the same'; and be aware of the 'mind of Europe' more than of their own individual mind. Eliot's notion of the 'mind of Europe' was akin to his concept of 'tradition' in that it retains its eternal shape and its cumulative form while also being slightly modified by ongoing shifts – the 'mind which changes, and that this change is a development which abandons nothing *en route*, which does not superannuate either Shakespeare or Homer or the rock drawing of the Magdalenian draughtsmen'.[26]

So we see here that Eliot's notion of 'tradition' contains both an *historical* element (namely the idea that the past, present and future are mutually constitutive); as well as an *aesthetic* element (namely the idea that 'great art' – which is 'new' in the eternal sense – conforms with a cumulative ideal of 'great art'); and a *personal* element (namely the idea that the artist must cultivate their 'consciousness' or 'awareness' of the tradition of art and its past and current manifestations).

Crucially, this process of personal cultivation, according to Eliot, could be achieved through practices of what he called 'depersonalisation', which in turn left the artwork with the desired attribute of 'impersonality'. The high value placed on such artworks was rationalized via a critical tradition that was to become highly influential – a critical tradition in which it was considered legitimate and desirable to examine the text or work apart from the personality of its creator. And, of course, the legacy of this tradition and its underlying assumptions about aesthetic autonomy can still be felt in the analytical practices of both literary studies and musicology today.

There is a clear irony in this process of de-subjectification, in that a concern for personality or its negation seems contrary to the values of aesthetic autonomy that it seeks to attain. Adorno's discussion of lateness in Beethoven is a case in point, with the formal stylistic attributes of lateness

---

[25] T. S. Eliot, 'Tradition and the Individual Talent' *The Egoist* 6.4 (1919): 54–5, 55.
[26] T. S. Eliot, 'Tradition and the Individual Talent', 6.4 (1919): 55.

being determined by the extent to which a work exhibits a detachment from the biographical experiences of its author – a detachment that he believed to be most attainable in later life. Indeed as Andrew Goldstone has noted, there is a 'recurrent pairing of lateness and impersonal aesthetics' that is in many ways paradoxical, resting the impersonality of the autonomous artwork on the level of personal discipline and professionalism of the artist, and thereby refocusing the notion of aesthetic autonomy on the '*process of autonomization*', or a particular form of self-cultivation.[27] As a form of cultivated distance from personality then, 'lateness' in the sense experienced by musical and literary figures within the milieu under investigation is not a chronological or biological category related to aging, but an ethos that is imbricated in both personal and artistic 'style' – with 'style' indicating not only musical or literary style, but also disposition, attitude and posture, as I noted earlier.[28]

In drawing this explicit link between tradition and impersonality – the latter being cultivated in order to achieve conformity with the former – Eliot created a powerful articulation of the intimate interconnection between the question of an artwork's relationship with its past and the question of an artist's relationship with the work. The emergence of impersonality as a doctrine of both artistic creation and criticism was shaped by historical conditions that impacted the thinking of our collection of musical figures as much as it did writers such as Eliot. Even in one of Heseltine and Gray's first collaborative ventures in 1916, when the former was twenty-two years old and just after his period living with the Lawrences, we see him already showing an emerging interest in the idea of de-subjectification as a direct expression of his attitude towards time. Heseltine wrote to Eugene Goossens about his and Gray's idea to produce an opera season at a theatre in the West End in terms that give something of an idiosyncratic sense of his early engagement with the stylistic implications of impersonality:

I am very busy with initial preparations for our opera season in the spring. It will take place in a very small theatre, and the main points about all the production will be: *Effective Simplicity – Absence of Realism. Symbolism rather than Representation – Subtlety and Intimacy* – the last two of which can only be obtained in a small theatre. A work like Delius's 'Village Romeo and Juliet', mounted realistically, falls utterly flat

---

[27] Andrew Goldstone, *Fictions of Autonomy: Modernism from Wilde to de Man* (Oxford and New York: Oxford University Press, 2013), 70–73 and 79–80. See also his references to other work that acknowledges this paradox, in fn. 11, at 73.

[28] See also Rebecca L. Walkowitz's description of style in *Cosmopolitan Style: Modernism Beyond the Nation* (New York: Columbia University Press, 2006), 2.

because, in the realistic stagy sense, there is no action: it is all psychological – all the action takes place in the hearts of the characters – Moreover the work is essentially symbolic rather than actual – I mean that it is more universal than the mere story it sets forth – So that it is not a mere talk of a *certain* pair of lovers whose love was thwarted by *particular* circumstances, but rather an expression of the emotions of *all* blighted lovers, an epitome, a quintessence – all great art is this, of course, to a certain extent, but in this work I am convinced that the actual characters *must* be made shadowy and unreal in order that they may be free to be pure emotional symbols – In a large theatre this is impossible. [...] Everything will be very simple as regards staging and lighting: plain curtain backgrounds for the most part, with a painted backcloth and painted screens (for trees, etc.) where necessary. No footlights or lights on or above the stage – all from behind, as in a Cinema – This can be immensely effective – No 'stars' but everyone efficient in an unostentatious way – *No vibrato singers!* You *must* help us – there are many more points (such as the robing of the orchestra in black Cassocks with hoods, by which a very disturbing illusion-spoiling element will be eliminated) but these must wait for explanation till we meet.[29]

Importantly, these stylistic features were twinned with a particular conception of time that shaped the overarching plan for the concert season. As Heseltine went on to explain in his letter to Goossens, the project was to include the performance of works by composers such as Monteverdi, Purcell, Pergolesi, Gluck, Mozart, Mussorgsky, Delius, Debussy and Ravel; 'ancient' pieces – old English string pieces from British Museum part books, orchestral works by Scarlatti, Lully, Rameau, Purcell, Vitali, Nardini and Bach; virginal music by Byrd, Giles Farnaby and Tisdall; early choral works by Dufay and Dunstable; madrigals English and Italian, including by Gesualdo;[30] and 'modern' works – including Ladmirault, Inghelbrecht, Stravinsky, Maurice Delage, Grainger and Goossens. 'Observe', Heseltine wrote after listing this indicative list of repertoire, 'ancient and modern: no intermediaries!'

Vividness, and its Implications

Impersonality has been viewed as a position of reaction against the subjective forms of expression that were valorized by Romantic and late-Victorian

---

[29] Philip Heseltine, letter to Eugene Goossens, 12 Sept. 1916, *GB-Lbl*, Add MS 57794. Original emphasis.

[30] Lawrence was later to read and translate the fiction of Giovanni Verga while travelling in Sicily and then on the ship for Ceylon in 1922, including the work *Mastro-Don Gesualdo*. Heseltine, Lawrence and Gray's shared interest in Gesualdo may in fact be a reflection of their shared preoccupation with impersonality (see Bell, 'Lawrence and Modernism', 229).

artists – forms of expression that no longer seemed desirable or even viable in the wake of wartime atrocities. However, the notion of impersonality has been construed by some as being politically reactionary, with scholars such John Harrison seeking to group together Yeats, Wyndham Lewis, Pound, T. S. Eliot and D. H. Lawrence into what he termed the 'anti-democratic intelligentsia'. Attributing to these figures a 'pragmatic support for fascism',[31] Harrison argued that their work was underwritten by a sense that democratic governance was a weakly non-interventionist form of political rule, seeking only to preserve freedom and not adequately protecting other types of value that were essential for human development. To these figures, according to Harrison, democracy was flawed in that it was open to manipulation, open to market whims, or sluggish and indecisive, which was especially pertinent in the context of the 1920s, with economic recession and then the failure of revolutionary action in the form of the General Strike of 1926.[32]

Impersonality – or indeed the related doctrine of aesthetic autonomy itself – was by no means necessarily politically motivated,[33] yet the reactionary tendencies that accompanied it were certainly antipathetic towards a certain set of values, as Baldick has also noted:

An apparently inconsequential preference for the work of certain seventeenth-century poets over most of the major nineteenth-century poets in fact dragged along behind it an extensive conservative condemnation of Western liberalism, Protestantism, Romanticism, democratic humanitarianism, individualism and their various conceptions of progress.[34]

These tendencies also often indicated a degree of sympathy towards the validity of natural hierarchy. For Lawrence, the working classes were not fit for self-rule because their imbrication in the system of labour and industry led them to valorize exchange value above all else.[35] By contrast, it was an ability to attain 'vividness' or 'hotness and brightness', that was the determining factor for Lawrence, and this libidinal charge could only be attained by some

---

[31] Harrison, *The Reactionaries*, 194.
[32] There will be further discussion of the link between anti-democratic politics and the ethos of lateness in the following chapter.
[33] This point is discussed by Goldstone in *Fictions of Autonomy*, 107.
[34] Baldick, *Criticism and Literary Theory 1890*, 65.
[35] 'It seems a strange thing that men, the mass of men, cannot understand that *life* is the great reality, that true living fills with vivid life […] They think that property and money are the same thing as vivid life. Only the few, the potential heroes or the "elect", can see the simple distinction' (D. H. Lawrence, *Selected Literary Criticism*, 312–13, qtd. in Harrison, *The Reactionaries*, 179).

and not others, and in relative degrees.[36] The implications of Lawrence's views in this respect led Gray to make the hyperbolic claim that Lawrence could have become a 'British Hitler',[37] and also prompted Bertrand Russell to claim that Lawrence's theory of 'blood consciousness' – which Lawrence conveyed to Russell in a letter written only a month after the former's first meeting with Philip Heseltine – had 'led straight to Auschwitz'.[38]

For Lawrence, the vividness of a person or an artwork was determined by its level of individuality or distinctness, its degree of difference from its surrounding community, or its ability to hold separate from the system of 'self-preservation' that he felt characterized the unthinking majority. To be vivid in this sense was to be an aristocrat. For Lawrence, aristocrats were heroic in that they could attain Being through cultivating individuality and distinction where others were mired in the form of consciousness associated with the industrial system. Aristocrats were supposedly not 'bound by conventional morality' and they were ideally detached, yet they suffered dissatisfaction for their detachment in a manner which aligns with the ethos of lateness. Lawrence viewed this dissatisfaction as leading to a necessary 'tiredness' – a 'touch of exhaustion' – to a true aristocrat.

With the men as with the women of old descent: they have nothing to do with mankind in general, they are exceedingly personal. For many generations they have been accustomed to regard their own desires as their own supreme laws. They have not been bound by the conventional morality: this they have transcended, being a code unto themselves. The other person has been always present to their

---

[36] 'Life is more vivid in the dandelion than in the green fern, or than in a palm tree/Life is more vivid in a snake than in a butterfly/Life is more vivid in a wren than in an alligator/Life is more vivid in a cat than in an ostrich' (D. H. Lawrence, 'Reflections on the Death of A Porcupine', in *Reflections on the Death of a Porcupine and Other Essays*, ed. by Michael Herbert (Cambridge: Cambridge University Press, 1988) 347–64, 357). Of this sentiment Daniel Albright has noted that 'Lawrence has in this way adapted his electrical concept of the body to show what happens when the self is destroyed: it is equivalent to a battery running completely down to a condition in which there is no voltage differential, no polarity, no internal distinctions, only pulpy confusion' (Daniel Albright, *Personality and Impersonality: Lawrence, Woolf and Mann* (Chicago: University of Chicago Press, 1978), 27–8).

[37] Cecil Gray, *Musical Chairs: or Between Two Stools* (London: Home & Van Thal, 1948; reprt. London: Hogarth Press, 1985), 131.

[38] Bertrand Russell, *Portraits from Memory and other Essays* (1956), 107, cited in John Beer, 'Lawrence's Counter-Romanticism', in *The Spirit of D. H. Lawrence*, ed. by Gāmini Salgādo and G. K. Das (Hampshire and London: Macmillan, 1988), 46–74, 61. Beer argued against this interpretation, though, tracing Lawrence's idea to 'a vision of independent growth in individual and free communication between them, grounded in the inward life of nature and criticizing those forces of industry and war which followed a mechanical and inhuman logic of their own', rather than to the militarism of German references to 'blood consciousness' (61).

imagination, in the spectacular sense. He has always existed to them. But he has always existed as something other than themselves.

Hence the inevitable isolation, detachment of the aristocrat. His one aim, during centuries, has been to keep himself detached. At last he finds himself, by his very nature, cut off [...] It may be, also, that in the aristocrat a certain weariness makes him purposeless, vicious, like a form of death. But that is not necessary.[39]

This intersection between notions of detachment, intensity and lateness had its roots in an English Romantic tradition that rejected sentimentalism – in 'Blake's visual imagery of flames and serpents' and 'Wordsworth's Prelude, with its moments of high insight following upon unusually intense fits of energy'[40] – but it was also indebted to late-Victorian aestheticism, and as much as both Lawrence and Heseltine attempted to distance themselves from this earlier tradition, their thinking about vividness was clearly related in some way to Walter Pater's influential provocation to 'burn always with this hard, gem-like flame, to maintain this ecstasy'.[41] Indeed Gray gave voice to a similar constellation of ideas in an extraordinary passage about Bartók in his autobiography:

Bartók, in short, was completely inhuman. He hardly existed as a personality, but his impersonality was tremendous – he was the living incarnation and embodiment of the spirit of music. He was pure spirit, in fact, and his frail, intense and delicate physique gave the impression of something ethereal and disembodied, like a flame burning in oxygen. No need to inquire, no need to know, the cause of his death: he consumed himself, burnt himself entirely away in the fire of his genius and of his selfless devotion to his art.[42]

Even for Eliot, impersonality was not a denial of or escape from emotion, or a paean to an austere, ironical or clinical form of art, but rather a call for

---

[39] D. H. Lawrence, 'Study of Thomas Hardy', in *Study of Thomas Hardy and Other Essays*, ed. by Bruce Steele (Cambridge: Cambridge University Press, 1985), 99–100. Lawrence's ideal community of Rananim was indeed intended as a community of 'new aristocrats': 'It is Communism based, not on poverty but on riches, not on humility but on pride, not on sacrifice but upon complete fulfillment in the flesh of all strong desire, not in Heaven but on earth. We will be Sons of God who walk here on earth, not bent on getting and having, because we know we inherit all things. We will be aristocrats, and as wise as the serpent in dealing with the mob. For the mob shall not crush us nor starve us nor cry us to death. We will deal cunningly with the mob, the greedy soul, we will gradually bring it to subjection. We will found an order, and we will all be Princes, as the angels are' (D. H. Lawrence, *Collected Letters*, 311–12, qtd. in Delavenay, *D. H. Lawrence: the Man and his Work*, 259).

[40] Beer, 'Lawrence's Counter-Romanticism', 64.

[41] Walter Pater, *The Renaissance: Studies in Art and Poetry* (1873; Berkeley: University of California Press, 1980), 188–9.

[42] Gray, *Musical Chairs*, 181.

a separation between the artist's emotions and the artwork, the latter being more rightly an intensified concentration of experiences, rather than the result of deliberate reflection upon how to render certain emotions in art. In other words, impersonality was not a quality of works of art, so much as a practice of artists who sought to create great works: 'it is not the "greatness", the intensity, of the emotions, the components, but the intensity of the artistic process, the pressure, so to speak, under which the fusion takes place that counts'.[43] Reading impersonality as a practice of vividness or as an epistemic virtue in this way made it directly relevant to the practice of criticism, linking it with the development of New Criticism and close reading. The close reader was charged with the authority of determining whether an artwork had indeed been created with the requisite intensity, or whether it exhibited spontaneous life or captured the flaming transience of immediate experience. Impersonality, therefore, had an intimate link with ideas about the vividness of being contemporaneous – of being present and immediate. Yet as we will see, this attribution of intensity and immediacy should not be equated with a desire for timeliness; rather it was a concern for *simultaneity of time* – of past, present and future viewed as one which found expression in a turn towards a spacialized conception of time.

Michael Bell has described the modernist preoccupation with time as 'inseparable' from the preoccupation with the self, especially in the work of writers such as Joyce, Proust and Woolf.[44] In the case of Lawrence, Bell discerned a more subtle time consciousness that emerges as a concern with the 'pure present' – 'One great mystery of time is *terra incognita* to us: the instant. The most superb mystery we have hardly recognized: the immediate instant self'.[45] Yet Bell does not tease out the significant implications of this connection for Lawrence, instead describing how Lawrence was more concerned with impersonality as a feature of the emotional lives of the characters in his novels than as a technique for the artist in the creation of an artwork, as was Eliot's meaning.[46] For Lawrence's characters, the moment of impersonal awareness – the 'non-moral awareness of a "beyond self"' which provides the ultimate imperative for all life decisions'[47] – had

[43] T. S. Eliot, 'Tradition and the Individual Talent: II' *The Egoist* 6.5 (1919): 72–3, 72.
[44] Bell, 'Lawrence and Modernism', 183.
[45] D. H. Lawrence, 'Introduction' to American Edition of *New Poems* in *Phoenix: The Posthumous Papers of D. H. Lawrence*, ed. by Edward D. McDonald (London: Heinemann, 1936), 222, qtd. in Bell, 'Lawrence and Modernism', 183.
[46] See also Bell's book *D. H. Lawrence: Language and Being* (Cambridge: Cambridge University Press, 1992).
[47] Bell, 'Lawrence and Modernism', 186.

an emancipatory or transformative function, allowing those characters to apprehend a broader non-teleological design beyond immediate moral consciousness.[48] On other occasions, however, the practice of impersonality led to a sense of spectatorship and an absence of vividness. This certainly became tragically true of Heseltine, yet it was also true of Lawrence. Gray later commented, perceptively as ever, that

The truth is that Lawrence was always inclined to treat his friends and acquaintances as if they were characters in one of his books, and sought accordingly to mould their characters and direct their actions as he desired. When he failed in this – and he invariable did fail – he took his revenge by putting the said friends and acquaintances recognizably into his books, and there worked his will upon them. In this respect Lawrence's life and his art were curiously intermingled; but whereas he was wont to claim that his art was a kind of overflow from his life; it was, in fact, the precise contrary, a substitute for life: to such an extent, indeed, that it is exceedingly probable that he would never have felt the urge to write his novels – the later ones at least – if he had been able to have his way with living personality. Practically all his novels are essentially a form of wish-fulfillment, an imaginary gratification of his desires. Throughout all the later ones he himself stalks, thinly disguised as the hero, surrounded by malevolent caricatures of those who, for some reason or other, had failed to respond completely or to submit themselves tirelessly to his will in actual life.[49]

Gray was not alone in viewing the autobiographical quality of Lawrence's works as a betrayal of the author's own ontological mandate to attain vivid Being.[50] Indeed it might be said that Lawrence's own pursuit of vividness led him to universalize his personal forms of experience, and thereby to live at one step removed from the present.

The tendency of the practices associated with impersonality and vividness to result in a disabling form of spectatorship and detachment was keenly felt by Heseltine, as we shall see below. Even as early as 1913, he was writing to Delius that

I have often felt myself to be a mere spectator of the game of Life: this, I know to my sorrow, has led me to a positively morbid self-consciousness and an introspectiveness

---

[48] For more on this type of practice see Amanda Anderson, *The Powers of Distance: Cosmopolitanism and the Cultivation of Detachment* (Princeton: Princeton University Press, 2001), but note that George Eliot's practices served an overtly moralistic purpose.

[49] Cecil Gray, *Peter Warlock: A Memoir of Philip Heseltine* (London: Jonathan Cape, 1935), 119–20.

[50] Daniel Albright gave a lucid diagnosis of this tendency in *Personality and Impersonality: Lawrence, Woolf and Mann.*

that almost amounts to insincerity, breeding as it does a kind of detachment from real life [...] Lately I have tried passionately to plunge into Life, and live myself, forgetfully.[51]

Heseltine's yearning to live forgetfully – burning and vivid in the present – which drew him initially into Lawrence's remit, was a personal expression that found resonance in Nietzsche's notion of eternal recurrence and its broader rejection of Christian morality and the belief in the possibility of an afterlife. The thought experiment that was involved in the idea of eternal recurrence, or repetition, aimed at just this outcome in fact, directing our attention away from past-oriented remorse or future-oriented desire, towards the presentness of our life as we live it. Bell has viewed this tendency as a 'mirror image' of 'Goethean acceptance' and therefore as transforming and in some ways continuing the tradition of lateness with which Goethe has become associated.[52] Lawrence's interaction with this tradition and its temporal implications can be traced in the development between *The Rainbow* (1915) and *Women in Love* (1920), as a 'transmutation of historical to spatial form', with the spatialization of temporality in the latter novel reflecting a type of superhistoricism – a resistance to assuming a correlation with the spirit of the time.[53]

Heseltine and Lawrence Meet

Heseltine was introduced to Lawrence's work by his close friend at Oxford, the poet Robert Nichols. The first evidence of Heseltine encountering Lawrence's work appears in a letter to Viva Smith on 27 February 1914 (written while he was still at Oxford), in which he makes it clear that he was most forcibly struck by Lawrence's use of language, more so than the emotion, content or form of the works. It was the words themselves and the author's turn of phrase (subsequently described as his 'allotropic style' – which had ontological implications) that excited Heseltine's initial interest.[54] This point is significant in the context of our discussion, because

---

[51] Philip Heseltine, letter to Frederick Delius, 17 Feb. 1913, qtd. in Barry Smith, *Peter Warlock: The Life of Philip Heseltine* (Oxford and New York: Oxford University Press, 1994), 41.

[52] Bell, 'Perceptions of Lateness', 138.

[53] Bell, 'Perceptions of Lateness', 138. Bell discusses this transformation further in his book *D. H. Lawrence: Language and Being*, 51–132.

[54] See Garrett Stewart, 'Lawrence, "Being", and the Allotropic Style', *Novel* 9.3 (Spring 1976): 217–42, which noted that critics for a long time did not pay attention to Lawrence's special use of language.

the life-force or the belief in cultivating an intensity of living that drew the men together after subsequent conversations was something that Heseltine clearly felt was visible on the surface of Lawrence's writing from the outset, bringing together literary 'style' and a particular 'style' of living. Heseltine wrote to Nichols of Lawrence's novel *Sons and Lovers* (1913), 'I know of no modern prose style so perfect as Lawrence's. Every word is weighed, and its precise effect calculated to the minutest nicety. Every adjective hits the mark exactly: it is almost uncanny'.[55] And to Viva Smith, of that same novel again, he wrote, 'the style is most uncannily sure: every word rings true, every adjective, every phrase is so startlingly apt and precise'.[56] And to Delius similarly he wrote, on 18 October 1914, that 'I have just read all the novels of D. H. Lawrence – three in number. They are to my mind simply unrivalled, in depth of insight and beauty of language, by another contemporary writer. Shall I send you one?'[57]

Heseltine withdrew from Oxford after only a brief period of study in order to pursue other interests in London, including music criticism – a move that his mother reluctantly supported owing to the outbreak of war and the reduced allowance that her son would require in the capital. Although Heseltine had very little formal training in music beyond boyhood,[58] his literary skill and perceptive mind, together with his obsessive valorization of Delius, had brought him to the attention of the conductor Thomas Beecham (who was Delius's primary champion in England), who contrived to secure Heseltine a post as music critic at a daily paper in London. The appointment did not last long though, as Heseltine felt unduly restricted by his editor, and he subsequently spent many of his days in the British Museum studying and editing early music manuscripts.

Heseltine had a personal interest in this idea of vividness, related both to a way of living or being, and to artworks. In the months before he first met Lawrence, for example, he spent some time in Gloucestershire in order to temporarily escape the tension of wartime London, yet he found himself unable to shake the feeling of living only faded reflections of past experiences, or living 'perpetually behind a veil':

---

[55] Qtd. in Copley, *A Turbulent Friendship*, 4, and in Gray, *Peter Warlock: A Memoir of Philip Heseltine*, 98.

[56] Qtd. in Copley, *A Turbulent Friendship*, 4.

[57] Qtd. in Gray, *Peter Warlock: A Memoir of Philip Heseltine*, 98.

[58] Indeed, he resolutely avoided entering study at the RCM or RAM, which Balfour Gardiner had apparently advised him were 'so effete and antiquated that it is merely a waste of time to study there' (Philip Heseltine, letter to Frederick Delius, 18 Oct. 1914, qtd. in Gray, *Peter Warlock: A Memoir of Philip Heseltine*, 96).

My mind at the present moment is fitly comparable to the blurred humming of the distant peal of bells, whose slow, monotonous droning seems to blend with the grey, listless sky and the still trees and the far-off, shadow-like hills, in an atmosphere of intolerable dejection and lifelessness […] My head feels as though it were filled with a smoky vapor or a poisonous gas which kills all the finer impressions before they can penetrate to me, and stifles every thought, every idea, before it is born […] I watch the sun go down behind the hills, flooding the broad valley with a glory of golden light that would in former days have made my whole being vibrate with its beauty – but I wait in vain for the old, ecstatic feeling. The colour and intensity of these pictures have become things external to me – they are no longer reflected in me, I can no longer merge myself in the *Stimmung* of nature around me, I can only gaze wistfully, from afar, at her beauteous pageantry. I can no longer take part in it, and so I am debarred from the greatest – perhaps the only – source of joy, solace, and inspiration that life offers me.[59]

Lawrence's appeal to Heseltine in this state would become even clearer when he met Lawrence personally in the coming months, and also as he became involved in the plans for Lawrence's ideal community of Rananim.[60] This was Heseltine's opportunity, or so he thought, to once again find inspiration and clarity by living 'forgetfully' in a community of artistic souls removed from the restless tension of wartime Britain.

It was during this time that Heseltine contrived to meet Lawrence through a mutual acquaintance,[61] and this first meeting occurred at a dinner party

---

[59] Philip Heseltine, letter to Frederick Delius, 22 Aug. 1915, qtd. in Gray, *Peter Warlock: A Memoir of Philip Heseltine*, 100–101. Though Gray tempers this melancholic impression of Heseltine's time in Gloucestershire with other accounts, including the well-known anecdote about Heseltine riding naked on a motorcycle through village streets in the middle of the night at top speed (103).

[60] The idea for a utopian community by this name is thought to have consolidated in Lawrence's mind during a Christmas party in 1914, an event which was also attended by Katherine Mansfield and John Middleton Murry, Gordon and Beatrice Campbell, Mark Gertler and Koteliansky. Lawrence wrote to Kotel. on 3 January 1915 about his idea for the name Rananim, see George J. Zytaruk, 'Rananim: D. H. Lawrence's Failed Utopia', in *The Spirit of D. H. Lawrence*, ed. by Gāmini Salgādo and G. K. Das (London: Macmillan, 1988), 271. He later also approached E. M. Forster and perhaps also Bertrand Russell and Lady Ottoline Morrell to be involved in the community (274). Lawrence went so far as to design a flag and write a constitution for Rananim. The community was initially conceived as a project of social regeneration in England, but later he turned his sights to America, and attempted to enlist a new younger set of adherents, including Heseltine, Robert Nichols and Aldous Huxley. These plans were thwarted not only by Delius's refusal to agree to the use of his Florida orange plantation as a venue, but also by the War and the limitations on international movement.

[61] Copley points out that 'in Nichols's account of the meeting contributed to Cecil Gray's biography he implies that it was Heseltine who, in the autumn of 1915, brought Lawrence to see him' (Copley, *A Turbulent Friendship*, 83). Kinkead-Weekes gives a different account, writing that 'it is unclear how he came to meet Lawrence now, but it was probably through

on 15 November 1915. The next day Lawrence wrote a letter to Heseltine that gives a sense of the tone and content of their first conversation:

I hope you didn't mind the holding forth of last night. But do think about what we were saying of art and life [...] It is so important that now, the great reducing, analytic, introspective process, which has gone on pure and interrupted since the Renaissance – at least since Milton – should now give way to a constructive, synthetic, metaphysical process. Because now, reduction, introspection, has reached the point when it has practically no more to reveal to us and can only produce sensationalism. One must fight every minute, at least I must, to overcome this great flux of disintegration, further analysis, self analysis. If it continues, this flux, then our phase, our era, passes swiftly into oblivion [...] In physical life, it is homosexuality, the reduction process. When men and women come together in love, that is the great immediate synthesis. When men come together, that is immediate reduction: these complex states, the finest product of generations of synthetic living, are reduced in homosexual love, liberating a conscious knowledge of the component parts [...] And it is necessary to overcome the great stream of disintegration, the flux of reduction, like a man swimming against the stream. Otherwise there is nothing but despair [...] This is why I am going to Florida. Here the whole Flux is deathly. One must climb out on to a firm shore [...] and I believe that music too must become now synthetic, metaphysical, giving a musical utterance to the sense of the Whole. But perhaps I don't know enough about it.[62]

Only a few days after their first meeting, Lawrence received the suppression order from the Courts about his novel *The Rainbow*,[63] with the Magistrate Sir John Dickinson ordering the destruction of all copies of the book that had been confiscated by police from the publishers Methuen.[64] Although there were a number of notable authors and playwrights who indicated that they would speak out on behalf of the novel and protest against its suppression, apart from a few minor voices of protest 'not a single well-known writer [who] stood up for *The Rainbow*' or for Lawrence, except Arnold Bennett.[65]

---

writing to denounce the suppression of what he assured Delius was a "a perfectly magnificent book" [...]As it happened, the 22-year-old Nichols was then in the Lord Knutsford Hospital for Officers, suffering from what was not yet recognized as shell-shock. He too must have written to Lawrence who visited him there' (Kinkead-Weekes, *D. H. Lawrence: Triumph to Exile, 1912–1922*, 288). Nichols also only spent a year at Oxford, in Trinity College, before volunteering for military service.

[62] This letter is reproduced in Nigel Heseltine, *Capriol for Mother: a Memoir of Philip Heseltine* (London: Thames, 1992), 101–4.

[63] Mark Kinkead-Weekes reports the date as 16 November (Mark Kinkead-Weekes, *D. H. Lawrence: Triumph to Exile, 1912–1922*, 288.

[64] Kinkead-Weekes, *D. H. Lawrence: Triumph to Exile, 1912–1922*, 282. The book was not available again in England for another eleven years (282).

[65] Kinkead-Weekes, *D. H. Lawrence: Triumph to Exile, 1912–1922*, 285.

This event ingrained in Lawrence a sense of being dispossessed by his native country, and led to his decision to leave London for New York immediately (the date was set at 24 November) to begin a new life and cultivate a new audience.

Lawrence was resolute, if pained, in his plans to leave England at this time – commenting to his literary agent Pinker when the police raided Methuen, 'it is the end of my writing for England'[66] – yet there were several circumstances that held the plans at bay over the coming months. First, there was the possibility that the Committee of the Author's Society would consider Lawrence's case on his behalf based on the fact that he was not given the right to defend himself in the proceedings (which was likely a decision taken by Methuen), and the possibility that the Lady Ottoline's husband Philip Morrell, who was a Liberal MP, would raise the issue with the Home Secretary.[67] While Lawrence waited for these possibilities to play themselves out, he also began to receive some supportive letters responding to the trial, but another decisive factor was his discovery of the admiration of a collection of younger readers, such as Heseltine and Nichols, who were both at the time in their early twenties.[68]

With this injection of energy and the possibility of these new young adherents, Lawrence delayed his plans to depart. Lawrence's vision of Rananim was evidently one of the topics of his first conversation with Heseltine, because the very next day, Heseltine wrote a letter to Delius asking whether Lawrence could live in the house on the property in Florida that Delius once inhabited in his failed attempt at managing an orange plantation. Unsurprisingly, Delius put Heseltine off, saying that the property was not in a habitable state: 'I should have loved to be of use to Lawrence, whose work I admire, but to let him go to Florida would be sending him to disaster.'[69] Heseltine persisted, and in a further letter he described what

---

[66] Qtd. in Kinkead-Weekes, *D. H. Lawrence: Triumph to Exile, 1912–1922*, 282.

[67] He did so during question time on 18 November, and then again via a written question to the Home Secretary (Kinkead-Weekes, *D. H. Lawrence: Triumph to Exile, 1912–1922*, 286–7).

[68] Kinkead-Weekes argued, for example, that 'with such ardent young adherents, Lawrence rapidly recovered a faith in the future that he could never quite lose. He wanted very much to believe that there was a life-force in people which his words could liberate; and though his elders and most contemporaries had proved too hardened in "corruption" to listen, and had felt so threatened by his work that they had banded together to destroy it, here seemed proof that Rananim was still possible with a younger group. Immediately the dream revived' (288–9). Possible members of the new colony included Heseltine and his Oxford acquaintance the 'Muslim Indian Shahid Hasan Suhrawardy' and perhaps also Dikran Kouyoumdjian (Michael Arlen), and Boris de Croustchoff, a Russian bibliophile and anthropologist (who later married Phyl Crocker).

[69] Frederick Delius, letter to Philip Heseltine, 24 Nov. 1915, qtd. in Copley, *A Turbulent Friendship*, 6.

the purpose of the colony would be – 'to have at least a year or two of *real life*', with a group who wanted to 'detach themselves from harassing surroundings and endeavor for a while to till the soil of their natures in a congenial atmosphere'.[70]

The immediate pre-history to the initial encounter between Heseltine and Lawrence is important, because Lawrence's suppression order came during a period of personal uncertainty, displacement and illness during the first years of the Great War, providing the bitter catalyst for the development of his 'philosophy'. Lawrence had begun sketching his philosophy in early 1913 in the personal 'Foreword' to his novel *Sons and Lovers*, which was not initially intended for publication.[71] He then spent nine months at Fiascherino in Italy with his lover Frieda Weekley, arriving back in England on 24 June 1914 with a full version of his novel *The Rainbow*, which he had promised to the publisher Methuen. Lawrence and Frieda were to marry on 13 July that year. A few weeks before this, Lawrence had been contacted by another publisher, James Nisbet and Co., with the idea of writing a study of Thomas Hardy. Lawrence began making preparations for the study, but very shortly afterwards Britain declared war. Lawrence was therefore unable to travel, either to Ireland or to Italy where he had intended to return, and he and Frieda were forced to ask friends for housing. Lawrence's feeling of precariousness was aggravated by his persistent illness.

The declaration of war also meant that Methuen returned Lawrence's book manuscript because they were postponing publications, making his financial situation all the more tenuous.[72] It was in this situation – financially insecure, without fixed accommodation, trapped in England and feeling greatly aggrieved by the senselessness of the War in all respects – that Lawrence pursued his work on the study of Thomas Hardy. It is unsurprising then that this study became less about the works of Thomas Hardy, and more about what he called 'the Confessions of my Heart'.[73] Lawrence spent the rest of 1914 completing this 'philosophicalish' manuscript, as he put it, and re-writing sections of *The Rainbow*.

---

[70] Philip Heseltine, letter to Frederick Delius, 15 Dec. 1915, qtd. in Copley, *A Turbulent Friendship*, 6, and in Gray, *Peter Warlock: A Memoir of Philip Heseltine*, 107. Emphasis added.

[71] Bruce Steele, 'Introduction', in *Study of Thomas Hardy and Other Essays*, xxiv.

[72] Some scholars have speculated that the manuscript was returned on the basis of obscenity, but others point out that most publishers returned manuscripts when the war was declared (see Steele, 'Introduction', in *Study of Thomas Hardy and Other Essays*, xxi, fn. 10).

[73] D. H. Lawrence, *Letters*, Vol. 2, 235, qtd. in Steele, 'Introduction', in *Study of Thomas Hardy and Other Essays*, xxiii.

The tenor of the philosophy contained in Lawrence's 'Study of Thomas Hardy' is reflected in his decision to change the title of the work to 'Le Gai Savaire', which was Lawrence's modified French for 'The Gay Science' or 'Skill'. Steele notes that the term was 'invented by the medieval troubadour poets for their poetic craft' and speculates that 'while [Lawrence] may have heard it from Ezra Pound […] the use of it as a title seems more likely to have come through Nietzsche's title *Die fröhliche Wissenschaft* (1882–7)'. The term is also used in Nietzsche's *Beyond Good and Evil*, and Lawrence is thought to have read Oscar Levy's English translation of this work (1909) during his time at Croydon. Steele also speculates that Lawrence may have also read Oscar Levy's 1888 translation of *The Case of Wagner*, where the term is further defined.[74] Heseltine was no doubt drawn to the Nietzschean quality of Lawrence's thinking during this time, given his ongoing correspondence with Delius at just the moment of his acquaintance with Lawrence, and consequent inurement in Delius's own brand of Nietzscheanism. Yet I would argue that it was not merely an 'atmospheric Nietzsche' that brought together Heseltine's obsession with Delius and his feeling of creative impotence with Lawrence's ideas about vividness. Rather, this intersection was supported by a specific understanding of vividness – Lawrence's own 'gay science' – as requiring a form of untimeliness.

The Spirit of Delius, and Lawrence's Poppy

To give a sense of how Heseltine evoked the idea of lateness both in terms of a conception of time and a conception of the self, it will be useful to examine at some length his description of the 'spirit' of Delius's music in his major book on the composer, published after his youthful obsession had cooled quite substantially.[75] Heseltine described the 'spirit' of Delius's music, taken as a whole, in the following terms:

The art of Delius belongs to the evening of a great period. It has its roots upon the descending arc of life; it is cadent but not decadent. Its image is rather to be

---

[74] Steele, 'Introduction', in *Study of Thomas Hardy and Other Essays*, xxiii, fn. 20. See also Explanatory Note 7.2, which mentions that others have incorrectly translated Lawrence's title as the 'Gay Saviour', perhaps with Lawrence's Messianic pretensions in mind. See also Delavenay, *D. H. Lawrence: the Man and his Work*, which notes that when Lawrence moved from Eastwood to Croydon in 1918, he began to explore the Croydon public library and there discovered Whitman and Nietzsche, among others (58).

[75] Peter Warlock [Philip Heseltine], *Frederick Delius* (London: John Lane, The Bodley Head; rev. ed. with annotations by Hubert Foss, Oxford and New York: Oxford University Press, 1952).

seen in the rich colours of the sunset fires than in the cool dim rays of twilight from which all fire and brightness has faded away. But it is neighbour to night: it looks before and after, seeing the day that is past mirrored upon the darkness that is approaching. […]

[…his art is a part of the] brief period immediately preceding the setting-in of decadence and decay in art when the body can yet bear, and bear nobly, the weight of all the magnificence and splendour that the soul would put forth; and it is this golden hour that Delius has realized more fully than any musician that ever lived. […]

[…in his music] The emotion [is] recollected: and the process of recollection, in this sense of the word, is creative rather than reminiscent. For the initial emotion will have called into activity an impulse that had long lain dormant in the soul's recesses, awaiting the word of sacred correspondence which alone could waken it into action, and it is from the union of these two principles, the initial emotion and that unknown correlative which it finds in the creative mind, that the work of art comes into being […]

One feels that all Delius's music is evolved out of the emotions of a past that was never fully realized when it was present, emotions which only become real after they had ceased to be experienced.[76]

The themes that Heseltine is evoking here could not be clearer. Delius's art – which corresponded with Heseltine's conception of the ideal art, at least for a time – had the attributes of 'lateness' in that it was not the apotheosis of a golden age, nor a blazing herald of a new age, nor an expressionist disintegration – Delius's art was on the very crest of decline, occupying a moment of pure intensity just prior to the excess of decadence; a moment 'when the body can yet bear, and bear nobly, the weight of all the magnificence and splendour that the soul would put forth'. It was 'late' in the same sense that Georg Simmel described Leonardo da Vinci's 'Last Supper', in one of the classic formulations of late style – 'as if, at this precise moment before its last glow will finally die out, its full force and inner permanence would yet shine forth resplendent from behind the broken exterior surface'.[77] It was also impersonal in the sense of being always one step removed from intimacy – namely it recollects emotions rather than being overcome by immediate

---

[76] Warlock, *Frederick Delius*, 130–33.

[77] Georg Simmel, 'Leonardo da Vinci's Last Supper' [first published in Georg Simmel, *Zur Philosophie der Kunst: Philosophische und Kunstphilosophische Aufsaetze* (Potsdam, 1922), 55–60], trans. Brigitte Kueppers and Alfred Willis, in *Achademia Leionardi Vinci*, Vol. 10, 1997, 141–4, 143, qtd. in Sam Smiles 'From Titian to Impressionism: the Genealogy of Late Style', in *Late Style and its Discontents*, 15–30, 28. Although Smiles notes that the 'Last Supper' was in fact not a chronologically 'late' work for the artist, and that Simmel was likely relying on Goethe's misinterpretation.

emotion; it acknowledges the simultaneity of past and future as a mirror of each other; and it illuminates the shadow-like nature of experiences.

The rather extraordinary collection of themes, values, historical conceptions and aesthetics that are evoked in this passage about Delius were the product of many years of development in Heseltine's thinking, and were at least partially fuelled by his association with D. H. Lawrence. But more than that, the coincidence of his ideas here with the notion of vividness articulated by Lawrence can tell us something about the broader cultural milieu and the motivations underlying the aesthetic preferences and politics of this milieu.

Lawrence's preoccupation with vividness in the works that he was drafting around the time of his acquaintance with Heseltine circulated around the image of the poppy. Indeed, he used the analogy of the poppy in his 'Study of Thomas Hardy' to describe the attitude of the ideal artist in strikingly similar terms to those used by Heseltine to describe Delius. For Lawrence, as we have seen, vividness was the greatest criterion of worth in both personal and artistic terms, and the relative merits of all things were directly proportionate to their ability to attain vividness. To be vivid was for Lawrence to attain a state of Being, and any deviation from this state was tantamount to having no life at all. In his 'Study of Thomas Hardy', the symbol of the poppy is made to emblemize the ideal state of vividness, and through this symbol, we learn that Lawrence's notion of vividness *as* Being relies upon an explosion of excess that is simultaneously used up in the process of explosion – a kind of extreme brightness before complete annihilation:

The excess is the thing itself at its maximum of being. If it had stopped short of this excess, it would not have been at all. If this excess were missing, darkness would cover the face of the earth. In this excess, the plant is transfigured into flower, it achieves at last itself. The aim, the culmination of all is the red of the poppy, this flame of the phoenix, this extravagant being of Dido, even her so-called waste. […]

[…The poppy's] fire breaks out of him, and he lifts his head, slowly, subtly, tense in an ecstasy of fear overwhelmed by joy, submits to the issuing of his flame and his fire, and there it hangs at the brink of the void, scarlet and radiant for a little while, imminent on the unknown, a signal, an out-post, an advance-guard, a forlorn, splendid flag, quivering from the brink of the unfathomed void, into which it flutters silently, satisfied, whilst a little ash, a little dusty seed remains behind on the solid ledge of the earth. […]

And the day is richer for the poppy, the flame of another phoenix is filled in to the universe, something is, which was not.

> That is the whole point: something is which was not. And I wish it were true of us. I wish we were all like kindled bonfires on the edge of space, marking out the advance-posts. What is the aim of self-preservation, but to carry us right out into the firing line, where what *is* is in contact with what is not.[78]

Lawrence's description of the poppy maps fairly closely onto Heseltine's conception of his ideal artist in the form of Delius – an artist, or a type of art, that is just prior to decadence, just prior to self-consumption, with no sense of self-preservation or safety. The related image of the phoenix held an ongoing fascination for Lawrence, and its appearance on his design for the flag of Rananim and his repeated references to it in creative and critical writings made it into something of a personal symbol for Lawrence.

In Lawrence's novel *The Rainbow*, the character Will Brangwen carved a wooden butter seal for his step-cousin Anna (whom he was later to marry) during their courtship. The seal was adorned with 'a mythological bird, a phoenix, something like an eagle, rising on symmetrical wings, from a circle of very beautiful flickering flames that rose upwards from the rim of the cup […] every piece of butter became this strange, vital emblem'.[79] Given the distinction between Will's urban social position and Anna's experience at the Marsh farm,[80] and the role of the seal as a marker of their courtship, the design of the seal held a dual meaning. On the one hand, it symbolized the ominous encroachment of industrial modernity – indeed, the Brangwen parents view the butter seal as beautiful but they are troubled by the image, and for them it becomes an emblem of a form of social mobility to which they had no access. On the other hand, the seal's design emblemized the possibilities of a new world created with the impending union of the couple – a union that is described in transformative terms as facilitating a new form of Being. In describing Will's realization about marriage, Lawrence wrote that 'it was true as they said that a man wasn't born before he was married […] It was as if the surface of the world had been broken away entire: Ilkeston, streets, church, people, work, rule-of-the-day, all intact; and yet peeled away into unreality, leaving here exposed the inside, the reality: one's own being'.[81]

Lawrence's counter-image to the poppy and the phoenix was the 'cabbage' – an image through which he described the non-being state occupied by those unable to attain vividness. In Lawrence's account, the cabbage

---

[78] Lawrence, 'Study of Thomas Hardy', 12–13, 18–19.

[79] D. H. Lawrence, *The Rainbow* (1915; Harmondsworth: Penguin, 1958), 116.

[80] Will was 'interested in churches, in church architecture' and 'the influence of Ruskin had stimulated him to a pleasure in the medieval forms' (Lawrence, *The Rainbow*, 113).

[81] Lawrence, *The Rainbow*, 150.

as a plant is the antithesis of the poppy, because its value lies in its ability to be consumed before it goes to seed, and therefore before it is able to achieve its full flowering self – the ecstatic realization of its flower just prior to its death, as with the poppy.

We dare not fulfill the last part of our programme. We linger into inactivity at the vegetable, self-preserving stage. As if we preserved ourselves merely for the sake of remaining as we are. Yet there we remain, like the regulation cabbage, hide-bound, a bunch of leaves that may not go any farther for fear of losing market value [...]. But the flower, if it cannot beat its way through into being, will trash destruction about itself, so the bound-up cabbage is beaten rotten at the heart.[82]

There is a clear parallel here with Lawrence's disdain for market-driven rationality, in the sense that the cabbage symbolizes all that is ill with basing worth on exchange value alone. But Lawrence's cabbage also carries a clear ontological argument, and one that has particular relevance to our discussion of lateness, and also of Heseltine. To be cabbage-like in the sense just described was to balk at the opportunity of achieving the extinguishing excess that is required of vividness, and hence of life and Being. To be cabbage-like is therefore tantamount to non-life, and a betrayal of the quest for Being. Other images that Lawrence used to describe this state – the state of the 'herd' – included sheep, the 'living dead', 'self-preservation' and the idea of being 'enclosed and complete'. These were used to contrast the images of the poppy and phoenix, as well as the tiger, fire, burning, and swift death, which were the requirements for creativity, in Lawrence's account.

Within Lawrence's metaphysic, the possibility of Being was not necessarily available to everyone. Many, indeed, are 'spent before they arrive; their life is a slow lapsing out, a slow inward corruption.'[83] Like the cabbage, they 'lapse into green corpulence', as with domestic sheep and pigs –

They frisk into life as if they would pass on to pure being. But the tide fails them. They grow fat; their only *raison d'être* is to provide food for a really living organism.

---

[82] Lawrence, 'Study of Thomas Hardy', 12. Steele notes how this was a reference to the practice of binding the outer leaves of the cabbage to stop it from going to seed (257, note 12:9). Lawrence wrote, further, that 'we are each one of us a swamp, we are like the hide-bound cabbage going rotten at the heart. And for the same reason that, instead of producing our flower, instead of continuing our activity, satisfying our true desire, climbing and clambering till, like the poppy, we lean on the sill of all the unknown, and run our flag out there in the colour and shine of being, having surpassed that which has been before, we hang back, we dare not even peep forth, but, safely shut up in bud, safely and darkly and snugly enclosed, like the regulation cabbage, we remain secure till our hearts go rotten, saying all the while how safe we are. No wonder there is a war' (15).

[83] D. H. Lawrence, 'The Reality of Peace (III)' *English Review* 25.1 (July 1917): 24–9, 24.

They have only the moment of first youth, then they lapse gradually into nullity. It is given us to devour them [...] thank God for the tigers and the butchers that will free us from the abominable tyranny of these greedy, negative sheep. [...][84]

To the null, my rose of glistening transcendence is only a quite small cabbage. When the sheep get into the garden they eat the roses indifferently, but the cabbages with gluttonous absorption.[85]

For organisms that are 'spent before they arrive' there was no possibility of redemption, in Lawrence's schema, confirming the notion that for Lawrence there was natural hierarchy. Equally, however, there were specific practices involved in achieving one's ecstatic full bloom – one's 'poppy-self' – and thereby becoming an artist and creating something that was truly not in existence before. This practice involved achieving lateness (i.e. being on the crest of decadent decay) and vividness, and all others were merely fodder for this vital achievement of the few. Lawrence went so far as to articulate this point as one of the 'inexorable law[s] of life', writing that 'the primary way, in our existence, to get vitality, is to absorb it from living creatures lower than ourselves'.[86]

This extreme vision of artistic individuality was no doubt the source of many of the acrimonious endings to Lawrence's personal relationships, as acquaintances were sequentially drawn in to his circle, made privy for a moment to his passionate vision for a new world and a new way of truly 'Being', only to subsequently discover their foibles being caricatured and ridiculed in Lawrence's fiction, where they were made to play the part of emblemizing some kind of pervasive ill of modernity. In essence, Lawrence's acquaintances became the cabbage-like fodder to be used up in the production of his own creative blossoming. This was certainly the case for Heseltine, as we can see early on in a letter he wrote to Delius on 6 January 1916, less than a week after he moved into the Lawrences' house at Cornwall. Clearly inured in the symbolism of Lawrence's thinking, yet wary of its broader implications, the young Heseltine wrote that:

I don't want you to identify myself with him in anything beyond his desire for an ampler and fuller life – a real life as distinct from the mere mouldy-vegetable exist-ence which is all that is possible here. Here is a very great artist, but hard and auto-cratic in his views and outlook, and his artistic canons I find utterly and entirely unsympathetic to my nature. He seems to be too metaphysical, too anxious to be

---

[84] Lawrence, 'The Reality of Peace (III)', 25.
[85] D. H. Lawrence, 'The Reality of Peace (IV)' *English Review* 25.2 (Aug. 1917): 125–32, 127.
[86] D. H. Lawrence, *Reflections on the Death of a Porcupine and Other Essays* (Bloomington: Indiana University Press, 1963), 210–11.

comprehensive in a detached way and to care too little for purely personal, analytical, and introspective art [...] his passion for a new, clean untrammelled life is very splendid.[87]

Lawrence's 'hard and autocratic' commitment to the activity of his own self-becoming was also reflected in Albright's point that Lawrence never lived a personal moment that could not be extrapolated into a universal, and Gray's observation that Lawrence's art was not an 'overflow' of life but a 'substitute' for life, cited above.

It is somewhat ironic, in this sense, that in the quest for Being and individuality beyond the cabbage-like herd, Lawrence became a spectator on his own life and remained at a distance from real experience. Heseltine no doubt suffered from a similar condition, yet his continuing inability to achieve the kind of clarity of being that Lawrence so persuasively and evocatively described ultimately led to the crippling realization that vividness would never be available to him in the way promised, neither in Florida, nor via his occult investigations in Ireland, nor in his treasured sixteenth- and seventeenth-century masters.

Heseltine the Unborn

Around the time of his first meeting with Lawrence, Heseltine also gained a reputational association with the Café Royal and a particular circle of artists who met at that venue, including Augustus John, Jacob Epstein, Aldous Huxley and others. Although Lawrence was taken enough with Heseltine initially to allow him to move in with him and his wife in Cornwall, to include him in plans for his ideal community of Rananim, and to introduce him to Lady Ottoline Morrell and her social circle of artist friends at her Garsington home,[88] he was also clearly sceptical of Heseltine's circle

---

[87] Philip Heseltine, letter to Frederick Delius, 6 Jan. 1916, qtd. in Copley, *A Turbulent Friendship*, 10. This letter is also qtd. in Kinkead-Weekes, *D. H. Lawrence: Triumph to Exile, 1912–1922*, 298, and also in Gray, *Peter Warlock: A Memoir of Philip Heseltine*, 110.

[88] Delavenay described Lady Ottoline (or Ottoline Bentinck) as a member of the 'radical aristocracy' (*D. H. Lawrence: the Man and his Work*, 251), descending from the 'ancient family of the Dukes of Portland, yet emancipated from 'aristocratic taboos' (for example she studied at St Andrews University). In 1902, Ottoline married Philip Morrell, who became a Liberal MP, and during his time in Parliament he defended Lawrence against the suppression of *The Rainbow* (Kinkead-Weekes, *D. H. Lawrence: Triumph to Exile, 1912–1922*, 290). In their country estate, Garsington Manor (near Oxford), Ottoline gathered about her an 'artistic, literary, radical and socialist elite' (251), many of whom were pacifists and conscientious objectors. Frequent visitors to Garsington included Lawrence and Frieda,

of acquaintances. It is not surprising then, that the character in *Women in Love* that is thought to be modelled on Heseltine – Julius Halliday – became a vehicle for Lawrence to voice his concern with the proliferation of an inauthentic style of being associated with Bloomsbury and bohemian London more generally.[89] In this context, Heseltine might be thought to be implicated in the clinging 'long-faced sheep' who pull upon Lawrence's individuality with their attitude of negation. For example, in an early chapter in *Women in Love*, the character Rupert Birkin (a character who shares characteristics with Lawrence himself)[90] is travelling to London on a train with Gerald Crich (the 'germ' of whose character may have come from John Middleton Murry).[91] Birkin expresses his feeling of foreboding at entering the maelstrom of London life, describing the deadening effect of a society driven by the market and novelty. Of the types of people whom Birkin stays with in London, Gerald asks:

'What kind of people?'

'Art – music – London Bohemia – the most pettifogging calculating Bohemia that ever reckoned its pennies [...]. They are really very thorough rejecters of the world – perhaps they live only in the gesture of rejection and negation – but negatively something, at any rate.'

'What are they? – painters, musicians?'

'Painters, musicians, writers – hangers-on, models, advanced young people, anybody who is openly at outs with the conventions, and belongs to nowhere particularly. They are often young fellows down from the University, and girls who are living their own lives, as they say.'[92]

Bertrand Russell, John Middleton Murry and Gertler, Augustus John, Charles Conder, Henry Lamb, Aldous and Julian Huxley, and Sidney and Beatrice Webb (252). During Heseltine's visits he sometimes also brought along his Oxford friend Hasan Shahid Suhrawardy (whom Kinkead-Weekes noted 'claimed direct descent from the Prophet'), as well as other associates such as Dikran Kouyoumdjian (the novelist known as Michael Arlen), and a Russian anthropologist Boris de Croustchoff. Together with Heseltine, these three young men were also candidates for Lawrence's Rananim (Kinkead-Weekes, *D. H. Lawrence: Triumph to Exile, 1912–1922*, 289).

[89] Although Fernihough has argued that Lawrence was more in sympathy with Bloomsbury aesthetics than he seemed. See Anne Fernihough, *D. H. Lawrence: Aesthetics and Ideology* (Oxford and New York: Oxford University Press, 1993).

[90] D. H. Lawrence, *Women in Love*, ed. by David Farmer, John Worthen and Lindeth Vasey (Cambridge: Cambridge University Press, 1987), 531, see explanatory note 16:6.

[91] Lawrence, *Women in Love*, ed. by Farmer, Worthen and Vasey, 530–31, see explanatory note 12:38.

[92] Lawrence, *Women in Love*, 60. The editors note that 'young fellows down from the university' was substituted for the phrase 'mostly Oxford fellows' in an earlier version of the novel. Heseltine had been at Oxford, as had other members of the group, such as Robert Nichols and Hasan Shahid Suhrawardy (535).

Birkin invites Gerald to meet him at the Pompadour – a depiction of the Café Royal ('it's a bad place, but there is nowhere else')[93] – to meet Halliday and his crowd.[94] As the train approaches London, Birkin is 'filled with a sort of hopelessness'[95]

'I always feel doomed when the train is running into London. I feel such a despair, so hopeless, as if it were the end of the world.'
  'Really!' said Gerald. 'And does the end of the world frighten you?'
  Birkin lifted his shoulders in a slow shrug.
  'I don't know,' he said. 'It does while it hangs imminent and doesn't fall.'[96]

And getting off at the station and moving with the crowd through the station building: 'Don't you feel like one of the damned? [...] It is real death.'[97]

  In the next chapter (Chapter VI, titled 'Crème de Menthe'), Lawrence's characters Birkin and Gerald meet at the Pompadour and encounter 'Miss Darrington', or 'the Pussum', a character thought to be based on the model Minnie Lucy Channing. Minnie Lucy Channing was also known as Puma, and was romantically involved with Heseltine – albeit acrimoniously – and ultimately bore him a child, Nigel Heseltine. When Heseltine stayed with the Lawrences in Cornwall from 1 January 1916 until approximately 21 February 1916, Puma visited for some of the time.[98]

---

[93] Lawrence, *Women in Love*, 60. The editors note that this is a reference to the Café Royal, which Lawrence felt had 'sordid' implications (536). Later in the book, Lawrence gave a fuller description of the curious fascination that the venue held – 'Gudrun hated the Café, yet she always went back to it, as did most of the artists of her acquaintance. She loathed its atmosphere of petty vice and petty jealousy and petty art [...] It was almost as if she *had* to return to this small, slow, central whirlpool of disintegration and dissolution: just give it a look' (380). The younger Heseltine, recently released from his studies at Oxford, and living for the first time an independent life in London, had a different impression of the area, seeing in its sordidness an exciting potential – 'I am living in a very jolly part of London – in a quite secluded square in Bloomsbury, near St Pancras Station. The neighborhood is thoroughly alive – which is essential, for my liking – and unrespectable; at night the streets swarm with whores and hot-potato men and other curious and interesting phenomena, and the darkness which the fear of hostile aircraft has enforced upon the city makes everything doubly mysterious, fascinating and enchaining' (Heseltine, letter to Delius, 18 Oct. 1914, qtd. in Gray, *Peter Warlock: A Memoir of Philip Heseltine*, 96).
[94] Lawrence apparently admitted to Donald Carswell that the character of Julius Halliday 'is Heseltine [...] taken from life' (qtd. in Lawrence, *Women in Love*, 536).
[95] Lawrence, *Women in Love*, 60.
[96] Lawrence, *Women in Love*, 61.
[97] Lawrence, *Women in Love*, 61.
[98] The character was described by Lawrence as being based on 'a model called the Puma [...] taken from life' (*Letters of D. H. Lawrence*, Vol. 3, 36) qtd. in Lawrence, *Women in Love*, 536, explanatory note 62:22. Puma stayed with Heseltine at the Lawrences' residence in Cornwall from 26 January to c. 21 February 1916.

When we encounter Halliday for the first time in *Women in Love* it is at his old haunt the Pompadour, where he is surprised to see Pussum after the break-up of their initial affair, because he had directed her to stay away from London, presumably for his own reputational purposes. Halliday is described in the first edition of *Women in Love* as 'a pale, full-built young man with rather long, solid fair hair hanging from under his black hat, moving cumbrously down the room, his face lit up with a smile at once naïve and warm, and vapid'.[99] At this moment in the book, Pussum informs the group that she is pregnant with Halliday's child, and she appears to relish Halliday's awkward response – ' "Julius is the most awful coward you've ever seen" she cried. "He always faints if I lift a knife – he's *tewwified* of me" '.[100]

A little earlier in this scene, Lawrence uses the character of Pussum to make an observation of Halliday that becomes important for our discussion of the interaction between time and the self: ' "He hasn't any mind, so he can't know it," she said. "He waits for what somebody tells him to do. He never does anything he wants to do himself – because he doesn't know what he wants. He's a perfect baby" '.[101] This quip about Halliday being somehow uncreated or babyish and having not attained his full state of being is significant, because it echoes Lawrence's own diagnosis of Heseltine's untimeliness and helps us discern what this condition of an aestheticized life entailed. Lawrence's description of Halliday in these terms, via the character of Pussum, was in fact not as wholly pejorative as his description of the bohemian set at the Café Royal, and it was also not confined to the pages of his novels.

In the weeks after the suppression of Lawrence's *The Rainbow*, Lawrence re-envisioned his community of Rananim as something that could be located within England, in Porthcothan in Cornwall. Frieda and Lawrence moved into the house of the novelist J. D. Beresford while he was temporarily away, settling in on 30 December 1915, with Heseltine joining them there two days later, on New Year's Day 1916, and living with them as a paying boarder.[102] Heseltine continued to live with the couple for seven weeks, despite clear tensions from the outset. During this period both men analysed each other's mode of living and being. Lawrence repeatedly described Heseltine as unborn, uncreated, and somehow one step removed from the essence of things. It was not that he believed Heseltine to be detached or withdrawn, but that the young composer's passionate rejection

---

[99] Lawrence, *Women in Love*, 65. This description was modified to better conceal the basing of the character on Heseltine, after he threatened legal action, as mentioned above.

[100] Lawrence, *Women in Love*, 71.

[101] Lawrence, *Women in Love*, 67–8.

[102] Kinkead-Weekes, *D. H. Lawrence: Triumph to Exile, 1912–1922*, 297.

of prevailing attitudes resulted in a form of spectatorship, and an inability to access a sense of vividness, and the 'new'. Lawrence's analysis of this position was not wholly pejorative, because it served the function of promoting and circulating the vividness that it failed to attain itself. A number of letters that were posted from the house in the first few weeks of their co-habitation begin to provide a sketch of this analysis. For example, on 9 January Lawrence confided to Lady Ottoline that

Tomorrow Kouyoumdjian is coming for a while, I hope we shall like him. He is at any rate more living than poor Philip Heseltine, who really seems as if he were not yet born, as if he consisted only of echoes from the past. But he will perhaps come to being soon; when the new world comes to pass. Meanwhile, conscription hangs over his head like a sword of Damocles.[103]

Lady Ottoline never took to Heseltine. Kinkead-Weekes surmises that from her perspective, his 'manners and conversation were distinctly un-Bloomsbury. Neither undergraduatish beer-drinking and motor-bikes, nor Café Royal wine-and-womanising would have appealed to her'.[104] It is true that Heseltine must surely have seemed like an impudent young upstart. Having recently withdrawn from Oxford and reeling against his Eton education, he was filled with the youthful spirit of passionate rejection, while still begrudgingly relying on the financial support of his mother. His debauched activities in London, his bawdy humour, and his association with Gray and others would not have recommended him as a guest with a refined aesthetic sensibility. Still, Heseltine was undoubtedly an interesting character and would have been somewhat of a party asset, and indeed it may have been this very 'un-Bloomsbury' character of Heseltine that attracted Lawrence to him in the first place.

On 10 January Dikran Kouyoumdjian (later Michael Arlen)[105] arrived at the Lawrences' and 'brought the atmosphere of London with him'.[106] Lawrence was becoming ill, and tensions rose. Three days later, on 13 January, Lawrence wrote again to Ottoline:

It is such a bore, about these young people, that they must be either tacitly or noisily asserting themselves [...] But why do they want to assert themselves, nobody wants to obliterate them. They are quite free; then why assert themselves. They spend their time in automatic reaction from everything, even from that which is most

---

[103] D. H. Lawrence, letter to Lady Ottoline, 9 Jan. 1916, qtd. in Copley, *A Turbulent Friendship*, 9.

[104] Kinkead-Weekes, *D. H. Lawrence: Triumph to Exile, 1912–1922*, 291.

[105] Author of *The Green Hat* (1924), *The London Venture* (1920) and other novels.

[106] Qtd. in Kinkead-Weekes, *D. H. Lawrence: Triumph to Exile, 1912–1922*, 298.

sympathetic with them. It is stupid. It is crass. It is as stupid as the wholesale self-submergence of bygone young men – it is the same thing reversed. Why can't they be simple, fallible like other mortals.[107]

Shortly afterwards Kouyoumdjian was told to leave.

During Heseltine's stay in Cornwall he proposed the establishment of a subscription-based publishing venture to be called *The Rainbow Books and Music*, which would begin by printing Lawrence's novel *The Rainbow* ('unex-purgated, from the original MS')[108] and then proceed to 'issue privately such books and musical works as are found living and clear in truth; such books as would either be rejected by the publisher, or else overlooked when flung into the trough before the public'.[109] Included in these longer term plans were a 'sequel to *The Rainbow*', a philosophical work 'Goats and Compasses' – 'a verit-able soul-bomb, a dum-dum that will explode inside the soul!'[110] – and a novel by John Middleton Murry. Heseltine was clearly taken by Lawrence's magnetic personality, and campaigned on his behalf in terms that were directly taken from Lawrence's own thinking:

There is no discrimination, none whatever, and the bloody herd will only read those who uphold them as they are, in their stinking, Christian self-complacency! [...]

I am getting a circular printed – it will be ready next week – in order to ascertain whether there be a substratum of genuine appreciation and love of the quest of truth in this country, underneath all the smug moral assurance, the unspeakably loathsome acquiescence in the existing social system – In the circular, we dwell upon the utter impossibility of publishing advanced books or music, since more and more popularity is becoming the sole test of a work's value.[111]

Although Lawrence clearly valued Heseltine's youthful enthusiasm, and particularly his passionate support[112] he had already begun to depersonalize

---

[107] D. H. Lawrence to Lady Ottoline, 13 Jan. 2016, qtd. in Copley, *A Turbulent Friendship*, 9–10.

[108] Philip Heseltine, letter to Viva Smith, 16 Feb. 1916, qtd. in Copley, *A Turbulent Friendship*, 11.

[109] Philip Heseltine, Circular to promote his subscription venture, qtd. in Copley, *A Turbulent Friendship*, 12–13. Heseltine printed 1000 copies at his own expense, and distributed 600. He received only thirty replies.

[110] Heseltine, letter to Viva Smith, 16 Feb. 1916, qtd. in Copley, *A Turbulent Friendship*, 11.

[111] Heseltine, letter to Viva Smith, 16 Feb. 1916, qtd. in Copley, *A Turbulent Friendship*, 10–11.

[112] Writing to Heseltine during a brief visit to London, Lawrence implored him to 'come back soon, free. Then in our retreat we will make the bombs to site the Philistine. Oh to bust up the Philistine-only that. I feel a new life, a new world ahead for us – down towards Lands End there we will be a centre of a new life, a centre of destruction of the old. I believe in the Rainbow books and music, quite gaily' (D. H. Lawrence, letter to Philip Heseltine, 24 Feb. 1916, qtd. in Copley, *A Turbulent Friendship*, 14–15). Also, in a letter to Lady Ottoline, Lawrence sincerely admitted that Heseltine 'is really very good and I depend on him and

Heseltine and construe his character as a universal exemplar of a particular state within his broader system of thinking. He wrote to Lady Ottoline at around this same time describing Heseltine as 'one of those people who are born to be conveyers of art: they are next to the artist and they convey art to the world',[113] and then he wrote a few days later to John Middleton Murry, describing Heseltine similarly as 'one of those people who are transmitters, and not creators'[114] and as someone who had 'some queer kind of abstract passion which leaps into the future'.[115] In this sense, for Lawrence, Heseltine's uncreated nature was a quality that was not synonymous with the untimely 'poppy-self' of the artist, but neither was it akin to the vegetative state of the 'herd'. It was a state of passionate spectatorship, or of passionate reaction that would never be fully consummated in Being.

Similarly, in *Women in Love*, Halliday's babyish inability to know his own mind (as described by the character Pussum) was not akin to the vacuity of London bohemianism (described by Birkin on the train into London). Indeed, in his uncreatedness, Halliday held a similar fascination to that of primitivism in the book, and the powerful unknowingness of 'savages'. In his interactions with the Pussum, Halliday is described as looking 'foolish. One glass of wine was enough to make him drunk and giggling. Yet there was always a pleasant, warm naiveté about him, that made him attractive'.[116] And when Pussum asks the character of Gerald (who is introduced to the groups as an 'explorer') whether he is afraid of 'savages', Gerald's reply is illuminating: 'No – never very much afraid. On the whole they're harmless – they're not born yet, you can't feel really afraid of them. You know you can manage them'.[117] When the group return to Halliday's apartment later that evening much is made of the fact that he has some 'African carvings',[118] comprising 'several negro statues, wood-carvings from West Africa, strange

---

believe in him' (D. H. Lawrence, letter to Lady Ottoline, 25 Feb. 1916, qtd. in Copley, *A Turbulent Friendship*, 22). The letter continues, 'but he is exasperating because he is always in such a state of mad reaction against things – all mad reactions. It is a terrible cyclonic state, but he will be worth having with us, oh, very much' (22).

[113] D. H. Lawrence, letter to Lady Ottoline, 15 Feb. 1916, qtd. in Copley, *A Turbulent Friendship*, 15.

[114] D. H. Lawrence, letter to John Middleton Murry, 24 Feb. 1916, qtd. in Copley, *A Turbulent Friendship*, 14. The idea of certain modernists acting as 'circulators' was further explored by Sydney Janet Kaplan in *Circulating Genius*.

[115] Lawrence, letter to Murry, qtd. in Copley, *A Turbulent Friendship*, 14–15. Indeed Heseltine later described himself in this way – 'I am afraid I was really meant to be a contemplator, a bystander not an actor' (Philip Heseltine, letter to Augustus John, 16 Oct. 1921, *GB-Lbl*, Add MS 57785).

[116] Lawrence, *Women in Love*, 69.

[117] Lawrence, *Women in Love*, 66.

[118] Lawrence, *Women in Love*, see explanatory note 74:10, 538.

and disturbing, the carved negroes looked almost like the foetus of a human being'.[119] In the morning, viewing Halliday crouching in front of the fire 'stark naked'

Gerald looked at him, and with a slight revulsion saw the human animal, golden skinned and bare, somehow humiliating. Halliday was different. He had a rather heavy, slack, broken beauty, white and firm. He was like a Christ in a Pietà. The animal was not there at all, only the heavy, broken beauty. And Gerald realized how Halliday's eyes were beautiful too, so blue and warm and confused, broken also in their expression. The fireglow fell on his heavy, rather bowed shoulders, he sat slackly crouched on the fender, his face was uplifted, degenerate, perhaps slightly disintegrate, and yet with a moving beauty of its own.[120]

And indeed the character of Halliday himself gives expression to this notion of the primitive being closer to vivid living. Halliday envies Gerald's experiences in 'hot countries where the people go about naked':[121]

Oh but how perfectly splendid! It's one of the things I want most to do – to live from day to day without *ever* putting on any sort of clothing whatever. If I could do that, I should feel I had lived [… because] one would *feel* things instead of merely looking at them. I should feel the air move against me, and feel the things I touched, instead of having only to look at them. I'm sure life is all wrong because it has become much too visual – we can neither hear nor feel nor understand, we can only see.[122]

Following through with this imagery, the 'bohemian set' are described as only 'half men' in contrast to the explorer Gerald, who is a 'real man' – an outsider, both on his missions to South America and in the context of Halliday's London party. And in describing why Halliday's African carving of a woman in childbirth is a work of art, Lawrence's character Birkin tells Gerald that

It conveys a compete truth […] it contains the whole truth of that state, whatever you feel about it […] pure culture in sensation, culture in the physical consciousness, really *ultimate* physical consciousness, mindless, utterly sensual. It is so sensual as to be final, supreme.[123]

Although the sense of uncreatedness of the image of the African woman in childbirth was clearly different from Halliday's and Heseltine's uncreatedness,

---

[119] Lawrence, *Women in Love*, 74. He also has some 'new pictures […] in the Futurist manner', and a 'large piano' (74).

[120] Lawrence, *Women in Love*, 77.

[121] Lawrence, *Women in Love*, 78.

[122] Lawrence, *Women in Love*, 78.

[123] Lawrence, *Women in Love*, 79.

there is clearly a link between them as both being fodder for the artist's creation of himself. Pussum's description of Halliday as being unable to decide anything for himself is clearly linked with Gerald's description of why he is not afraid of 'savages' (i.e. because their unborn quality makes them easy to 'manage'). And Lawrence used a related temporal image to describe the character of Hermione Roddice in the book – a caricature of Lady Ottoline – 'She was rather pale and ghastly, as if left behind, in the morning'.[124]

To cast the African wood carvings and the character of Halliday as alike 'unborn' and 'uncreated' in a way that attains a 'broken beauty', and the character of Hermione as occupying a state of being that is 'left behind, in the morning', in addition to the lateness of the aristocrat artist – the phoenix, the poppy – is to evince a preoccupation with characters who are for one reason or another not legitimate components of the system of relations that make up the contemporary moment. Both the unborn and the late are outside this system and do not seek after timeliness. Indeed, they are resolutely untimely and seek out and feed off others who are as well. For Gray and Heseltine, Delius held a similar fascination, not being the culmination or rejection of tradition, but a rule unto himself – indeed self-created and entirely individual, in their account – and taking no part in the requirements of the contemporary. These types of description should not be viewed for their truth-content, but rather for their position within a wider discursive field.

Blood Consciousness

My great religion is a belief in the blood, the flesh, as being wiser than the intellect. We can go wrong in our mind. But what our blood feels and believes and says, is always true.[125]

Lawrence's thinking undoubtedly had an influence on the young Heseltine, as we have seen, though Heseltine's presence in Lawrence's life can also be seen to have substantially shaped the latter's thinking, especially on the topics of union and blood consciousness. Lawrence's close observation

---

[124] Lawrence, *Women in Love*, 98. See also explanatory note 15:22, at 531, where the editors show that Hermione 'owes a good deal to Lady Ottoline Violet Anne Morrell', and that 'Lady Ottoline herself saw the character as a malicious and potentially libelous portrait', against Lawrence's general denials of the coincidence in character and description.

[125] D. H. Lawrence, letter to Ernest Collings, reprt. in *Letters of D. H. Lawrence* Vol. 1, 503, qtd. in Beer, 'Lawrence's Counter-Romanticism', 61.

of, and entanglement with, Heseltine's relationship with Minnie Channing helped him further develop his ideas on 'Love and Law', as he described it, which provided the blueprint for his social ideas.[126] Lawrence's critique of the frame of mind that he attributed to the industrial system – a frame of mind that based human freedom and individuality on the possession of property – was intimately related to his project of living vividly, such that he sought 'to recover of the human spirit from the base forcing of industrialism' via the process of rediscovering 'the creative reality, the actual living quick itself'.[127] It is for this reason that his response to the relationship between Heseltine and Puma is illuminating.

Lawrence's voyeuristic interest in Heseltine's relationships with women had a disquieting effect on Heseltine. In the first week of March 1916, Lawrence was still writing to Murry about the possibility of them 'all be[ing] friends together'[128] and suggesting that Heseltine could live with Murry and Mansfield while they were in Cornwall. But in the same week, Heseltine was writing to Robert Nichols to the effect that

I am not returning to Lawrence; he has no real sympathy. All he likes in one is the potential convert to his own reactionary creed. I believe firmly that he is a fine thinker and a consummate artist, but personal relationship with him is almost impossible. At least so it appears at present.[129]

In a letter to Delius, Heseltine conveyed a similar impression that 'Lawrence is a fine artist and a hard, though horribly distorted, thinker. But personal relationship with him is impossible – he acts as a subtle and deadly poison'.[130]

The rift between Heseltine and Lawrence was evidently caused by a specific incident involving Lawrence secretly attempting to intervene in some way with Heseltine's personal affairs by attempting to pair Heseltine (and Nichols) with a woman in Hampstead, knowing that Heseltine was already begrudgingly betrothed to Puma.[131] Heseltine responded to Lawrence's

---

[126] Raymond Williams has noted how Lawrence's 'vital study of relationships [...] is the basis of his original contribution to our social thinking' (Williams, 'The Social Thinking of D. H. Lawrence', 295). Williams also noted two popular misunderstandings of Lawrence's contribution – first, the idea that he believed that 'sex solves everything' and second that he was a 'precursor of the Fascist emphasis on blood' (295).

[127] Williams, 'The Social Thinking of D. H. Lawrence', 310.

[128] Qtd. in Copley, *A Turbulent Friendship*, 17.

[129] Qtd. in Copley, *A Turbulent Friendship*, 17, and in Gray, *Peter Warlock: A Memoir of Philip Heseltine*, 116.

[130] Philip Heseltine, letter to Frederick Delius, 22 April 1916, qtd. in Copley, *A Turbulent Friendship*, 17, and in Gray, *Peter Warlock: A Memoir of Philip Heseltine*, 117–18.

[131] The details of the falling out are not quite clear. See Copley's discussion: *A Turbulent Friendship*, 17–23.

intrusion by cutting ties with him, and according to varying accounts, by destroying the only manuscript of one of Lawrence's philosophical essays, either 'Goats and Compasses' or 'At the Gates'.[132]

While the manuscript is now either lost or destroyed, there is evidence to suggest that the philosophical musings contained in 'Goats and Compasses' were developed directly in relation to Heseltine's relationship with Puma, which would have been observed by Lawrence at close hand during their stay with him at Cornwall (Puma joined Heseltine there towards the end of January 1916). Lawrence wrote of their relationship to Lady Ottoline at length, describing the potential of Heseltine's relationship with Puma as a 'blood connection, the dark, sensuous relation'.[133] This idea might be viewed as an extension of Lawrence's comment to Heseltine in the first letter he wrote after their initial meeting, about homosexuality as being somehow 'reductive' and a force of 'disintegration', as well as a development of Lawrence's critique of Bloomsbury and his derision of over-intellectualization. Kinkead-Weekes observed how 'by late 1915 his broodings on "Cambridge" and "Bloomsbury" had traced close links between the hard brittleness of intellectual, egotistic will, irreverence, self-enclosure and homosexuality'.[134] Through the discussion of how all humans are bisexual in *Hardy*; the exploration of the transformative power of marriage in *The Rainbow* and the destructive force of an individuality that refused to give itself over to the union; and from comments made to Bertrand Russell after Lawrence met E. M. Forster in February 1915, it seems likely that the new text extrapolated the creative potential of the union of the self (the man) with the other (the woman), as an expression of the necessity to temper intellectual consciousness with sensual perception, as we saw in our earlier discussion of Halliday's relationship with themes of primitivism in *Women in Love*.[135]

---

[132] Gray, Copley and Nigel Heseltine give differing accounts of the fate of these manuscripts. Kinkead-Weekes admits that 'whether PH thus destroyed two works by the same method, or whether Gray confused them, cannot be known' (*D. H. Lawrence: Triumph to Exile, 1912–1922*, 835, fn. 9).

[133] Qtd. in Kinkead-Weekes, *D. H. Lawrence: Triumph to Exile, 1912–1922*, 302.

[134] Kinkead-Weekes, *D. H. Lawrence: Triumph to Exile, 1912–1922*, 304. Kinkead-Weekes speculated on what the context of 'Goats and Compasses' may have been. While noting that 'the only descriptions we have are from hostile witnesses', it seems clear that it dealt in some way with what Lawrence believed to be the spiritual limitations of homosexuality: 'To understand the concern with homosexuality we need to recall the whole process of self-examination which began in 1913 by acknowledging homoerotic feelings, unworried, because his relation with Frieda had saved *him* from Middleton's tragic solipsism. He knew himself to be bisexual, but was convinced that a greater degree of "otherness" made heterosexual relationship the more reactive and transforming, if more difficult' (303).

[135] Kinkead-Weekes, *D. H. Lawrence: Triumph to Exile, 1912–1922*, 303.

There was also another shaping factor in the development of Lawrence's thinking during this period, which related to the shifting make-up of his circle of acquaintances in Cornwall. Heseltine and Puma's son was born on 13 July 1916 and they married on 22 December in what Heseltine described as a concession, making 'her a final present of forty shillings worth of respectability'.[136] In early March 1917, Heseltine returned to Cornwall alone, taking up residence close to Lawrence, much to the latter's chagrin.[137] Gray then also moved to the area in May 1917, assisted by Lawrence.[138] While in Gray's autobiography he claims that he met daily with the Lawrences, Kinkead-Weekes has shown that this was far from the case, though this is not to deny that there was a sympathy and semi-regular contact between the parties.[139] There was also another figure who joined them at Cornwall at this time – Meredith Starr, who amplified the occult sensibilities of Heseltine and Lawrence, marking a shift in Lawrence's intellectual milieu away from the Murrys and Ottoline at Garsington. By 17 June Lawrence had counselled Heseltine into quite a different view on Puma – indeed as a 'fulfillment of my own being'[140] – though Heseltine later repudiated his own 'idiotic emotionalism' in this thought, attributing this lapse to his experimentation with 'Black Magic'.[141] Heseltine had harboured an interest in occultism and psychical research since his time at Oxford, but it was the presence of Meredith Starr at Cornwall – whom Robert Nichols described as an 'imposter' with 'long hair, bulbous rings etc.' and as an 'infernal gas bag'[142] – that accelerated his experimentation in this area. There is

---

[136] Philip Heseltine, letter to Crocker, 19 April 1917, qtd. in Kinkead-Weekes, *D. H. Lawrence: Triumph to Exile, 1912–1922*, 384.

[137] See Copley, *A Turbulent Friendship*, 23–4. Lawrence wrote to Murry and Mansfield on 5 May 1917 that 'I don't like him anymore; it can't come back, the liking'. Kinkead-Weekes positions Heseltine's return to Cornwall as being in 'late March', settling finally in April (Kinkead-Weekes, *D. H. Lawrence: Triumph to Exile, 1912–1922*, 381).

[138] Kinkead-Weekes noted that Gray took out a five-year lease on Bosigran Castle, which was the name of the 'rocky headland on which it stood, with disused tin-workings at its side. It had seven rooms and a great view out to the Scilly Islands in front [...] Lawrence threw himself enthusiastically into getting furniture and liaising with workmen about colour schemes, just as for the Murrys the previous year; and went over himself to scrub and clean and get the house ready' (*D. H. Lawrence: Triumph to Exile, 1912–1922*, 385).

[139] Kinkead-Weekes, *D. H. Lawrence: Triumph to Exile, 1912–1922*, 386.

[140] Philip Heseltine, letter to Robert Nichols, 17 June 1917, qtd. in Kinkead-Weekes, *D. H. Lawrence: Triumph to Exile, 1912–1922*, 385.

[141] Kinkead-Weekes, *D. H. Lawrence: Triumph to Exile, 1912–1922*, 387.

[142] Qtd. in Kinkead-Weekes, *D. H. Lawrence: Triumph to Exile, 1912–1922*, 387. Also discussed in Smith, *Peter Warlock*, 118. From the accounts of Gray and Nichols we can glean that Heseltine had already read, during his time at Oxford, the works of Boehme, Trismegistus, Paracelsus, Eliphas Lévi, Havelock Ellis, Carpenter and Weininger. Kinkead-Weekes notes that Delius also

evidence of Starr's influence on Lawrence as well; and Lawrence maintained a guarded interest in the work of Blavatsky and in Pryse's description of the *chakras*, both of which seemed to offer him a new collection of images, symbols and ideas to describe aspects of his thinking that had been present in his work since some of his earliest novels.

The reason that this interest is relevant to us is that it again brought together a particular conception of the self and a non-teleological conception of time. While the Lawrence of *Hardy* and *The Rainbow* had posited a broadly developmental conception of time, by late-July 1917 he began to move away from evolution to the idea of the existence of a universal ancient wisdom that had been progressively sullied by modern forms of knowledge dating back to Socrates and following a slow degeneration throughout the development of modern humankind, resulting finally in the carnage of the War. In essays such as 'The Whistling of the Birds' and 'The Reality of Peace' (particularly part IV), Lawrence begins to develop a notion of time that is static and eternal, within which cycles of degradation and renewal play out in a constant state of return to or rediscovery of eternal truths. This notion was broadly consonant, in fact, with Heseltine's treatment of 'old' and 'new' works as existing on a single plane of vitality, discussed above.

In highlighting these aspects of Lawrence and Heseltine's thinking it is important to avoid imposing an artificial uniformity of concerns on the modernist interest in primitivism, the occult and ancient wisdom. In the case of Lawrence at least, the symbolism offered by some of these earlier sources was paired with his interest in the physical body and the potency of sexual communion to generate spiritual union, as against the transcendental spiritualism of traditions such as theosophy. In other words, the syncretic nature of theosophy and related esotericisms made their central symbols into convenient catchwords for a range of divergent ideas; and in Lawrence's case it was very much in this sense of strategic borrowing to support his developing ideas on the body, on sexual union and blood consciousness. Lawrence's diagnosis of Heseltine as uncreated and unborn, and his attempts to intervene on his personal affairs with Puma, issued from a belief in the importance of balancing the 'white', 'spiritual' consciousness of man, or of the 'Son' (who forsook his body), and 'dark', 'physical'

---

had mentioned 'table turning & spirit rapping' in a letter to Heseltine in 1912, and Delius's own collaboration with Papas surely entered their ongoing discussions. Kinkead-Weekes also speculates that 'it was probably in Cornwall that he immersed himself in S. T. Klein's *Science and the Infinite*, J. M. Pryse's *The Apocalypse Unsealed* and the *History of Magic* by Eliphas Lévi' (Kinkead-Weekes, *D. H. Lawrence: Triumph to Exile, 1912–1922*, 387).

consciousness of woman, or of the 'Father' (the focus of Roman Catholicism as against English Protestantism), in order to attain Being. This did not mean a reconciliation of these forces, but what Lawrence described as an 'equipoise' between them:

I am born uncreated. I am a mixed handful of life as I issue from the womb. Thenceforth I extricate myself into singleness, the slow-developed singleness of manhood. And then I set out to meet the other, the unknown of womanhood. I give myself to the love that makes me join and fuse towards a universal oneness, I give myself to the hate that makes me detach myself, extricate myself vividly from the other in sharp passion; I am given up into universality of fellowship and communion, I am distinguished in keen resistance and isolation, both so utterly, so exquisitely, that I am and I am not at once; suddenly I lapse out of the duality into a sheer beauty of fulfillment, I am a rose of lovely peace.[143]

Failed Utopias and False Messiahs

When the first complete draft of *Women in Love* was completed in July 1916,[144] Lady Ottoline and Gray were both made privy to the manuscript. It was at this time that they would have become aware of the unflattering caricatures presented in the book – Ottoline in the character of Hermione, Heseltine in the character of Halliday, and Minnie Channing in the character of Pussum. Gray alerted Heseltine to the content of the book, yet it was not until the first edition of *Women in Love* was released and nearly all copies sold, that Heseltine began to consider legal action. As a result of the negotiations between Heseltine's solicitor and Secker (during September 1921), the first English edition of the book was eventually withdrawn, and further printing and distribution was paused. Lawrence was in Italy, and when Secker sent him the marked-up manuscript he grudgingly agreed to slightly modify the physical descriptions of Pussum and Halliday, making Pussum blue-eyed and fair-haired, and Halliday 'black and swarthy'.[145] Heseltine refused to accept these minor alterations and continued to threaten legal action, though eventually he agreed to a monetary settlement of £50, which

---

[143] D. H. Lawrence, 'The Reality of Peace (IV)', 132.

[144] Copley, *A Turbulent Friendship*, 24. The revised text (modified according to Secker's instructions) can be seen in the Phoenix Edition, produced by Heinemann in 1954, and the original text is the Penguin English Library Edition of 1982 (which was the edition available in America). Copley noted some of the changes in descriptions and names (28).

[145] For further details see Farmer, Worthen and Vasey, 'Introduction' to *Women in Love*, xlix; and Copley, *A Turbulent Friendship*, 25.

Lawrence referred to as 'hush money': 'Really, one should never give in to such filth'.[146]

It is of course somewhat ironic that Heseltine would seek a legal remedy to suppress Lawrence's work, given his rhetoric of free speech that littered the circular advertising the *Rainbow Books and Music* venture. Heseltine even went to the trouble of asking his solicitors to contact Scotland Yard and encourage the suppression of the book by police force ('every day's delay is bound to make a difference to the circulation of the book'), in much the same terms against which he had previously fought the suppression of Lawrence's *The Rainbow* only a few years earlier.[147] In reality though, Heseltine's disillusionment with Lawrence's project, and particularly the means by which he sought to execute that project, was clear far earlier in their relationship. As early as 16 April 1917, Heseltine wrote a poem that he sent to Robert Nichols (written from Zennor) casting Lawrence as a lonely grotesque figure with messianic delusions:

> On a cross set by the roadside
> Stands a dismal man,
> While a lark above him, fluttering and twittering,
> Asks how he can
> Play at such a queer game [...]
>
> Do you suppose I'm Jesus
> Saving humanity,
> Or Judas Iscariot, expiating himself?
> (What vanity!)
> For you know it's all the same.
>
> No, I'm only an ordinary
> Thief, an old Pirate
> Never caught me, yet here I am! Now isn't that
> Something to smile at?
> Down with this bloody frame! [...]

---

[146] D. H. Lawrence, letter to Mountsier, 26 Nov. 1921, qtd. in Farmer et al., l.

[147] 'Apart from the chapters containing the libels, this second edition does not differ in any way from the first, and if ever a book afforded grounds for prosecution on a charge of morbid obscenity in general and the glorification of homosexuality in particular, this one does [...] If Scotland Yard proves dilatory, could you not address a communication to the National Council of Public Morals, urging them to take the matter up and press for police action?' (Philip Heseltine, letter to his solicitor, 1921, qtd. in Copley, *A Turbulent Friendship*, 26–7, and in Gray).

And whenever we see a signpost
With white arms – a pose
Like a blooming crucifix, trying to lead
Wild girls and boys
By the hard road to the town

Of smoke and sacrifices, pretending
Moors and trespassers' land,
We'll climb up the bank behind it, when
It's not looking,
Into the sunshine, and
Pull the bloody thing down![148]

It bears noting at this point that both Heseltine and Lawrence were exempt from war service on medical grounds – Lawrence for his persistent chest infections (later ascribed to tuberculosis), and Heseltine for a 'nervous stricture'.[149] Both felt disgusted by the War and its material as well as cultural effects – jingoism and patriotism, its stultifying effects on the arts, and its tendency to intensify the mobbish mentality of a public towards whom they were already ill-disposed. Yet despite their abhorrence of the War, and the pacifist inclinations of both, neither Lawrence nor Heseltine would have been conscientious objectors, by their own admission. Heseltine admitted that 'the general public pressure would probably have driven me to enlist myself',[150] and Lawrence had commented in 1916 that he would 'rather be a soldier than a schoolteacher', though he later railed against the idea of entering service – feelings that were intensified by the way in which he came under suspicion of espionage in Cornwall for his wife's links with Germany, leading ultimately to their eviction. Delavenay gave a particularly evocative

---

[148] Reprt. in Gray, *Peter Warlock: A Memoir of Philip Heseltine*, and qtd. in Copley, *A Turbulent Friendship*, 29.

[149] Smith, *Peter Warlock*, 64–5. The 'nervous stricture' was described as related to 'undue mental fatigue after moderate effort, and inability to carry out consistent daily work without distress, having to work in an irregular manner', amounting to 'functional neurosis'. Cecil Gray had been exempted from conscription three times before being called up, in August 1918 for the mildest category of service, which he associated with 'cleaning lavatories'. Though even then, with the end of the War in sight, Gray 'absented' himself and spent the final months of the War studying Palestrina in the British Museum (Gray, *Musical Chairs*, 135). Neither Yeats, Pound, Eliot nor Joyce fought in the War either.

[150] Philip Heseltine, letter to Frederick Delius, 18 Oct. 1914, qtd. in Gray, *Peter Warlock: A Memoir of Philip Heseltine*, 95. Despite this expressed sentiment, and Heseltine's escape to Ireland to avoid being called up, Barry Smith describes him as a 'conscientious objector' in his entry in Grove.

summary of the kinds of wartime social pressures that shaped the period in Cornwall for the Lawrences, Heseltine and Gray in this regard:

by 1917, England had no more illusions concerning the nature of the war [...] public opinion turned indignantly against 'shirkers' and conscientious objectors. A minority of pacifists persisted, some (like Bertrand Russell, Clifford Allen or E. D. Morel) going to prison, others (like Ramsay MacDonald) risking their political careers. [...] Lawrence and his wife, very probably unaware of the facts, had come to live in a theatre of naval operations, in a forbidden military zone of the Salisbury Command. Both were notably unrestrained in language; she was German-born, he had a German uncle; the company they kept may well have surprised the local people. American visitors, young men like Heseltine and Cecil Gray, for no apparent reason not in uniform. They received letters and newspapers from Germany. Cecil Gray has reported how Lawrence talked to all and sundry of going to the industrial North to campaign for pacifism and to bring the war to a speedy end [...] The circumstances ending in his summary expulsion from Cornwall are fully documented: the old piano that served to accompany their German singsongs; the warnings of neighbours who knew that they were being watched; the arrest and search by the police in London of the American Mountsier after his visit to the Lawrences in Cornwall at Christmas 1916; the various occasions on which either soldiers searched a knapsack full of groceries, or coastguards watched outside their windows at night; the incident of the badly blacked-out light at Cecil Gray's house at Bosigran; the eruption of armed men into the sitting-room where Gray and his friends were singing in German; Gray's sentence to a heavy fine for this offence; the subsequent search of the Lawrences' cottage in their absence.[151]

After the Lawrences were evicted from their Cornwall residence in late 1917 due to suspicions of espionage, they returned to London and were offered lodgings by H. D. and also Dollie Radford, Cecil Gray's mother, whose residence at Hermitage, Bucks, became their home from May to November 1919. Delavenay describes this period as 'a time of increased uncertainty and wounded self-respect' for Lawrence.[152] At Lawrence's final army medical examination in September 1918, when he was classified as 'fit for non-military service', he seemed somewhat more pragmatic in his attitude to non-cooperation, asking Lady Cynthia Asquith if she could organize a job for him in the Ministry of Education.[153] Though as Delavenay noted,

---

[151] Delavenay, *D. H. Lawrence: the Man and his Work*, 246–7.

[152] Delavenay, *D. H. Lawrence: the Man and his Work*, 213. Lawrence stayed in nine different houses between 1914 and 1919, and during this period his 'health was consistently poor' – a condition that was later diagnosed as tuberculosis. 'Heseltine told Delius he was afraid Lawrence was "rather far gone with consumption", which suggests that among his friends, if not actually in his presence, the name of his illness was openly mentioned' (218).

[153] Delavenay, *D. H. Lawrence: the Man and his Work*, 248.

'fortunately for his self-respect, the war ended without his having either to execute these threats [of desertion and non-cooperation], or to face the consequences of a total capitulation by accepting some sort of educational work.[154] Heseltine left for Ireland before he could be called up for further examination.

In some ways, Lawrence and Heseltine's attitude to conscription reflected what Terry Eagleton and John Harrison have bemoaned of the reaction-aries in terms of their having called for radical change without being willing to engage in political action. More generously, Raymond Williams has attributed Lawrence's failure to consolidate a viable social alternative to the ills of the industrial mindset to his own close personal embroil-ment with the implications of that mindset. Lawrence's escape from the fate of working-class 'replacement' was not achieved through his upward mobility in quotidian terms (i.e. his university education, acceptance into London literary circles, and adoption of a middle-class lifestyle), but rather through his intensive project to reform his own mindset and consciousness:

He was deeply committed, all his life, to the idea of re-forming society. But his main energy went, and had to go, to the business of personal liberation from the system. [...] What he lived was the break-out, not theoretically, nor in any Utopian con-struction, but as it was possible to him, in immediate terms.[155]

Both of these interpretations are undoubtedly illuminating, yet neither acknowledges that this unwillingness, or more likely inability, to engage in political action was a central and necessary element in shaping the ethos of lateness. The sense of passionate impotence – of radical renewal just out of reach – of being filled with anger and disdain and ideas for change but at the same time resigned to the certain failure of these ideas – these were the founding elements of the types of attitudes to time, history and the self that emerged from the cultural formation described here. Indeed, Lawrence criticized the 'women suffragists' for the concreteness of their demands for equal treatment, so that even though they were

certainly the bravest, and, in the old sense, most heroic party amongst us, even they are content to fight the old battles on the old ground, to fight an old system of self-preservation to obtain a more advanced system of preservation [...whereas]

---

[154] Delavenay, *D. H. Lawrence: the Man and his Work*, 248.

[155] Williams, 'The Social Thinking of D. H. Lawrence', 301. Williams also noted that Lawrence acknowledged the value of community, and was not a simple isolationist or iconoclast: 'he was rejecting, not the claims of society, but the claims of industrial society' (302).

I would wish that many laws be unmade, and no more laws made. Let there be a parliament of men and women for the careful and gradual unmaking of laws.[156]

This commitment to non-action also conditioned both Lawrence and Heseltine's attitudes towards their native Britain more generally, whereby their disillusionment with the internal reaction to the War and the public discourse that arose from the War was expressed as a feeling of being, as Heseltine put it, 'out of sympathy with the general temper of the country'.[157] At the same time they were dedicated to the regeneration of national cultural life and an older vision of communal relations. In other words, while both Lawrence and Heseltine sought to distance themselves from their cultural and political climate, their governing attitude was not one of detachment *per se*, or cosmopolitanism, but rather of a deep desire for change coupled with an awareness of necessary failure. This ethos continuously tempered their utopianism and hope for renewal, yet it did not amount to pessimism – it was a kind of bleak hope that sustained their ecstatic vision of the possibility of living life vividly:

One cannot even raise one's voice in protest – and such is the temper of one's countrymen, if one does, it only hardens their hearts in their own conceptions. Well did Blake say that unacted desires breed pestilence. For impotence is always a pestilential thing.[158]

This sense of impotence was a central shaping force for both Lawrence and Heseltine, and it conditioned their respective expressions of lateness.

---

[156] Lawrence, 'Study of Thomas Hardy', 14. In an explanatory note on this passage, the editor Steele noted that the term 'self-preservation' was 'in wide circulation' and that Lawrence had read as a student Herbert Spencer's *Education* (1861) in which Spencer specified that the first category of activity for the constitution of human life was one that ministered to 'self-preservation' (255, note 7:22).

[157] Philip Heseltine, letter to Colin Taylor, 12 Nov. 1915, qtd. in Gray, *Peter Warlock: A Memoir of Philip Heseltine*, 105.

[158] Philip Heseltine, letter to Colin Taylor, 12 Nov. 1915, qtd. in Gray, *Peter Warlock: A Memoir of Philip Heseltine*, 105.

Figure 4.1 'Kaikhosru Sorabji c. 1919', photograph by Alvin Langdon Coburn, image courtesy of the George Eastman Museum, © 'The Universal Order'. Coburn contributed to Heseltine's journal *The Sackbut* the following year.

4 | Modernism, Democracy and the Politics of Lateness: Kaikhosru Sorabji and *The New Age*

> The only vital creative work still being produced to-day is either the work of men well over middle age, such as Sibelius, Ernest Bloch or Medtner, or that if and when the work of any younger men shows any real creative vitality and drive, as opposed to a cheap-jack smart-Alec musical wisecrackery, it is the work of men creating in comparative obscurity, unknown, boycotted or both, and for one reason or another *personae ingratissimae* with the organized gangs, cliques, rings and institutions of music. 'The Future of Music' … What then? If what we see has happened to our wretched Art after the first of the Free Democratic Blood Orgies, what does anyone with any imagination suppose is likely to be its state now?[1]

Artists within the milieu of late modernism who were troubled by the aging of the 'new' often attributed this process of calcification to the consumer market. This assumption led them to denounce initiatives or aesthetic tendencies that expanded public access to art. In some ways this attitude towards the public conforms to the institutional caricature of the artist of high modernism – elite, intellectual, specialized, and prizing difficulty and complexity as a bulwark against accessibility or easy consumption. Yet as we have seen, post-World War I lateness was characterized by a reaction against these same tendencies. The approach to the public that I will describe in what follows as an expression of 'lateness' is perhaps better viewed within the constellation of ideas encapsulated by Ezra Pound's advice to imagist poets to 'go in fear of abstractions'.[2] In its immediate context, this advice warned against the use of conceptual language in poetry – for example, where an abstract or ineffable idea is evoked by the use of an inexact substitute term such as 'peace', as in the expression 'the dim lands of peace'. Pound counselled against this practice, as part of his agenda to fashion a more direct poetic language that harnessed the symbolic power of the 'natural object' alone. Pound's advice was not then about formal abstraction, and it was certainly not an embrace of realism. Rather, it applied to conceptual abstractions,

---

[1] Kaikhosru Shapurji Sorabji, *Mi Contra Fa: The Immoralisings of a Machiavellian Musician* (London: Porcupine Press, 1947), 100.

[2] Ezra Pound, 'A Few Don'ts by an Imagiste' *Poetry* 1.6 (1913): 200–206.

or ideas that required further explication beyond the artwork – it was a plea for autonomy and immediacy. This opposition to 'abstractions' was also directed towards a broader range of processes associated with modern rationalization, including the drive of 'democracy' towards 'equality', the drive of 'capitalism' towards standardization, and the sense that terms such as 'equality' and 'liberty', as much as a term like 'progress', were categories devoid of any substantive content. Importantly, this concern with abstractions was also expressed in polemics against certain artistic techniques, such as realism and imitative language, intellectual practices, such as music analysis and the theory of musical forms, and processes of professionalization and institutionalization, including public education and musical training. These phenomena were viewed as threats to individuality, reducing individual expression and experience to equivalent units within a system of exchange through processes of standardization and rationalization. Such processes were thought to have an atomizing social effect, but they could be resisted by propagating a type of art that was not amenable to replication or to conventional analysis – art that was irreducible to other forms of knowledge.

A 'fear of abstractions' shaped discussions on an even broader range of topics within the periodical press. The journal *The New Age* published contributions by a number of the leading literary modernists of the early twentieth century, and included music criticism written by Cecil Gray, Kaikhosru Sorabji and Ezra Pound.[3] Within its pages, essays on literary and musical style appeared alongside essays devoted to issues such as vegetarianism, eugenics, suffragism, maternity, birth control, diet reform, national efficiency, urban degeneracy, realism, free verse, geometric sculpture, socialism, the 'intermediate sex', state education, the minimum wage, theosophy, psychoanalysis, feng shui, mesmerism and, of course, aesthetics. As

---

[3] Pound contributed music criticism to *The New Age* from 1917 to 1921 under the pseudonym William Atheling. Atheling was particularly sympathetic to the revival of early music; he championed the work of Arnold Dolmetsch and, like Gray and Heseltine, appreciated Elizabethan music. He also supported Bernard van Dieren, and became interested, like Gray, in Marjory Kennedy-Fraser's 'Songs from the Hebrides' (published with texts in both Gaelic and English in three volumes in 1909, 1917 and 1921); he viewed these, similarly, as more vital and new than many 'modern' musical trends: 'with all the talk of modern music, I cannot see that the "freedoms" have amounted to much more than a rather timid reaching out from, let us say, Mozart, toward a few rhythms older than Gregory, older than the pietising [sic] and general taming of music during the Middle Ages' (William Atheling [Ezra Pound], 'The Gaelic' *The New Age* 22.22 (28 March 1918), 434, reprt. in *Ezra Pound and Music: the Complete Criticism*, ed. by Murray Schafer (London: Faber, 1977), 90–94). Kennedy-Fraser was personally acquainted with both Yeats and Pound.

Anne Fernihough has observed, the full extent to which these discourses were intimately intertwined often goes unrecognized in scholarship on cultural modernism:

What stands out so clearly is the way in which the languages used to address these diverse concerns blend into one another and indeed feed off each other. On reading these magazines, the critical concepts which subsequently became so central to our understanding of modernism are reinvigorated: concepts such as Imagism, Vorticism, impersonality, the 'objective correlative', the 'dissociation of sensibility' and the stream of consciousness all draw their life-blood from the social, cultural and political discourses surrounding them. Yet too often, by the time they reach the standard textbooks on modernism, their complex social and political overtones have been bleached out of them.[4]

While it is common enough to think about how the relationship between art and politics was viewed during this period, we must also comprehend how these discourses were firmly embedded in and intermingled with other concerns about 'modern life', and it is with this in mind that we are able to view the late modernist approach to the public as part of a broader constellation of concerns about rationalization.

There were several key events that influenced the consolidation of this attitude among certain thinkers in Britain in the first decades of the twentieth century, but many trace its immediate origin to the 1906 General Election – an election which delivered a landslide victory to the Liberal Party and its Labour Party allies after almost two decades of near-continuous Conservative Party rule.[5] The reforms that followed under the banner of 'New Liberalism' signalled the Liberal Party's move away from the classical liberal conception of the government's role as ensuring the liberty of its subjects against threats of domination, towards a view of the State as protecting its subjects against hardship and other threats to quality of life, such as poor health or unemployment. In other words, the reform policies of the New Liberals after the 1906 election marked the emergence of what would become the modern British welfare state. This change proceeded from an emerging public awareness of the living conditions of the urban poor and the working classes, prompted by influential surveys conducted by late-Victorian and Edwardian social reformers and culminating in the Royal Commission on the Poor Laws after

---

[4] Anne Fernihough, ' "Go in Fear of Abstractions": Modernism and the Spectre of Democracy' *Textual Practice* 14.3 (2000): 479–97, 480–81.
[5] The Labour Representation Committee (which was re-named the 'Labour Party' after the 1906 election) had only been constituted for five years, yet it won a total of twenty-nine seats in the House of Commons in 1906.

1909, and the robust national discussions that ensued. The Military Service Acts of 1916 and 1918, which dealt with conscription, heralded a period of increased state intervention into and regulation of the activities of ordinary citizens across a range of areas during wartime. And of course the entrance of women into the political sphere as voters in two stages – an Act of 1918 allowed certain women over the age of thirty the right to vote, and then in 1928 all adult females gained the right to vote – engendered a radical change in the make-up of the voting population, and therefore in political discourse, in the interwar period.

The coincidence of an increasingly interventionist government programme and the achievement of near universal adult suffrage made some sense in democratic terms, of course – just as the State had a greater role in the lives of its citizens, so more of those citizens were able to have a hand in determining by whom they would be governed. Yet to some these developments represented the culmination of a malevolent process whereby a 'Ruling Class' of bureaucrats controlled the lives of an increasingly servile populace. They viewed this process in broadly capitalistic terms – particularly after the War – seeing ideas about equal opportunity and public institutions as serving to degrade individuality and standardize experience.[6] The political alternatives explored by writers who held this view tended to favour locally focused forms of self-organization, voluntarism or cultural philanthropy, as a means of cultivating a sense of self-reliance (which was conceived as a central feature of national character).

The politics involved in the attitude towards the public that will be extrapolated here has sometimes been described as 'reactionary'.[7] Indeed T. S. Eliot celebrated T. E. Hulme as 'Classical, reactionary, and revolutionary

---

[6] This was a concern they shared, in fact, with a number of the *supporters* of state-sponsored social welfare who nonetheless were sceptical of how initiatives such as the national insurance system offered mechanistic and centralized welfare provision divorced from social relationships and the ethical components of citizenship or collective spirit. Jose Harris traced the idealist and Hellenistic foundations of this view, and charted its demise in the 1940s and 50s as social theory and moral philosophy became increasingly separate from the realm of social policy. With this increasing professionalization, the earlier idealism of social welfare policy was gradually replaced by functionalist and descriptive language (see Jose Harris, 'Political Thought and the Welfare State 1870–1940: An Intellectual Framework for British Social Policy' *Past & Present* 135 (1992): 116–41). For the writers in the milieu of late modernism, however, the remedy for the encroachment of rationalization lay in a range of political alternatives that were markedly different from the democratic politics that informed much of the discourse in favour of social reform.

[7] See for example John Harrison, *The Reactionaries* (London: Victor Gollancz, 1966), and Charles Ferrall, *Modernist Writing and Reactionary Politics* (Cambridge: Cambridge University Press, 2001).

[...] the antipodes of the eclectic, tolerant, and democratic mind of the last century';[8] and the figures who fostered this stance have also been described as 'revolutionary conservatives', or 'reactionary modernists', the latter term having been applied to W. B. Yeats, Ezra Pound, Wyndham Lewis and D. H. Lawrence to describe their combination of 'a radical aesthetic modernity with an almost outright rejection of even the emancipatory aspects of bourgeois modernity', including liberalism, equality, democracy, industrialism and 'progress'.[9] Yet it is important to note that this attitude was distinct from other conservative or counter-revolutionary tendencies – such as emblemized by Edmund Burke and given contemporary expression by Stanley Baldwin and others – as well as being distinct from reformism, such as that of the Fabian Socialists. Similarly, the ideological skirmishes that were fought across political, economic and artistic discourses in early-twentieth-century Britain had no clear battle lines, and we must be wary of suggesting any necessary connection between, for example, conservative politics and conservative aesthetics, or between a concern for social welfare and a leftist progressivism, or between modernist aesthetics and proto-fascist tendencies. Equally, it is important to acknowledge the institutional interests at play in construing the anti-liberal politics of interwar modernisms with the benefit of post-World War II hindsight. This perspective tends to flatten out the variety of expressions of dissatisfaction with the technocratic expression of liberalism in the early decades of the twentieth century. It is important to note that although the figures in this milieu were indeed 'reactionary' in the sense of rejecting the social reform initiatives of New Liberalism and advocating medieval modes of organization, the temporal implications of that term – the sense of wanting to 'go back' or return – are not an accurate reflection of lateness as I conceive it here. These artists were undoubtedly future-oriented, and the musical figures involved in this milieu were deeply engaged with the question in the opening quotation – 'What then?' – namely, with the project of constructing a musical future (or a concern with that future's judgement of the present) in light of the aging of modernism.

In addition to the political and religious implications of the stance of the so-called 'reactionary modernists', their position also relied on a sense of the simultaneity of time. With the past, present and future all a part of a single spatial frame, the primitive might be conceived in terms of a heightened

---

[8]　T. S. Eliot, 'A Commentary' *Criterion* 3.7 (1924), cited in Rachel Potter, *Modernism and Democracy: Literary Culture 1900–1930* (Oxford and New York: Oxford University Press, 2006), 144. The article was a review of Hulme's posthumously published *Speculations*.

[9]　Ferrall, *Modernist Writing and Reactionary Politics*, 2.

form of subjectivity, or the work of the seventeenth-century masters might be seen as being more alive and vivid than that of contemporary artists. Stylistically, this position encompassed a combination of contemporary artistic languages and a so-called 'consciousness' of tradition – a modernist surface underpinned by a Classical sensibility.

In the course of the following I will investigate the way in which certain ideas about music and literature participated in the interwar politics of lateness, via concerns over processes of rationalization inherent in liberal progressivism – concerns that in fact targeted the work of pre-war modernists as much as it derided developments in modern democracy. I take as my focus a set of discussions reflected in the journal *The New Age*, and position the music critic and composer Kaikhosru Sorabji's critical work in relation to them. I will focus on three types of argument that proceeded from the anti-democratic rhetoric associated with the reactionary modernists. The first is what I have described above in terms of the 'fear of abstractions', or scepticism towards processes of rationalization. The second is an association between anti-humanism and what T. E. Hulme described as a 'classical' temperament. And the third is a sceptical association of egalitarian initiatives (and the notion of 'equality' more broadly) with imitative forms of art that lack individuality and vitality, or with forms of mimicry and ritualized behaviour. This last type of argument has been linked with the pervasive rhetoric of eugenics during the 1920s and 30s; and in the final part of this chapter I shall examine this idea further with respect to music via the notion of the 'death of the spectator'.

In so doing I hope to demonstrate that a certain stream of modernist opposition to cultural democratization was not simply a pose of the intellectual elite bent on preserving its own cultural authority, or indeed a withdrawal from political engagement in the public sphere. Rather, I will show how an ambivalent attitude towards the public rested equally on a concern with what were perceived to be the tainted motivations of a reformist elite (both political and artistic) and with the bureaucratization of authority (namely, with the deadening effects of codification), and that their opposition in this regard was an expression of lateness.

Anti-Democratic Politics and Modernist Aesthetics in *The New Age*

The New Age was central in the discussion of artistic modernism from the time of the 1906 General Election to well into the interwar period.

It included contributions by leading literary modernists, reproductions of modernist artworks, and discussions of music and theatre, but it was also explicitly a political weekly, publishing articles by social reformers, economists and political commentators. The journal was particularly important to the collection of figures involved in the milieu described here, as many of these figures either wrote for the journal or were influenced by or associated with the circle of writers who supported it, particularly during Alfred Orage's editorship (1907–22). Two of our musical essayists of interest – Cecil Gray and Kaikhosru Sorabji – contributed to this journal, and the writings of Heseltine and Van Dieren also appeared in its pages.[10] The journal encapsulated a set of politico-aesthetic discourses that will allow us to better construe the wider positioning of certain ideas about music and literature associated with 'late modernism'.

The overall political positioning of *The New Age* has been a point of contention. The initial impetus behind the journal came from the Left – its purchase was partly funded by George Bernard Shaw,[11] and the founding editors, Orage (editor from 1907 to 1922)[12] and Holbrook Jackson (co-editor for the first eight months of its New Series),[13] were also sympathetic to Fabian Socialism, at least initially; and the journal supported Guild Socialism.[14] H. G. Wells and Arnold Bennett wrote for the periodical in its early issues, and it was initially supportive of the Liberal government and the Labour Party after their 1906 election success – an outcome that was viewed as a long-awaited triumph for Left-wing radical politics in Britain. However, a rift developed in the journal's first year of operation that reflected a broader division within the Fabian Society at the time, between those who were

---

[10] Sorabji's two large books of essays, *Around Music* (1932) and *Mi Contra Fa* (1947), contain material reproduced from the criticism he wrote for *The New Age* as well as for the *Musical Times*, the *Musical Mirror and Fanfare* and the *New English Weekly* (the last also edited by Orage).

[11] The journal had been launched in 1894 as a Christian Socialist periodical, but was re-launched in its New Series, subtitled 'Independent Socialist Review of Politics, Literature, and Art', in May 1907, and then later the subheading was changed to simply 'Weekly Review of Politics, Literature and Art'. Lewis Wallace – who had known Orage in Leeds when the latter organized the Leeds Art Club with Holbrook Jackson – provided the other half of the purchasing price for the journal.

[12] After editing *The New Age*, Orage went on to edit the *New English Weekly* (1932–34), a journal for which Sorabji also contributed music criticism (from 1932–45).

[13] Beatrice Hastings claimed that she was also an unacknowledged co-editor between 1907 and 1914 (see Beatrice Hastings, *The 'Old New Age': Orage – and Others* (London: Blue Moon Press, 1936)).

[14] Ardis has noted that the journal only fully gave up its socialist identity in 1919, 'when Orage's disappointment with the political trends post-World War I led him from National Guild Socialism to C. H. Douglas's theory of social credit, psychoanalysis, and Gurdjieffian

committed to gradualist change through the parliamentary mechanism, such as the older Executive Committee, emblemized by Sidney and Beatrice Webb and G. B. Shaw, and those who had become frustrated with the compromise and centrist tendencies of the parliament, such as G. K. Chesterton and Hilaire Belloc, who criticized the Fabian Society's focus on achieving political democracy over economic or industrial democracy.[15] Orage and Jackson supported the latter view, and although Wells had argued for the reform of the Fabian Society in opposition to its conciliatory approach to parliamentary politics, both he and Shaw (and eventually Bennett as well) ultimately became alienated from the journal.

So while a number of commentators and scholars have construed *The New Age* as being oriented towards the political Left, others have highlighted its alienation from these tendencies, with scholars such as Charles Ferrall arguing that the journal was 'actively hostile' towards the Left, even before the War, in a such a way as to suggest an early link between modernist aesthetics and anti-Left politics.[16] Still others have viewed *The New Age* as a 'neutral' platform for a range of opposing views,[17] or a dialogic forum for all manner of cultural radicalisms, where opposing sides of debates were given space as part of an agenda on the part of Orage and Jackson to expose (and some suggest, to propagate) divisions within the Fabian Society and socialist discourse more broadly.[18] Tom Villis has persuasively argued,

mysticism' (Ann L. Ardis, 'The Dialogics of Modernism(s) in the *New Age*' *Modernism/Modernity* 14.3 (2007): 407–34, 419).

[15] For a useful outline of the background to this rift and its articulation in the early issues of *The New Age* see Lee Garver, 'Neither Progressive nor Reactionary: Reassessing the Cultural Politics of *The New Age*' *The Journal of Modern Periodical Studies* 2.1 (2011): 86–115. Garver described Belloc as a 'catholic controversialist and author [...] an independent-minded Liberal MP who had already made a considerable name for himself as a poet, travel writer, essayist, and popular historian', and who together with Oscar Levy took the journal further away from socialism (108). Belloc edited the *Eye-Witness* until 1912, with Chesterton taking over the editorship of the then *New Witness* after him (from 1912 to 1917). Cecil Chesterton was the brother of G. K. Chesterton, who was involved in some notable debates in the early issues of *The New Age*. Belloc had been a Liberal MP from 1906 to 1910, but he resigned his seat 'out of despair for the party system' (Tom Villis, 'Elitism and the Revolt of the Masses: Reactions to the "Great Labour Unrest" in the *New Age* and *New Witness* Circles' *History of European Ideas* 31 (2005): 85–102, 87, fn. 12).

[16] Charles Ferrall, 'The *New Age* and the Emergence of Reactionary Modernism Before the Great War' *Modern Fiction Studies* 38.3 (1992): 653–67.

[17] See for example Wallace Martin, *The New Age Under Orage: A Chapter in English Cultural History* (Manchester: Manchester University Press, 1967).

[18] Garver has shown how *The New Age* differed in this respect from other British radical magazines during the pre-war era, such as the *Eye-Witness* (1911–14), *The Freewoman* (1911) and *The New Freewoman* (1911–13), *The Egoist* (1914–19) and the *New Statesman* (1913 onwards), which were all mouthpieces for specific political agendas (Garver, 'Neither

however, that while the 'loose editorial policy' made the journal a forum for a broad range of often-conflicting political viewpoints, its primarily oppositional status meant that we can in fact discern a reasonably coherent strain of political impetus in the journal, shaped by a desire to 'move towards a new constellation of values that both reflect the crisis of liberalism and anticipated the intellectual response to fascism. [...*The New Age*] searched for politics that were beyond right and left.'[19]

The oppositional politics of *The New Age* was shaped by two other intellectual trends that gave it a reactionary inflection. The first was Guild Socialism, which was outlined in *The New Age* by G. D. H. Cole and further discussed by writers such as Hilaire Belloc. Belloc's *The Servile State* became an influential text for Sorabji's thinking, as well as reflecting a particular stream of counter-socialist thought in the early part of the twentieth century that illuminates the politics of lateness. Some advocates of Guild Socialism in *The New Age*, such as A. J. Penty, envisaged the restoration of the guilds of medieval Europe – 'associations of small masters where relations of personal devotion and service prevailed'[20] – to return to an imagined past of organic society based on personal relationships rather than larger industrial or bureaucratic structures. While Orage warned against idealizing the feudal past, he did claim that 'the influence of the medieval guilds remained, humanizing feudal conceptions of work, which under the large industry became always non-human and often inhuman.'[21]

Belloc, a former Liberal MP, argued that the collectivism of both New Liberalism and State Socialism were complicit in the logic of capitalism. He believed that rather than leading to a society where the means of production were collectively owned (in opposition to the individualism of *laissez-faire* capitalism), New Liberal reform initiatives that focused on ensuring personal security and sufficiency would leave the means of production in

Progressive nor Reactionary', 111–12). Ardis also forwarded this view, describing the journal's 'Bakhtinian dialogics in the public sphere' (Ardis, 'The Dialogics of Modernism(s) in the *New Age*', 409). Ardis used this phrase to describe 'the kind of exchanges [*The New Age*] orchestrates, both within individual issues of the journal and diachronically, over multiple issues, between its editors, regular contributors, and correspondents in its "Letters to the Editor" column' (428, fn. 12).

[19] Villis, 'Elitism and the Revolt of the Masses', 87–88. Villis was primarily concerned here with the way *The New Age* and the *New Witness* responded to the unprecedented series of strikes and industrial action between 1910 and 1914, which became known as the 'labour unrest' of this period.

[20] Villis, 'Elitism and the Revolt of the Masses', 95.

[21] Villis, 'Elitism and the Revolt of the Masses', 95, qtd. from Orage, 'The Great Industry and the Wage System' *The New Age* 11.2 (9 May 1912), 29.

the hands of an elite corporate and political minority who would be charged with the power to regulate the lives of the masses, who in turn worked for a wage far removed from the purchase value of the product they produced.

Belloc presented an idealized vision of social organization in the Middle Ages, when the serf was 'bound in legal theory to the soil upon which he was born'. Serfs avoided becoming a transferable commodity – as slaves had been, and as modern wage workers were also, according to Belloc. In Belloc's account, apart from supplying a minimum of produce to their lord, serfs were relatively independent and socially mobile, as well as being free to use the surplus of the produce of their labour to their own ends. Guilds arose around small industry in the towns, and these Guilds were partly co-operative and self-governing, and they 'jealously' safeguarded 'the division of property, so that there should be formed within its ranks no proletariat upon the one side, and no monopolizing capitalist upon the other'.[22] For Belloc, New Liberalism, socialism and other forms of modern collectivism that he argued were complicit in capitalism would lead to a revival of the 'Servile State' – a mode of organization that for him pre-dated the Guild system and propagated forms of slavery, including 'wage slavery'.

Belloc's book is regularly seen as being a part of an intellectual lineage between Herbert Spencer's *The Man Versus the State* (1884) and F. A. Hayek's *The Road to Serfdom* (1944), though some argue that Belloc aimed primarily to critique capitalism rather than to equate New Liberalism or State Socialism with slavery in the same way that Spencer did, and that his lineage from Spencer was a malicious invention of Shaw.[23] The book was extremely influential for *The New Age* circle, and despite the fact that Sorabji only wrote for the paper after Orage's period of editorship had come to an end, he still referred frequently to Belloc's book, and it clearly continued to be influential in his thinking even in the years after World War II.[24]

---

[22]   Hilaire Belloc, *The Servile State* (London: Foulis, 1912; 3rd ed. London: Constable, 1927), 47–9.

[23]   Edward McPhail, 'Does the Road to Serfdom Lead to the Servile State?' *European Journal of Political Economy* 21 (2005): 1000–1011.

[24]   For example, he praised the book in a chapter he contributed to a volume in commemoration of Ananda Coomaraswamy's seventieth birthday in 1947, tellingly titled 'The Validity of the Aristocratic Principle' (in *Art and Thought* (London: Luzac, 1947), 214–18). Incidentally, although Sorabji wrote for two years under Orage's editorship at the *New English Weekly*, he wrote for far longer under Orage's posthumous successor, Orage's close friend and fellow supporter of Social Credit, Philip Mairet, whose wife Ethel had at one time been married to Coomaraswamy. It is important to remember the extent to which intellectual sympathies in these types of milieu also often carried personal investments (as we saw in the previous chapter in the case of Lawrence and Heseltine, and as we shall see in the next chapter, in the case of Gray and H. D.).

The second intellectual trend that gave a reactionary inflection to the radical politics of *The New Age* was English Nietzscheanism. Orage himself had only just published *Friedrich Nietzsche: The Dionysian Spirit of the Age* (1906) when he took over the editorship of the journal, and he invited a number of like-minded writers to contribute, including one of the central proponents and translators of Nietzsche's work in England, Oscar Levy. Levy edited the complete English-language edition of Nietzsche's works, which appeared between 1907 and 1913, but prior to this time the translation of Nietzsche into English had been intermittent and uneven, and the belated arrival of Nietzsche's ideas into the wider intellectual landscape in Britain gave English Nietzscheanism a particular – and decidedly conservative – character all its own.[25] One of the main factors in this uneven reception was that it was Nietzsche's later works that appeared in English translation first, with *Thus Spake Zarathustra* and *The Case of Wagner* appearing in 1896 and *The Genealogy of Morals* in 1899, translated by Thomas Common and W. A. Hausmann, and then a second group of translations of his earlier works only appearing between 1907 and 1913 (including *Beyond Good and Evil* in 1907, and *The Birth of Tragedy* in 1909), funded and translated by Oscar Levy. Writers who were sceptical of the advent of mass democracy in the early decades of the twentieth century, and who were dissatisfied with New Liberalism's mandate for social reform and greater state provision of social welfare, found a persuasive critique ready to hand in Nietzsche's *Zarathustra*, whose hero derided the 'herd' and looked upon the masses from a height; and in *Beyond Good and Evil* and *The Genealogy of Morals*, which cast moralistic abstractions as being akin to religious doctrine in their effect of standardizing experience, favouring the weak and demonizing the strong and the individual.

Although a number of the contributors to *The New Age* criticized the faddish nature of the English craze for Nietzsche before the War, many of their central ideas in support of 'organic society', hierarchy and aristocracy, as well as their criticisms of Christianity and capitalism, were very clearly shaped by the same intellectual tradition, as was their support of eugenics, their anti-Semitism, and their preference for classical aesthetics. Garver

---

[25] The classic text on this topic is David Thatcher, *Nietzsche in England 1890–1914: the Growth of a Reputation* (Toronto and Buffalo: University of Toronto Press, 1970), yet there are some who have criticized or expanded upon Thatcher's approach to the topic. See for example in John Burt Foster, *Heirs to Dionysus: A Nietzschean Current in Literary Modernism* (Princeton: Princeton University Press, 1981); Michael H. Levenson, *A Genealogy of Modernism: A Study of English Literary Doctrine 1908–1922* (Cambridge: Cambridge University Press, 1984); and Potter, *Modernism and Democracy*.

observed that Orage's appointment of Levy showed that he was 'willing to promote forms of Nietzschean critique that went well beyond the kind of humorous and reformist assaults on conventional morality popularized by Shaw'.[26] As we saw in the previous chapter too, Nietzsche's work was also more than a passing interest for Heseltine and Delius, and although Sorabji – always wary of faddish ideas – denied ever reading Nietzsche, his writing is saturated with the rhetoric of this discourse.

A further point to highlight here about the intellectual culture of *The New Age* circle is that the convergence of increased state intervention and female enfranchisement in the early decades of the twentieth century led to the rhetorical feminization of the masses and of market mechanisms more generally in the work of many of these figures. This association shaped the vaunted misogyny of a number of male modernists. Sorabji was certainly complicit in making this alignment, and like other male modernists of this era his comments about women can be read as an extension of his fear of abstraction and distain for democracy.[27] In an essay with the typically pro-vocative title 'Against Women Instrumentalists', Sorabji argued that women could never be great musicians or artists because they are unable to view a composition 'as a whole', instead making 'of it an agglomeration of small sections that may be individually charmingly played, but that is all – no current of organic life flows through the whole, no architectonic sense of the whole conveyed'.[28] He also criticized women musicians for appealing to their audience through bodily and facial movements, praising male performers for maintaining a barrier between themselves and the audience – a point which evokes the idea of the 'death of the spectator' that will be further discussed below, and the related fear of the breakdown of distinctions in democracy. The terms Sorabji used to castigate female musicians readily invite a political interpretation, being directly aligned with his view that mass democracy (achieved through the enfranchisement of women) was descending into a form of commodity culture. He described women instrumentalists as superficial, childish, without strength, feeble and prac-tically 'physically degenerate', and with no discernible original talent[29] – all to be contrasted with the strong, vital, authentic, original masculinity.

Thus women's enfranchisement, mass democracy and the market became associated terms of derision, even, as it happens, for some female writers

---

[26] Garver, 'Neither Progressive nor Reactionary', 110.

[27] For more on this point see Potter, *Modernism and Democracy*.

[28] Kaikhosru Sorabji, 'Against Women Instrumentalists', in *Around Music* (London: Unicorn, 1932), 138–141.

[29] Sorabji, 'Against Women Instrumentalists', in *Around Music*, 140–41.

such as H. D., Dora Marsden and Beatrice Hastings. After a period identifying with the suffragette cause, Beatrice Hastings (who helped edit *The New
Age* from 1907 to 1914) and Dora Marsden (who edited *The Freewoman*
from 1911) both moved towards fashioning a modernist feminism that was
sceptical of that political project – a change that was influenced by their
reading of Nietzsche and Max Stirner. Disillusioned by the emphasis on
sentimentalism and sexual purity that they discerned in the equality discourse, these women turned their focus towards creating a modern femin-
inity via a new poetic language that would allow them to produce 'images of
the self as an aesthetic, rather than a juridical or moral unity'.[30]

One final point to note about the background to these discussions is that
while the music critics within this milieu such as Sorabji, Heseltine and
Gray were each from reasonably wealthy family backgrounds and benefitted from varying degrees of private income, very few of the other figures
within the milieu of late modernism enjoyed a similar level of independence, and indeed the critics of the New Liberal reforms to social welfare did
not necessarily come from privilege. Ardis noted that the readership of *The
New Age* was '*not* Oxbridge-educated or socially elite', and that its 'rank-
and-file readers were the socialist autodidacts and left-leaning graduates
of Mechanics Institutes, working men's colleges, teachers' colleges and
extension lecturing circuits that Orage set out to uplift socially when he
and Holbrook Jackson first founded the Fabian Arts Group in 1906'.[31]
Neither Orage nor Jackson themselves came from moneyed backgrounds.
And indeed, T. E. Hulme's influential linking of anti-democratic politics
and Classicism (an idea that became important for both T. S. Eliot and
Ezra Pound) rested on the idea that democracy was a relic of middle-class
romanticism which had fooled contemporary reformers into believing that
it served the interests of the working classes. For Hulme, as for the French

---

[30] Potter, *Modernism and Democracy*, 14–15. Potter argues that Andreas Huyssen's attempted
reversal of the understanding of modernism as masculine and misogynist by viewing it from
the perspective of the masses and from the feminist perspective served in fact to further
strengthen this perception of modernism, with the feminist 'alternative' being pitched against
the masculine authoritarian dominant modernist culture, further consolidating the cultural
authority of the male modernists. By focusing on the work of anti-suffragette feminist
modernists, Potter's approach presents a challenge to this tendency.

[31] Ardis, 'The Dialogics of Modernism(s)', 417–18, 409. Orage had estimated that the circulation
of *The New Age* was 4500 copies a week in August 1913, but that it had reached 22,000 in
November 1908 (Villis, 'Elitism and the Revolt of the Masses', 86; and also Ardis, 'The Dialogics
of Modernism(s)'). Paul Selver commented, however, that 'the circulation of the *New Age* was
small (so small was known to very few), but it was widely read' (Paul Selver, *Orage and the New
Age Circle: Reminiscences and Reflections* (London: Allen & Unwin, 1959), 21).

Syndicalist Georges Sorel (whose work he translated) and the right-wing French nationalist group L'Action Française (who were also influential in his thinking), the interests of the proletariat would only be served by violent revolution, which in turn would revive the 'classical spirit'.[32]

It also bears remembering that many Fabian Socialists were closely involved in the Independent Labour Party and later the Labour Representation Committee, which finally became the Labour Party after the 1906 election success. Even after many writers in *The New Age* turned against the new government, it was the militant trade unions that were seen by some within *The New Age* circle as providing a potential basis for the achievement of Guild Socialism, and the journal was broadly supportive of the workers involved in the 'labour unrest' of 1910–14. Still, as Villis noted, the support of the workers by reactionary writers such as Belloc was mainly for the reason that they showed a 'healthy revolt against the parliamentary system he so despised'.[33] In other words, *The New Age* used the strikes as evidence that the parliamentary system, and the Labour Party with it, did not serve workers' interests.

A number of the contributors to *The New Age* found themselves in the conflicted position of being intellectual elites from working-class backgrounds proposing to serve the interests of those subject to 'wage slavery' by rejecting social reform measures designed to alleviate poverty, and by criticizing political mechanisms designed to give equal voice to those with less privilege. Villis provides an apt summary of the tensions at play, noting an inherent discord 'between the libertarian motives of the writers and the reactionary values that underpinned their alternatives', and contextualizing this position as a 'British example of the European crisis and rethinking of Marxism' in that it 'borrowed from the language of social revolutionary thought, but its conclusions were a bastardisation of the Marxist legacy'.[34] As we shall see, Villis's idea that 'disgust with both liberal and socialist politics could lead to a reactionary position in the belief that it was more honest' applies as much to Hulme, Eliot and Pound as it did to Heseltine, Sorabji and Gray.

Although Sorabji only joined *The New Age* as music critic after Orage's departure as editor, the two men were clearly acquainted. Orage wrote a glowing endorsement of Sorabji's critical abilities in his foreword to *Around*

---

[32] T. E. Hulme, 'Translator's Preface to Sorel's *Reflections on Violence*' *The New Age* 17.24 (14 Oct. 1915), 569–71.

[33] Villis, 'Elitism and the Revolt of the Masses', 88.

[34] Villis, 'Elitism and the Revolt of the Masses', 86–92.

Music (1932), and Sorabji's period writing for the *New English Weekly* over-
lapped by two years with Orage's editorship of that paper.[35] In addition,
it is clear that Sorabji had been following the discussions in *The New Age*
even prior to his acquaintance with Orage, because his writings appear in
the 'Letters to the Editor' section of the periodical in earlier issues. Indeed,
in the year 1917 there were two controversies within the pages of *The New
Age* involving a number of the figures within the milieu sketched here.
The first debate was prompted by an article written by Bernard van Dieren
defending Jacob Epstein against his critics;[36] and the second was prompted
by an article written by Cecil Gray defending Bernard van Dieren against
his own critics, in the wake of a concert of his music at The Wigmore Hall
in early 1917.[37] These two articles prompted a series of exchanges in the
'Letters to the Editor' section of the journal in the following months, within
issues that also contained the writings of Belloc, a serialized essay by G. D.
H. Cole on 'Reflections on the Wage System', and articles with titles such as
'Some Considerations of Class Ideologies' in close proximity to these artistic discussions.[38]

By this time Sorabji had become a satellite figure in Heseltine's circle,
having corresponded with Heseltine on the basis of their shared sympathy
with 'ultra-modern' music since October 1913. In the early period of their
correspondence Heseltine was still reluctantly at Oxford and Sorabji had the
benefit of being in London and able to attend the latest post-impressionist
exhibitions and contemporary music concerts – which he did voraciously.
It was Sorabji who recommended to Heseltine the music of Bartók, Kodály,
Scriabin, Schoenberg and Berg, among others, and who introduced
Heseltine to the latest in literary modernism, such as providing him with
a copy of the journal *BLAST* in late 1914. This landmark publication was
edited by Wyndham Lewis and supported by Ezra Pound, and reproduced
work by Jacob Epstein and others – figures whom Heseltine would come to

---

[35] Orage edited *The New Age* from 1907 to 1922 and Sorabji wrote music criticism for the journal
      from 1924 to 1934. Orage edited the *New English Weekly* from 1932 until his death in 1934,
      and Sorabji contributed music criticism to that journal from 1932 to 1945. For a discussion of
      Sorabji's music criticism in these two journals see Nazlin Bhimani, 'Sorabji's Music Criticism',
      in *Sorabji: A Critical Celebration*, ed. by Paul Rapoport (Aldershot: Scolar Press, 1992), 256–84.

[36] Bernard van Dieren, 'Epstein' *The New Age* 20.19 (8 March 1917), 451–3. Van Dieren
      argued that Epstein's critics were blinded by their preference for realism, and in contrast he
      highlighted the humanity of Epstein's formal abstractions.

[37] Cecil Gray, 'Bernard van Dieren: a Reply to Critics' *The New Age* 20.22 (29 March 1917),
      516–17.

[38] See also, for example, the relevant 'Letters to the Editor', in *The New Age* on 5 April 1917, 550;
      19 April 1917, 26; and the May 3 issue also included an interview with Epstein.

know in the Café Royal when he moved to London at the outset of the War, and some of whose work had already appeared in the pages of Orage's *New Age*.[39] Although Heseltine's view of Sorabji was at times circumspect, they were close enough for Heseltine to include Sorabji on one of his visits to Lady Ottoline Morrell's gatherings at Garsington, at which D. H. Lawrence and his wife Frieda were also present.[40] Sorabji continued to correspond with Heseltine until 1922, and wrote for Gray and Heseltine's radical music journal *The Sackbut* during the period of the latter's editorship (1920–21).[41] A few years later, in 1924, Sorabji reputedly met with another of the influential contributors to *The New Age*, Havelock Ellis – a meeting evidently instigated by Sorabji's mother in order for him to be able to discuss his homosexuality.[42] Sorabji dedicated his *Concerto per pianoforte e piccolo orchestra, 'Simorg-Anka'* (1924) to Ellis, 'in respectful admiration, homage and gratitude'.

Sorabji's political convictions are not easy to ascertain – his critics point to his rabidly anti-democratic views, diatribes against the working classes and outspoken misogyny, while his advocates choose to highlight his pacifism,

[39] In a letter to Heseltine, Sorabji wrote that he 'left with the Porter at 32 a parcel for you containing "Blast"' (27 Dec. 1914, reprt. in Kenneth Derus, 'Sorabji's Letters to Heseltine', in *Sorabji: A Critical Celebration*, ed. by Paul Rapoport (Aldershot: Scolar Press, 1992), 195–255, 216). Sorabji also evidently attempted to expand Heseltine's theosophical and spiritualist readings, and at the same time that he requested Heseltine return his copy of *BLAST*, he also asked for the return of books on 'esoteric Buddhism' and 'Christianity and Buddhism' (Kaikhosru Sorabji, letter to Philip Heseltine, 2 March 1915, in Philip Heseltine Papers, *GB-Lbl*, Add MS 57963, 78). He also took it upon himself to engage Heseltine in contemporary political issues, sending him pamphlets published by the Independent Labour Party with titles such as 'British Militarism', 'Britain and the War', 'Nationality and Patriotism', 'Is Britain Blameless?' and 'How the War Came' (Kaikhosru Sorabji, letter to Philip Heseltine, 24 Aug. 1915, in Philip Heseltine Papers, *GB-Lbl*, Add MS 57963, 98).

[40] See Ottoline Morrell, *Ottoline at Garsington: Memoirs of Lady Ottoline Morrell, 1915–1918* (New York: Knopf, 1975), 77, cited in Derus, 'Sorabji's Letters to Heseltine', 219.

[41] There are thirty-eight letters from Sorabji preserved in the Heseltine papers in the British Library (Add MS 57963), mostly dated between 1913 and 1916 and some from 1920 to 1922, the latter around the time of Sorabji's contributions to *The Sackbut*. In a letter to Kenneth Derus, Sorabji claimed to have destroyed the letters that Heseltine sent him (Kaikhosru Sorabji, letter to Kenneth Derus, n.d. (mid-September 1984), cited in Derus, 'Sorabji's Letters to Heseltine', 196).

[42] Kaikhosru Sorabji, letter to Paul Rapoport, 25 Jan. 1975, cited in Paul Rapoport, 'Sorabji: A Continuation', in *Sorabji: A Critical Celebration*, ed. by Paul Rapoport (Aldershot: Scolar Press, 1992), 58–87, 70. Rapoport goes on to make a range of highly speculative and by now discredited links between Sorabji's sexual orientation and his general outlook (links that are not entirely absent even from more recent literature on Sorabji, such as in Nalini Ghuman, *Resonances of the Raj: India in the English Musical Imagination, 1897–1947* (Oxford and New York: Oxford University Press, 2014)), yet Rapoport's chapter is still useful for documentary purposes.

his anti-imperial views and his commitment to yogic asceticism. He was known to have followed the writings of the Labour Party during the War,[43] yet like other anti-parliamentarians, Sorabji was frustrated with the centrist tendencies of parliament, and viewed the Left and the Right (the 'Red Ranter' and the 'Belowing Blimp', as he called them) as 'roaring the selfsame sentiments in the self-same words'.[44] In what follows I will show how positioning his thinking in relation to the set of discourses that circulated through *The New Age* can illuminate how interwar modernist aesthetics and a certain brand of ambiguously reactionary politics were mutually reinforcing components of the ethos of lateness during this period.

Against 'Equality'

The most obvious social fact of the last forty years is the failure of liberal capitalist democracy, based on the premises that every individual is born free and equal, each an absolute entity independent of all others; and that political equality, the right to vote, the right to a fair trial, the right of free speech is enough to guarantee his freedom of action in his relations with his fellow men. The results are only too familiar to us all. By denying the social nature of personality, and by ignoring the social power of money, it has created the most impersonal, the most mechanical and the most unequal civilization the world has ever seen, a civilization in which the only emotion common to all classes is a feeling of individual isolation from everyone else, a civilization torn apart by the opposing emotions born of economic injustice, the just envy of the poor and the selfish terror of the rich.[45]

One of the central aspects of the politics of late modernism was a general hostility towards egalitarian initiatives – in terms of both the promotion of public access to art and broader democratic reforms. Yet the sources of this hostility, not to mention its aesthetic implications, are far more complex than is often acknowledged, and markedly different from those of the prewar avant-garde. A recurring theme in expressions of this hostility was the

---

[43] For example, Sorabji describes the 'extremely absorbing pamphlets published by the ILP' in 1915 about political power relations in wartime Europe (Kaikhosru Sorabji, letter to Philip Heseltine, 24 Aug. 1915, cited in Derus, 'Sorabji's Letters to Heseltine', 219).

[44] Kaikhosru Sorabji, 'Organic and Inorganic Form', in *Mi Contra Fa*, 47–61, 54.

[45] W. H. Auden, 'The Public v. the Late Mr. William Butler Yeats', qtd. in Michael North, *The Political Aesthetic of Yeats, Eliot, and Pound* (Cambridge: Cambridge University Press, 1991), 2. North notes that in fact what Auden diagnoses is not the decline of liberalism but a condition of liberalism itself – a political tradition that prized the neutrality of procedures over values and was premised on the idea of freedom from constraint, as opposed to the idea of freedom to participate in society according to classical political theory.

view that notions such as 'equality' and 'liberty' were just as abstract and devoid of content as a notion like 'progress', and that one should be sceptical of the way in which these abstractions were often presented as having inherent merit or a singular meaning. Thomas Mann had voiced a similar concern in 1917 over the problematic implications of democratic reform that assumed a standardized version of human reason as the basis of 'virtue', referring sarcastically to the 'three-part equation of democratic wisdom, "reason = virtue = happiness"', and advocating the merits of being an intellectual 'gypsy' who tolerates 'not settling down on any truth'.[46] Mann cast his critique against the figure of the Jacobin politician, and indeed anti-democratic discourses in Britain also drew from contemporary debates in France over the ongoing effects of revolutionary politics and the ideas of Rousseau. The rhetoric associated with anti-Rousseauian sentiment in France became particularly important for certain literary modernists such as T. E. Hulme, whose ideas in this area were highly influential for the late modern milieu. After the War, the terms of anti-democratic discourse shifted somewhat, and the concerns became much more focused on the controlling nature of 'Big Business and High Finance' under the guise of democracy.[47] The supposed abstractions of democratic discourse were viewed as sentimental relics of Romanticism, propagated anew as modern 'progress'.

In aesthetic terms, the scepticism towards conceptual abstractions extended to artistic works that seemed to consciously pursue the 'new', or which relied on pre-formulated devices or theories, in favour of works that were seen to have achieved a more vital newness simply by following the intuitive logic of their material. Writing in the early 1930s about Busoni's music, for example, Sorabji rationalized Busoni's lack of popular success on the basis that he was neither consciously modern, nostalgically sentimental or academically conservative, reflecting 'his power of infusing some absolutely new original and unmistakably personal quality into what is apparently a quite ordinary sequence of harmony or turn of phrase' – an ability that was 'disconcerting to audiences and critics accustomed to two conventions: the "academic" and "modern"'.[48] In this description and others, Sorabji clearly sought to distance Busoni from the institutions of modernism as much as

---

[46] Thomas Mann, 'On Virtue', in *Reflections of a Nonpolitical Man*, trans. Walter D. Morris (New York: Frederick Ungar, 1983), 273–314, 290. I discuss this essay further in Sarah Collins, 'What is Cosmopolitan?: Busoni and Other Germans' *Musical Quarterly* 99.2 (2017): 201–29.

[47] For more on this point see Potter, *Modernism and Democracy*, 7.

[48] Kaikhosru Sorabji, 'Busoni', in *Around Music* (London: Unicorn, 1932), 21–30, 25.

from either professional composition or the popular realm – each of which he viewed as products of rationalization. Busoni's 'aloof, haughty and aristocratic outlook on music' and his 'emotional coldness' kept him 'undefiled and untainted by popular success, or, what is worse, fashionable success among the Art Snobs and the high Bohemia Circus Riders'. This was a particularly heroic achievement, according to Sorabji, 'in a day that has drunk itself besotted on "democracy" and democratic ideals'.[49]

Cecil Gray cast Sibelius in a similar way, writing that his music demonstrates how 'it is still just as possible as it ever was to say something absolutely new, vital, and original, without having to invent a new syntax, a new vocabulary, a new language, or order to do so', while also highlighting that Sibelius was 'no reactionary'.[50] And Heseltine made a similar claim for Delius, as we have seen. Each of these composers was valorized by the music critics in the late modern milieu for their music's apparent resistance to analytical abstraction, or to attempts to determine a singular conceptual motivation – such as 'universal brotherhood' or 'the new' – for their work. These critics positioned their ideal composers somewhere between, or perhaps beyond, both the avant-garde and the rear-guard in the same way that politically they sought after alternatives beyond the Right and the Left.

In political terms, the scepticism described above shaped the view that the conceptual abstractions that informed liberal 'progressivism' had the effect of degrading individuality and difference, promoting a form of false consciousness that concealed democracy's slow creep towards 'totalitarianism'. Sorabji, once again, was particularly explicit in drawing a link from what he described as 'modern democracy and mob-man rule' to 'its hideous and unspeakable logical end, Red Fascist Totalitarianism',[51] or 'totalitarian bureaucratic control over the entire population'.[52] Like the proponents of Guild Socialism in the early years of *The New Age*, and following the Catholic medievalism of Hilaire Belloc, Sorabji idealized the social structures of medieval Europe, and elevated the 'ancient aristocratic-hierarchical ordering of organized human society' above what he called

---

[49] Sorabji, 'Busoni', in *Around Music*, 23.

[50] Cecil Gray, *Predicaments, or Music and the Future: An Essay in Constructive Criticism* (London: Oxford University Press, 1936), 278–88, self-quoting from his earlier book *Sibelius* (London: Oxford University Press, 1931).

[51] Kaikhosru Sorabji, 'The Validity of the Aristocratic Principle', in *Art and Thought* (London: Luzac, 1947), 214–18, 218.

[52] Kaikhosru Sorabji, 'Sentimentality and Contemporaneity: With Especial Reference to Music', in *Mi Contra Fa: The Immoralisings of a Machiavellian Musician* (London: Porcupine Press, 1947), 53–61, 54.

the 'myth' of a 'classless society', and as a way out of the 'democratic-totalitarian midden'.[53]

Sorabji joined the argument against the idea of equality (both class and gender equality) in a chapter contribution to a collection in honour of Coomaraswamy's seventieth birthday in 1947. Sorabji lighted upon the abstract nature of the idea of 'equality' and defended Coomaraswamy against the temporal assumptions underpinning the term 'reactionary' as follows:

The implication is, of course, of opposition to what is equally loosely and imprecisely called 'progress', 'advance' and such like fads. It will not escape the notice of any critical observer that these words too are just as loose, windy and imprecise. Progress? Towards what, from what? It is progress when a fruit from being merely bad, becomes a deliquescent mess – progress in the process of decomposition. The same thing is true of 'advance' though the fact that the word is often associated with an advanced stage of decay may in some small way act as a check upon the fantasies of modern sentimental 'Progressivist' cant.[54]

Sorabji contrasted Coomaraswamy with contemporary progressives such as Wells, who together with G. B. Shaw had become alienated from *The New Age* circle from early on, when the paper moved away from the statist Fabian Socialism to the anti-parliamentarian tendencies of Guild Socialism, as described above. Sorabji attributed to Coomaraswamy an interest in the reintroduction of the caste system 'as the way to that harmonious ordered civilization': 'The principle of caste is founded on the fact that all men are not equal'.[55] Similarly, for Sorabji, the notion of 'equality of opportunity' presented a sentimentalist threat to individualism.

I yearn to become a linguist like the late Father Ledochowsky, the great General of the Society of Jesus, but I have unfortunately no ear and no special ability in mastering languages. How can my opportunity be made equal to Father Ledochowsky's; [...] how are you going to secure my equality of opportunity without seeing to it that all potential Father Ledochowsky's [sic] are strangled at birth or liquidated before they can be a danger to my equality of opportunity.[56]

---

[53] Sorabji, 'The Validity of the Aristocratic Principle', 215–18. Sorabji wrote that Belloc had 'unerring political foresight and sagacity' and that 'every step, every development there set out has come to pass with unfailing precision in exactly the sequence that Belloc describes', observing that Hayek made a similar point in *The Road to Serfdom*, but with less clarity (215–16). For a further example of Sorabji's support and propagation of Belloc's theory, see ' "La Trahison Des Clercs": Music and War-Mongering', in *Mi Contra Fa*, 80–88.

[54] Sorabji, 'The Validity of the Aristocratic Principle', 214.

[55] Sorabji, 'The Validity of the Aristocratic Principle', 215.

[56] Sorabji, 'Sentimentality and Contemporaneity', in *Mi Contra Fa*, 54–5.

Sorabji's argument in his chapter on 'The Validity of the Aristocratic Principle' (1947) proceeds from the idea that humans have different talents, and that it makes sense to organize humans according to their talents and abilities, implying a disturbingly biological basis for guilds and professions, as in the caste system. His critique of the idea of the 'classless' society and progressivism stems from the progressivist's supposed inability to adhere to their own principles. So Sorabji criticizes the progressives' idea of the classless society not on the basis that it is inherently undesirable, but that it is not possible, because the bureaucracy required to organize the affairs of the populace will always constitute a 'Ruling Class'. In opposition to a democratically appointed 'ruling class', Sorabji follows Coomaraswamy's adherence to the idea of heredity in order to ensure that the governing class were less amenable to bribery, in his account. Also, in Sorabji's view, heredity allows more freedom of expression, because the aristocracy would not then feel threatened by dissenting political opinion. On this point, Sorabji offers several examples from Russian and European history that he argues show Imperial systems to be more lenient than liberal systems in tolerating dissent. Sorabji also compares the Treaty of Vienna with the Treaty of Versailles or Trianon as 'evidence' that aristocrats can secure a more peaceable agreement than 'the so-called "democratic" politicians'.[57] In reflecting upon these international agreements Sorabji laments the 'calamitous decline in International Good Manners' as

part and parcel of the same thing, the decline and disappearance of the aristocratic principles of an hereditary ruling caste. Metternich, Fleury, or Talleyrand would have been horrified and disgusted at the idea of locking a man up and robbing him of all his property for no other reason than that his and your Governments happen to be at variance; [....] The overthrow of the older aristocratic Ruling Classes of Europe and the usurpation of their place by the brigands of Big Business and High Finance has quickly brought in its train all the disasters of 'confusion of Cast'.[58]

Sorabji was writing here after World War II, but as Miller and Adorno have observed, many modernists viewed this second conflict as an inevitable unfolding of the post-trauma situation of the first. Very little had changed for them, and indeed the second conflict only served to strengthen this view. Thus we see Sorabji being highly sceptical of the British response to the atrocities perpetrated against Jews in Continental Europe during the

[57] Sorabji, 'The Validity of the Aristocratic Principle', 217.
[58] Sorabji, 'The Validity of the Aristocratic Principle', 218.

1930s and 40s, accusing the British of hypocrisy in a way that reflects his anti-parliamentarianism:

the shedding of tears over the wrongs of Poles or Jews by those who have been responsible for the almost complete disappearance of the Indians of North America, and the indigenous people of Tasmania, is similarly both sentimentality [because proceeding from a sentiment that is not truly felt] and hypocrisy [being a feigned respect for a principle that is ignored]. So, of course, is denunciation of racial discrimination against Jews by those who pass and enforce rigid discrimination by legal and social coercions against their negro fellow-citizens.[59]

Sorabji describes all political ideologies as sentimental and writes that the aim of both the Left and the Right political parties is 'totalitarian bureaucratic control over the entire population'. Yet the more immediate source of Sorabji's frustration on this point, perhaps, was his cultivated resistance to institutional forces or structures of professionalization – structures from which he may have felt disbarred by virtue of his minority self-identification both ethnically and in terms of sexual preference – which found expression in his aversion to doctrine or principle:

It seems that the English, when discussing the 'reform' of their public schools, need do no more than restore them to those to whom they rightfully belong, for whom they were built and endowed, namely the clever sons of poor men, whether these are dukes or dustmen. To exclude the duke's son merely because he is a duke's son, is as wholly illegitimate as to exclude the dustman's boy because he is the dustman's boy [...] and is the kind of inverted proletcult snobbery that is, if possible, even beastlier than the other sort.[60]

In essence, Sorabji viewed the ideal of equality, and democracy more generally, as a result of envy and an unwillingness to appreciate individual talents, describing egalitarian initiatives as a 'frenzy of factitious sympathy for the unfortunate'.[61]

Sorabji's views in this regard extended to his commentary on musical culture. He decried the democratization of London concert life and the expansion of the amateur music-making scene, not for the reason that these changes expanded access to music per se, but because they failed to expand the numbers of audiences willing to concentrate on the music itself rather than treating it as a mass social practice – a mere extension of what he construed as the malevolently imperialistic politics of democracy. Referring

---

[59] Sorabji, 'Sentimentality and Contemporaneity', in *Mi Contra Fa*, 53.
[60] Sorabji, 'Sentimentality and Contemporaneity', in *Mi Contra Fa*, 55.
[61] Sorabji, 'Sentimentality and Contemporaneity', in *Mi Contra Fa*, 57.

to the work of Hugh MacDiarmid in *The New Age*, Sorabji supported his view that 'too many people are interested in their own fiddling little abilities to take any interest in better work: they have no intention of forming an audience'.[62] There were also what he called 'musical manifestations' of democracy, which circulated around over-abundant easy emotional evocation ('sentimentality') and direct speech in song, sexual titillation without any robust vitality, and realism. These aesthetic implications are revealed in Sorabji's criticism of Shaw's play *Mrs Warren's Profession*, which he described as the very essence of sentimentality:

[Shaw] works up feelings that are ridiculous and false, over situations that are equally false; he lacks the mature ironic realism of a Pareto, the urbane humane skepticism of a Norman Douglas; he is a reformer, and mankind has rarely known worse scourges nor greater curses than those ferocious reptilian monsters, the reformers.[63]

Sorabji cited Oscar Levy's description of reformers in *The Idiocy of Idealism* as well as quoting from Norman Douglas's *Alone* (1921)[64] in support of this description of a reformer as one who 'graft[s] abstract principles of conduct upon natures devoid of sympathy [...] a monster, a sanctimonious fish, the coldest beast that ever infested the earth'.[65]

Underpinning this type of criticism against liberal reformism, then, was not only a concern about the compromised nature of parliamentary politics and about the expanding reach of the bureaucratic mechanism of the

---

[62] Kaikhosru Sorabji, 'The Decline of the Public Concert with Some Reflections on the Concert Problem', in *Around Music*, 78–91, 84. No original source given.

[63] Sorabji, 'Sentimentality and Contemporaneity', in *Mi Contra Fa*, 60.

[64] Norman Douglas was also closely acquainted with Cecil Gray, who described Douglas in his autobiography as 'my old friend' who was 'much more typically and representatively Caledonian than "the hairy old bore of Ecclefechan" [Thomas Carlyle]', and indeed who was the 'living embodiment of all that the pagan way of life represents' (Cecil Gray, *Musical Chairs, or Between Two Stools* (London: Home & Van Thal, 1948; reprt. London: Hogarth, 1985), 57 and 209). In the late 1940s Gray and Douglas both became residents of the island of Capri – 'the heart of Siren-land', and it was reputedly there, in Norman Douglas's house, that Gray first met his daughter by Hilda Doolittle, Perdita Schaffner (see Barbara Guest, *Herself Defined: the Poet H. D. and her World* (New York: Doubleday, 1984). Constant Lambert also visited Gray and Douglas in Capri (see Stephen Lloyd, *Constant Lambert: Beyond the Rio Grande* (Woodbridge: Boydell & Brewer, 2014), 358). Douglas was also acquainted with a number of other figures within the late modern milieu sketched here, including Augustus John, D. H. Lawrence and Michael Ayrton. Yet Douglas was far more than a personal friend and drinking companion – he was, for Gray and Sorabji both, a formative intellectual influence, and their writings are peppered with quotations from Douglas's work. Indeed Cecil Gray's Papers held in the British Library include a large photo album of images of Norman Douglas from childhood to old age.

[65] Qtd. in Sorabji, 'Sentimentality and Contemporaneity', in *Mi Contra Fa*, 60.

State, but also a view of humans as inherently unequal and inherently fallible, prejudiced, limited and mired in their historical context. This view – which Sorabji extrapolated as the early insight of the doctrine of original sin[66] – was derived from the anti-humanism of Nietzsche and developed further by Hulme and Yeats.[67] It follows from the belief that humans are by nature imperfect, and that not all are capable of reason, that behaviour and tastes should be regulated by an intellectual authority. This is in contrast to the reformist belief in the possibility of human perfectibility, resting on the idea of an *a priori* sense of humanity – a belief that also underpinned the arguments for greater participation in the political process, such as in the expansion of the franchise, and the notion of equality more generally.

The Classical Temperament

The distinction between a belief in human fallibility and human perfectibility was famously characterized by T. E. Hulme as a distinction between a 'classical' and 'romantic' temperament. Hulme's ideas became particularly influential within the milieu of late modernism. His work was significant for Pound and Eliot; for the consolidation of literary Imagism (propounded by H. D., who was associated with Cecil Gray) and Vorticism before the War; and for interwar modernists who positioned themselves against the prewar liberal Bloomsbury ethos (including both Gray, Heseltine and Sorabji, as well as many of the literary modernists with whom they associated). Jacob Epstein created a bust of Hulme, and Hulme wrote the beginnings of a book about Epstein, *The Sculpture of Epstein*, now lost.[68] Of Hulme's extraordinary influence on Wyndham Lewis it has been noted that 'many of Lewis's articles on art were almost paraphrases of Hulme's ideas'.[69]

Hulme wrote the essay 'From Romanticism to Classicism', most likely in 1911 or 1912, and he may have presented it as a lecture to a private

---

[66] Sorabji, 'Validity of the Aristocratic Principle', 215.

[67] For more on this, and especially the type of anti-humanism that favoured vitality and life-affirmation rather than being life-denying as it is usually viewed, see Elizabeth Kuhn, 'Toward an Anti-Humanism of Life: The Modernism of Nietzsche, Hulme and Yeats' *Journal of Modern Literature* 34.4 (2011): 1–20.

[68] For more on Hulme's support of Epstein, particularly of the latter's geometrical and abstract work in 1913–14, see Alan Munton, 'Abstraction, Archaism and the Future: T. E. Hulme, Jacob Epstein and Wyndham Lewis', in *T. E. Hulme and the Question of Modernism*, ed. by Edward P. Comentale and Andrzej Gasiorek (Aldershot: Ashgate, 2006), 73–91.

[69] Louise Blakeney Williams, *Modernism and the Ideology of History: Literature, Politics, and the Past* (Cambridge: Cambridge University Press, 2002), 143.

audience in 1912, though it was not until 1924, after his death during the War (in 1917), that the essay became more widely available as a part of his posthumously published *Speculations* (1924).[70] In Hulme's account, romantics held to the belief that 'man, the individual, is an infinite reservoir of possibilities: and if you can so rearrange society by the destruction of oppressive order then these possibilities will have a chance and you will get Progress'.[71] He associated this view with the principles of 'liberty' and 'equality' – principles that, in his opinion and that of many other 'reactionary modernists', were distastefully 'abstract' – that had propelled revolutionary sentiments in France. By contrast, classicists believed that it was 'only by tradition and organization that anything decent can be got out of [the human]'. On this latter view, because humans were static in time, without the promise of progression, there was no argument for increasing political participation in the sense that this was necessary to realize your humanity (such as in John Stuart Mill's argument in *The Subjection of Women* in 1869).[72]

Hulme's bleak summary of these two outlooks was that 'to the one party man's nature is like a well, to the other like a bucket'.[73] It is worth pointing out, though, that to view man's nature as a bucket was not necessarily

---

[70] T. E. Hulme, 'Romanticism and Classicism' (1911) in *Speculations: Essays on Humanism and the Philosophy of Art*, ed. by Herbert Read (London: Routledge & Kegan Paul, 1960), 179. The compositional history of this essay is uncertain.

[71] T. E. Hulme, 'From Romanticism to Classicism', reprt. in *The Collected Writings of T. E. Hulme*, ed. by Karen Csengeri (Oxford: Clarendon, 1994), 1999.

[72] Potter, *Modernism and Democracy*, 134–5.

[73] Hulme, 'From Romanticism to Classicism', 1999–2000. Hulme's thinking here explains his sympathy with the ideas of the Syndicalist Georges Sorel. Hulme's 'Translator's Preface to Sorel's *Reflections on Violence*' was published in *The New Age* on 14 Oct. 1915, where he sought to expose the flawed assumption of the 'liberal socialist' that democracy was the 'natural and inevitable equipment of the emancipated and instructed man'. Hulme described the basis of Sorel's argument in terms of the realization that democracy had little connection with the working-class or revolutionary movement, and was in fact 'an organic body of middle-class thought dating from the eighteenth century', observing the continuation of this doctrine in liberal socialism in strikingly similar terms to Orwell's image of the bisected wasp, which in turn relates to the concern with mimicry that will be discussed below under the heading 'the death of the spectator': 'When vulgar thought of to-day is pacifist, rationalist and hedonist, and in being so believes itself to be expressing the inevitable convictions of the instructed and emancipated man, it presents the pathetic spectacle of *an apparently exuberantly active being which is all the time an automaton without knowing it*' (emphasis added). In contrast to this fatuously passionate, sentimental and therefore 'romantic' figure, Hulme described Sorel's prediction positively as the 'return of the classical spirit through working-class violence' (569–70). It is therefore worth distinguishing Hulme's ideas from Sorel's, and highlighting the fact that not all anti-liberal discourses implied a sympathy with fascism (see Edward P. Comentale and Andrzej Gasiorek, 'On the Significance of a Hulmean Modernism', in *T. E. Hulme and the Question of Modernism*, ed. by Edward P. Comentale and Andrzej

pessimistic – rather, its adherents believed that it was a realistic acknowledgement of the historical situatedness of man, set against the supposedly sentimental view that phenomena such as equality, liberty and humanity were anything but empty categories. The alignments of these sets of terms – the temperament of the *romantic* or *sentimental* aligned with the *abstract* or *artificial* on the one hand; and the temperament of the realistic or pragmatic *classical*, aligned with the *organic* on the other – are surprisingly consistent throughout the writings of the literary and musical figures examined here, and will become important in the analysis below.

According to Hulme, these political views reflected a particular temperament, and in turn were manifest in artistic endeavours. Because the romantic was always searching after the infinite – an endeavour that was pejoratively attributed to Beethoven by both Sorabji and Gray, as well as by Edward Dent – and because there is always a gap between the potential and the actual, romantic art tended to be 'gloomy'; yet the classical attitude resulted in a sense of reserve, of an awareness of limitation, of a 'holding back'.[74] For Hulme, classical poetry – the poetry of Horace and Pope and 'most of the Elizabethans' – is 'dry' and 'hard' – while romantic poetry is 'damp' and 'sloppy' and 'moaning', exhibited in the work of Keats, Coleridge, Byron, Shelley and Swinburne. 'The awful result of romanticism is that, accustomed to this strange light you can never live without it. Its effect on you is that of a drug.'[75]

Hulme's ascription of aesthetic tendencies to certain political views, which itself was indebted to the right-wing L'Action Française, was influential for writers such as T. S. Eliot, who went further in describing the implications of this connection for the work of the artist in his essay 'Tradition and the Individual Talent' (1919). In a later essay, 'The Function of Criticism' (1923), Eliot described the Romantic temperament as a form of 'Whiggery'.[76] For Eliot, Romantic artists sought to follow their 'inner voice', searching for the universal within themselves and emphasizing intuition,

---

Gasiorek (Aldershot: Ashgate, 2006), 1–22; and Andrzej Gasiorek, 'Towards a "Right Theory of Society"?: Politics, Machine Aesthetics, and Religion', in *T. E. Hulme and the Question of Modernism*, 149–68). Tom Villis has made a similar point in *Reaction and the Avant-Garde: the Revolt Against Liberal Democracy in Early Twentieth-Century Britain* (London: Tauris, 2006).

[74] There was also a religious component to these designations (see Hulme, 'From Romanticism to Classicism', 2000–2001).

[75] Hulme, 'From Romanticism to Classicism', 2002.

[76] T. S. Eliot, 'The Function of Criticism', in *The Complete Prose of T. S. Eliot: The Critical Edition: The Perfect Critic, 1919–1926*, ed. by Anthony Cuda and Ronald Schuchard (Baltimore: Johns Hopkins University Press and Faber & Faber, 2014), 458–68, 463. First published in *Criterion*, 2 Oct. 1923, 31–42.

the unconscious, the personal and 'personality'. The Classical artist, by contrast, sought to discern external 'principles' via 'impersonality', in order not to pursue simply what they liked but what was 'right'. Classical artists relied on an external authority ('tradition'), rather than on personal intuition, marking a link between Classicism and Catholicism, and again a belief in the fallibility of man – 'the Catholic did not believe that God and himself were identical'.[77] 'In theory', Eliot wrote, this aspect of English national character 'leads to a form of pantheism which I maintain is not European – just as [John Middleton] Murry maintains that "Classicism" is not English'.[78] In other words, for Eliot, the task of both the artist and the critic is not simply to follow their own intuitive special sensibility – a liberal, Whiggish and pantheistic course – but to work tirelessly towards discovering 'truth', 'fact' or 'reality'. He does not define these terms, but specifies 'a scheme into which, whatever they are, they will fit, if they exist'.[79] The aspiration towards discovering 'reality', and the correction of taste thereby, is for Eliot the 'function of criticism', just as for Hulme it was 'accurate, precise and definite description'.[80]

Hulme also agreed with the link between the classical view and the Catholic view, even likening the political idea of human fallibility with the notion of original sin as equally justified beliefs, just as Sorabji was to do later. Both ideas of classicism linked it with deference to a centralized external authority (namely, God or monarch), which found expression in the interwar period in a rejection of mass democracy, and in anti-parliamentarianism. Eliot made a similar argument in a series of lectures on modern French literature in Oxford in 1916, drawing on an association that had been common in French literary debates since the establishment of parliamentary democracy in the 1870s – between romanticism, Rousseau and the political ideals of the French Revolution on the one hand, and between classicism, monarchism and anti-Rousseauian currents on the other.[81] Writing later, in 1924, Eliot defined the democratic mindset in terms of a 'meanness of spirit, that egotism of motive, that incapacity for surrender or allegiance to something outside oneself, which is a frequent symptom of the soul of man under democracy' – and it followed that this condition had a deleterious effect on the condition of art within a democracy, which,

---

[77] Eliot, 'The Function of Criticism', 461.
[78] Eliot, 'The Function of Criticism', 461.
[79] Eliot, 'The Function of Criticism', 466.
[80] Hulme, 'From Romanticism to Classicism', 2002.
[81] See Potter, *Modernism and Democracy*, 132–3.

without acknowledging 'tradition' as the only external authority, had lapsed into the preference for the 'derivative, the marginal'.[82]

For musical figures in the late modern milieu, the supposed 'sentimentality' of political abstractions held similar aesthetic implications, both in terms of musical style as well as the temperament of the artist. Although Sorabji never named Hulme as an influence (and indeed unlike Hulme, Sorabji favoured stylistic complexity), he did share with Hulme and his associates at *The New Age* the desire to politicize aesthetics in such a way as to cast the decline in taste as a result of certain political changes. Sorabji echoed T. S. Eliot in bringing together the conservative idea of human fallibility with the Catholic notion of original sin, seeking to rationalize the naturalness of a hierarchical society and the inequality of humans, against the progressive ideals of equality and liberty. Showing himself to be immersed in these discourses as they further intensified after the War, Sorabji valorized temperamental and aesthetic characteristics aligned with Hulme's – and then Pound and Eliot's – ideal, casting his exemplary artist as a steely, virile, honest and clear-seeing individual. And on this point Busoni once again seemed to shine most brightly. Busoni's playing, for Sorabji, evinced an 'extraordinary cold white fire of intellectualized and sublimated emotion',[83] and his works were

like burnished steel, and its edges are as finely defined and keen as a razor – idea and expression are fused into an instant lightning-like projection. There are no blurred, smudged outlines, no muddle headedness masquerading as 'colour' or 'atmosphere' a la Celtic fog or Maeterlinckian morass.[84]

For Sorabji, as for Gray and Heseltine describing Sibelius and Delius respectively, the true artist was ruthlessly individual without being idiosyncratic in a way that could be replicated in the form of mannerism, abstracted in the form of theory, or described in terms of its pursuit of any identifiable value – such as order, newness or the sublime. Sorabji viewed Nikolai Medtner as 'among the few masters of our time' for these reasons – namely for his 'remarkable individuality under a superficially ordinary exterior, and a harmonic scheme very conservative and restrained in character, but so thoroughly infused with Medtner's own personal flavour as to stamp it in every bar as his'.[85] In another essay he described Medtner as 'by far the most

[82] T. S. Eliot, 'A Commentary' *Criterion* 2.7 (1924), 231, cited in Potter, *Modernism and Democracy*, 144–5.
[83] Sorabji, 'Busoni', in *Around Music*, 21.
[84] Kaikhosru Sorabji, 'Music and Muddleheadedness', in *Around Music*, 18–40, 25.
[85] Kaikhosru Sorabji, 'The Modern Piano Concerto', in *Around Music*, 66–77, 71.

interesting and striking personality in modern Russian music' because of 'his absolute independence and aloofness from the Stravinsky group and its satellites on the one hand, and his equally marked detachment from the orthodox academics grouped around Glazounov and the inheritors of the Tchaikovsky tradition on the other'.[86] Sorabji's description of Medtner's qualities once again map squarely onto Hulme's description of the classical temperament – 'dignity and aloofness, a calm and sad austerity, a meditative anachronism', his personality 'is aristocratic and reticent, it shrinks from *profanum vulgus*, and hugs its reserve ever closer in their presence'.[87]

I have spent some time here looking at the views of Hulme not only because they were shaping forces on the milieu under investigation, but because these ideas emblemized the conflation of certain aesthetic preferences with particular political orientations and habits of mind that allows us to view a range of views under the banner of 'lateness'. Hulme's notion that aesthetic positions are attended by particular political positions that reflect a deeper temperament, character or mindset was broadly consonant with the rhetoric surrounding the tendencies of conservatism and progressivism. Indeed, while conservatism and progressivism were in no real sense polar opposites, the popular conception of their opposition supported a range of related binaries that are of interest in thinking about the politics of lateness. Taking a long historical view of this opposition, Emily Robinson has noted that '[mature] age, timidity and moderation were allied with supporting aristocratic interests, whereas youthful enthusiasm supposedly corresponded with representing the people. So the temporal and the ideological elements were seen to be necessarily entwined'.[88] While it is important to understand that lateness was by no means necessarily connected with 'old age' or, here, 'mature age', as I have argued elsewhere,[89] the metaphorical alignment between moderation and a support for pre-determined authority or hierarchy as attributes that succeed the ebbing away of 'youthful enthusiasm' is useful as a broad description of the sense of 'coming after' that I am ascribing to lateness. There was also a temporal element to parliamentarianism – one that favoured the gradual, incremental, institutionalized and regulated working out of contested topics – all

---

[86] Kaikhosru Sorabji, 'Medtner', in *Around Music*, 132–7, 132.

[87] Sorabji, 'Medtner', in *Around Music*, 132–3.

[88] Emily Robinson, *The Language of Progressive Politics in Modern Britain* (London: Palgrave Macmillan, 2017), 35–6.

[89] Sarah Collins, 'Review of *Late Style and its Discontents: Essays in Art, Literature, and Music*, ed. by Gordon McMullan and Sam Smiles (New York and Oxford: Oxford University Press, 2016)' *Music & Letters* 98.3 (2017): 489–92.

forms of abstraction that some late modernists believed would lead to a widening gap between the political elite and the servile populace.

The 'Mass Production of Minds, Tastes and Thoughts'[90]

The writers examined here tended to cast their rejection of mass democracy as an expression of their moderation as figures with 'classical' mindsets, in contrast to both the supposedly misguided youthfulness of the pre-war avant-garde, and the wayward and impressionable public. Still, these writers were not conservatives in the sense of wanting to shore up the status quo against progressive forces. Nor were they reactionary in the sense of wanting to recover a golden age from the past. They did not align with either of these positions, because both assume a linear and largely progressive view of history – a progressiveness that must be tempered, on these views, but nevertheless accepted that this is the direction of history. In addition, their radical conservatism was fed by an anxiety about state intervention for the purposes of social reform, because this kind of state intervention moved against their conception of history being driven by exceptional individuals, and it seemed to indicate for them an unpardonable intervention by the State into the every day lives of ordinary people.

This view had decidedly Spencerian overtones up until the mid-1880s (and indeed Herbert Spencer had a special interest in music) but its associated rhetoric was reconfigured around responses to the Dreyfus Affair, so that while conservatives rejected mass democracy and promoted individualism, they saw their views as being more closely attuned to the will of the people, in contrast to the supposedly 'artificial' or 'abstract' notions of liberty and equality forwarded by liberal progressives – these were intellectual constructs associated with a liberal elite.[91] In this respect, the 'fear of abstractions' outlined above was aligned with one of the central characteristics of lateness – namely, scepticism towards codification, or towards the setting down of principles in the form of a manifesto or a set of

---

[90] Kaikhosru Sorabji, 'Modern Popular Music as Part of a Plan of Progressive Besotment', in *Mi Contra Fa*, 128–32, 129. This comment appears just after a quotation of Norman Douglas describing the evils of 'compulsory education' which he viewed as destroying children's 'originality of outlook, their curiosity, the directness of their mental vision. They learn to see with eyes, and to think with brains, which are not their own. Their impulses, their conversations – their dreams, I daresay – are standardized…Education is a State-controlled manufactory of echoes' (128). No original source given.

[91] See Robinson, *The Language of Progressive Politics in Modern Britain*, 43.

norms. Although this scepticism came to be expressed in a way that pitted the authority of the aloof modernist artist against the irredeemable 'herd' (fuelling the notion of the 'Great Divide'), it was not towards the public itself that these writers directed their vitriol. Sorabji certainly adjured artists to bracket themselves off from others and wrote of wishing to inhabit not an 'ivory tower', but a 'Tower of Granite with plentiful supplies of boiling oil and molten lead handy to tip over the battlements onto the heads of unwanted and uninvited intruders on my privacy and seclusion'.[92] Yet some of his most impassioned expressions of this scepticism focused not on the public but on the deleterious effects of various types of *structured intellectual process* that he viewed in terms of abstraction, atomization and rationalization – a drive towards the standardized, the consumable and the mass-produced.

One such process that Sorabji viewed with disdain was 'musical appreciation', which he described as an 'unwholesome symptom' of the musical life of England. Sorabji believed musical appreciation did not encourage audiences to think critically or independently, but rather to have their tastes 'ready-made by means of the newspaper, by means of "Half Hours with the Best Authors", "Moments with the Masters", and all the peptonized predigested diluted pabulum of the sort'.[93] Another process that attracted Sorabji's ire on this basis was compulsory education. Sorabji endorsed Norman Douglas's view of public education as a 'State-controlled manu-factory of echoes', though he inflected these processes with an additional corporate malevolence:

In the Western and ultra-Western worlds, the principal incentive towards this mass production of minds, tastes and thoughts comes from vast – and sinister – combines for the mass-production of various commodities. Any adjunct to the pro-cess of benumbing, bemusing and besotment, so that all critical and discriminatory faculties shall be crushed and one man's meat turned into every man's poison, too, is, of course, welcome, and is sure to find Big Money and the Big Interests eager to make use of it.[94]

This comment is from Sorabji's later writings, where he increasingly framed his aesthetics in explicitly political terms. In his reactionary critique of 'modern dance music', tellingly titled 'Modern Popular Music as Part of a Plan of Progressive Besotment', for example, he described the hypnotic

[92] Kaikhosru Sorabji, 'Il Gran Rifiuto', in *Mi Contra Fa*, 141–8, 145. The essay is partitioned into 'Reasons for not going to Concerts'; 'Reasons for having nothing to do with Musicians'; and 'Reasons for living in a Granite Tower'.

[93] Kaikhosru Sorabji, 'Musical Appreciation', in *Around Music*, 112–14, 113.

[94] Sorabji, 'Modern Popular Music as Part of a Plan of Progressive Besotment', in *Mi Contra Fa*, 129.

effects of popular musical forms, which he viewed as depriving the audience of the capacity for individual thought. Sorabji derided this collection of music for its lack of

clean clearly-defined lines, its lack of any organic and cohesive form and sustained train of musical thought [… which turns] the victims still further into the mindless robots of preconditioned reflexes that is the aim and ideal of citizenship held up to these dolts by […] the Ruling Class armed with powers such as no hereditary aristocracy of an *ancient régime* ever possessed, or ever dreamed of claiming; the establishment, in fact, of that which forty years ago Hilaire Belloc foresaw with unerring political sagacity [i.e. the 'Servile State'], and whose advent approaches visibly at an ever increasing pace. All the while, of course, talk about Freedom and Democracy goes on unceasingly, thus bearing out what one of those in the conspiracy once said: 'We are denying with our mouths what we are doing with our hands'.[95]

Sorabji's rejection of codification as a form of rationalization and abstraction akin to liberal democratic politics also finds expression in his argument against formal analysis. In his scepticism towards analysis and towards prescriptions of formal design, he invoked the same types of positive tropes of the self-reliant, self-determining nature of the English national character – a character conceived in opposition to the Germanic, and historically rooted in the sixteenth and seventeenth centuries, before the Glorious Revolution and the end of the House of Stuart:

Few greater moral disasters could have overtaken this country than the ousting of the civilized, humane and urbane Stuart dynasty in favour of this crowd of beer-swilling usurpers and boors. […] Some of the results to which all this led are grotesque and pitiful. Thus, Charles Villiers Stanford, whose work here and there shows short glimpses, flashes of individuality, some small indication of a personality which are, however, soon smothered under a mountain of classroom lumber, used, it is said, in the course of 'teaching' people to compose, to instruct his pupils to compile a sonata, taking as a model a Beethoven work in the same genre. […] How anyone managed to survive this stultifying process is astonishing.[96]

With this 'Germanic pedantry' Sorabji associated an undue reverence for predetermined types of 'form' – a point that again sees him describe this pedagogical tendency and its effect on innovation in music culture as a type of pre-fabrication akin to mass production, where we see music 'forced or poured into a ready-made mould, as in the case of the Stanfords the Parrys, and often of the Brahms [sic] too, a form that does not really arise out of

---

[95] Sorabji, 'Modern Popular Music as Part of a Plan of Progressive Besotment', in *Mi Contra Fa*, 132.
[96] Kaikhosru Sorabji, 'Organic and Inorganic Form', in *Mi Contra Fa*, 47–52, 48–9.

any inner necessity of the music, in the other it moulds its own form, as in the case of Delius or Sibelius'.[97] For Sorabji, the former type of composer was a 'mechanistic mechanical practitioner' whose works replicate a 'meaningless manipulation of technical school room tricks' and whose ideas are so 'empty of any vitality or inner drive' that they 'pour the concoction into jelly and blancmange moulds'.[98] These processes – the Germanic, the Stanford-esque, the classroom-oriented, the pre-fabricated – are described as 'inorganic', as against composers who, 'pursuing intensely orderly cohesive trains of musical thinking instinct with vital and living ideas, mould and shape their forms in accordance with the growth, development, and proliferation of these ideas'.[99] And on this point Sorabji recalled nostalgically the 'mad Englishman' of the eighteenth century

that stimulating and engaging eccentric that this land used to produce when it was still inhabited by individuals, rather than the members of a cinema audience, and when a capacity to think and feel for themselves had not been roller-milled out of them by an educational process which leaves them with the correct ideas about everything and the right ideas about nothing.[100]

Mimicry and the Death of the Spectator

The curious alignment of modernist aesthetics with reactionary politics within this milieu has been described by Tyrus Miller in terms of a concern with the pre-war modernists' valorization of the 'new', which late modernists viewed as a form of rationalization that would have a deadening effect on culture. Miller pointed out that Adorno later cast this tendency as an effect of trauma, reflecting in *Minima Moralia* that 'the new, sought for its own sake, ... petrified into a conceptual scheme, becomes in its sudden apparition a compulsive return of the old, not unlike that in traumatic neuroses'.[101] Adorno's reflections, written in exile during and just after World War II, were of course themselves a product of trauma, and in this sense both the late modernist critique of the 'new' after World War I and Adorno's own critique in the context of the later war were both conditioned

---

[97] Sorabji, 'Organic and Inorganic Form', in *Mi Contra Fa*, 52.

[98] Sorabji, 'Organic and Inorganic Form', in *Mi Contra Fa*, 52.

[99] Sorabji, 'Organic and Inorganic Form', in *Mi Contra Fa*, 52.

[100] Kaikhosru Sorabji, 'Portmanteau Words: or Those "British" Composers', in *Mi Contra Fa*, 76–9, 76.

[101] Theodor Adorno, *Minima Moralia: Reflections from Damaged Life* (1951), qtd. in Tyrus Miller, *Late Modernism: Politics, Fiction and the Arts Between the World Wars* (Berkeley: University of California Press, 1999), 41.

by a sense of coming after – a 'postness'. This echo-effect was also reflected in the fact that the anti-humanism of late modernism found a later expression in developments in poststructuralism; just as the transformation of Hulme's ideas by Eliot and others found expression in later developments in New Criticism.

Miller describes the compulsive and repetitive tendencies of the pre-war modernist deference towards newness in terms of the 'mimetic contamination of subject and object'.[102] For Miller, the preoccupations of the late modernists of the late 1920s and 1930s were substantially shaped by the idea that these mimetic, ritualized or imitative practices were no longer only present in the sphere of art and religious ritual, but were also increasingly prevalent in broader social life – for example in its aestheticization in the forms of department stores, the cinema, and the spectre of the mass public in political and cultural events.

This distaste for the imitative also held darker implications. In Fernihough's account, the fear of abstraction and the critique of liberalism held a common basis in the support of eugenics, in the sense that eugenics presented a 'master discipline governing all others' and was therefore also a shaping force for this branch of modernist poetics. For example, she notes how Pound's Vorticism 'relies not upon similarity or analogy, not upon likeness or mimicry', and that his terms were drawn explicitly from the eugenicist discourse. Similarly, critiques of Romanticism in the modernist press, such as that of T. E. Hulme, were often cast in terms of degeneracy, or a fear of the unfitness of the sprawling masses to participate responsibly in political processes. They also betrayed a distaste for the conditions of the urban poor – the 'gas-lit, supposedly drug-infested slums of London' – and reflected anxieties about the physical readiness of British troops in the context of increasing Anglo-German tensions in the years leading up to World War I.[103]

So, just as we saw earlier with the idea of the 'fear of abstractions' playing into commentary on artistic style, aesthetic temperament or mindset, as well as on entire political and economic systems, the sense of a malevolent compulsive repetitiveness seemed to appear as much in the artistic forms of pre-war modernism as it did in social practices, political structures and economic tendencies of that period. For example, Sorabji described the unmusical music-loving amateur performer in a similarly mechanistic way, as practising 'for hours and hours, for years and years with a remorseless and imbecile persistence, like those robot automata of the insect world who

---

[102]   Miller, *Late Modernism*, 43.
[103]   Fernihough, 'Go in Fear of Abstractions', 483.

go on doing their piece when all reason for doing it has ceased to exist'.[104] Here we see Sorabji's anxiety about greater musical access resulting in tasteless replication, a sort of kitsch, in the name of mere desire – 'this man, too, like all his dreadful "amateur" tribe, "loves" music. How one wishes they *didn't!'*[105]

Sorabji's views on amateur performance, the democratization of the musical realm, the function of the music critic, the art of singing and a whole host of other concerns reflected his overarching anxiety with what Miller has described as the 'de-realization of reality, its progressive replacement with simulacra and spectacles'.[106] He laments that

the ever-increasing number of students at our academies and colleges of music appals [sic] one – appals one because one knows only too well that the vast majority of them are seized with the 'itch to do', as that brilliant Scotch critic and writer, Hugh M'Diarmid, said in the *New Age* some time ago, and that too many people are interested in their own fiddling little abilities to take any interest in better work: they have no intention of forming an audience – the one and only function in which they might be of any use – they all expect audiences themselves. Of true musical insight the far greater part of them possess none, but only an ape-like aptitude for imitation, a spaniel-like ability in picking up a few of the parlour tricks of music – a handful of the most hackneyed of pieces from a hackneyed répertoire.[107]

In a similar concern with automation, Sorabji casts concert culture in terms of a mechanism of self-interested parts. Here, mechanization or mechanical circularity stands in for mimesis, evoking a similar lack of substance, individuality or variation:

Thus A (a composer or player) is the spring of the mechanism of which D (a critic) is one of the wheels. Movement on this part sets D going, dealing out praise, or, if he happens to belong to an opposing mechanism, blame; and no defect or merit on the part of A will alter the working of D.[108]

What concerned these figures was that the focus on newness in cultural modernism had become reflected in social behaviours that replaced means–ends rationality with a type of bourgeois aestheticism, resulting in the propagation of 'ever-changing sameness' that reflected a 'loss of a stable, authentic social ground'.[109]

---

[104] Kaikhosru Sorabji, 'The Amateurs, or Thick Skins and Thicker Heads', in *Mi Contra Fa*, 41–6, 45.

[105] Sorabji, 'The Amateurs, or Thick Skins and Thicker Heads', in *Mi Contra Fa*, 45.

[106] Miller, *Late Modernism*, 43.

[107] Sorabji, 'Decline of the Public Concert', in *Around Music*, 84–5.

[108] Kaikhosru Sorabji, 'On the Value of Professional Criticism', in *Around Music*, 167–71, 169.

[109] Miller, *Late Modernism*, 42–3.

[Wyndham] Lewis views this perilous breakdown of distinction – between subject and object, between spectator and spectacle, between producer and consumer – and the subsumption of art into everyday life as expressed integrally in both social revolution (Lewis criticizes both communism *and* fascism on this point) and the revolutionary aesthetics of the avant-garde.[110]

While the boundary between subject and object can surely not be said to have ever been stable in the sense Miller seems to imply, it is true that many of the tenets of pre-war modernism – particularly those that took as their point of reference a rejection of artistic realism – tended to assume that this boundary was desirable.

Similarly, Wyndham Lewis's response to what he and others perceived to be a discarded boundary between art and social life that had resulted in a 'de-realization of reality' in the 1920s and 30s was not simply to reject this state of affairs – through pursuing ever-intensifying forms of complexity or indeed through complete withdrawal. Rather, he sought to disrupt this mimetic compulsion through what he termed 'nonethical satire', or ' "satire" for its own sake' – a practice that allowed him to critique the prevailing order or representation (emblemized, for Lewis, by Bloomsbury and the Sitwells) without also identifying with another group or viewpoint which itself would then ossify in a similar way.

Sorabji's literary style in his music criticism reflects a similar desire (a vitriolic wittiness surely intended to 'blast', in Lewis's meaning of the term), and his mimicking of modernist withdrawal *in extremis* with respect to his musical works – eventually banning any public performance of his work without his express consent – presented a similar form of parody. Similarly, despite living most of his life in metropolitan London – even while others within this milieu were moving either to the countryside or abroad – in rationalizing why he no longer attended public concerts as often as he once had he noted that:

As I grow older, I find my dislike of my fellow-creatures increases by leaps and bounds: I find my own failings and foibles as much as I can bear with a becoming equanimity; those of others added I find an intolerable burden. The sight of them in their various degrees and kinds of physical and mental ugliness is a distasteful and humiliating reminder that I am one of them; that displeases me.[111]

This stylistic form of disruption was thematized by Lewis in his fiction as a kind of convulsive laughter – a reflex that was intended to produce both

---

[110] Miller, *Late Modernism*, 43–4. Original emphasis.
[111] Sorabji, *'Il Gran Rifiuto'*, in *Mi Contra Fa*, 142.

a violent nonsynchrony in the symbolic fabric of the narrative, as well as allowing the character to re-assert their subjecthood against the tide of aestheticized surroundings. Laughter was also to be the result of the rhetorical and narrative form itself – a 'special type of de-formed "spatial" form'.[112]

Mirroring Lewis's concern about the lessening distinction between spectator and spectacle as a symptom of the de-realization of reality (which in turn was an outcome of liberal democracy, in their view) Sorabji conveyed his anxieties about what he took to be a subversive blurring of the line between audience and performer. For example, he lamented the way in which the competition festivals in Northern England and other parts of the country had resulted in music being considered like a sport – an 'athletics of music' whereby music was merely a vehicle for competitive success rather than a genuine interest. He worried that participation in these festivals did not result in higher numbers of audience members in concert halls. In response to this situation, he called upon music to be 'celebrated' rather than 'performed' – for music to be treated more like a religious ritual than an entertainment or sport. He advocated that

music and its public execution should, as Busoni wished, be surrounded with an atmosphere of peculiar sanctity and reverence – opportunities for hearing it decreased, not increased, and the approach to the art should be surrounded with every difficulty and obstacle, so that only the most worthy could ever reach to the level of priest – that is, as we now call it, public performer.[113]

As we have seen, these types of views were propelled by concerns over the broader effects of developments in 'mass' democracy, as well as by a scepticism towards the mimetic effects of the pre-war modernists' emphasis on 'newness'. In response, late modernists sought to mobilize distilled forms of expression as a way to shore up the subject–object boundary and recuperate an 'authentic' social realm.

---

[112] Miller, *Late Modernism*, 63.

[113] Kaikhosru Sorabji, ' "Performance" versus "Celebration" ', in *Around Music*, 198–200.

Figure 5.1 Photograph of Cecil Gray on the island of Capri, © The British Library Board, Cecil Gray Papers, MS 57803, pencil mark 72.

5 | Cycles, Rotation and the Image: Cecil Gray's Music History and H. D.'s Imagism

> We shall not even begin to understand the first thing about the history of music, or of any other art, until we dismiss from our minds every vestige and trace of the belief that there is such a thing as progress or regress *per se* to be found in it.[1]

So far I have argued that lateness in interwar modernism involved a particular attitude towards time, subjectivity and the public. I have described this form of relation in terms of ascribing epistemic value to autonomy and impersonality, and as involving intellectual practices associated with classicism. This form of relation, and the habits of mind through which they were manifest, exhibited lateness in the sense of enabling a withdrawal from narratives of either progress or revolution, and indeed from the terms of codification altogether. By viewing lateness as a form of relation, we can trace its manifestation across a range of cultural expressions – including music, literature, painting and history – without resorting to the problematic practice of making intermedial analogies, akin to the ambiguous ascription of 'impressionistic' features to music, for example. In what follows I will examine the way in which this form of relation shaped a concept of music history, but I will also suggest how this concept developed out of, or at least in sympathy with, a contemporaneous theory of poetry. This speculative link between a philosophy of music history and a theory of poetry – both as expressions of lateness – is bolstered by a level of personal interaction between the figures involved. Cecil Gray's close relationship with the poet and novelist Hilda Doolittle, or 'H. D.' – who has been described as a 'modernist classicist'[2] – will be particularly significant, as it suggests how Gray may have had direct exposure to the aesthetic presuppositions of Imagism.

Imagism was polemicized by H. D.'s one-time fiancé Ezra Pound, supported by the editorial work of her husband Richard Aldington, and embodied in the work of her close associates at the Café Tour d'Eiffel – many

---

[1] Cecil Gray, *Predicaments, or Music and the Future: An Essay in Constructive Criticism* (London: Oxford University Press, 1936), 49–50.

[2] Rachel Potter, *Modernism and Democracy: Literary Culture 1900–1930* (Oxford and New York: Oxford University Press, 2006), 10.

of whom admired the work of T. E. Hulme. The idea of poetry as 'image' – as a *visual* art concerned with direct communication rather than description or narrative – mirrored the cyclic conception of history shared by a number of prominent artists associated with this milieu such as W. B. Yeats, Ford Madox Ford, Pound, Lawrence, and Hulme himself. This sensibility involved an aspiration to look down upon history as if from a great height, in order to perceive all of the past and the future as a simultaneity existing in the present, at the immediate disposal of the artist.

Gray's philosophy of music history – developed across the widely read *A Survey of Contemporary Music* (1924), *The History of Music* (1928) and *Predicaments, or Music and the Future* (1936) – was emblematic of this temporal sensibility of late modernism, and ultimately resulted in his construction of a distinctive counter-canon. In 1931, Gray used his landmark study of Sibelius to pose a number of historiographical questions that had been troubling him for over a decade. They are striking for their continued contemporary relevance. Paraphrasing, they included: what is the relationship between art or artist and their context? What agents or forces shape the flow of history? and how can we understand the relationship between the past, present and future? These questions – which had also occupied a number of writers in the early issues of *The Sackbut* – reflect the unprecedented time-consciousness of the Edwardian generation, which intensified concerns that have re-emerged in recent years in the disciplinary re-evaluation of the context-driven mandate of 'new musicology'.

For Gray, Sibelius embodied the appropriate response to all three questions. He used the 'idea of Sibelius', as I will call it, as a means to challenge the emerging canon of modernist composers in a similar way to how recent Sibelian studies have been sites for challenges to the Schoenberg-centred history of musical modernism. Further, I will argue that not only was 'the idea of Sibelius' tied to an attempt to subvert the mainstream canon of musical modernism, but more broadly that it involved a rejection of the philosophy of history upon which this historical narrative was based. In other words, I will show how certain British Sibelius-sympathizers explicitly sought to subvert the teleological imperatives of modernist ideology itself, and to erect counter-canons based on different temporal imperatives – in this case, cyclic and what has been called 'sinusoidal' (referring to a periodic oscillation). Investigating counter-canons such as Gray's, and the philosophy of history upon which they are based, offers us not only the opportunity to disentangle the historiography of modernism from modernist ideology, but also an avenue for exploring alternative temporal sensibilities in the early-twentieth-century musical sphere.

Time and the Idea of Sibelius

From the aesthetic point of view, music is neither old nor modern: it is either good or bad music, and the date at which it was written has no significance whatever. Dates and periods are of interest only to the student of musical history. The cult of admiring old music merely because it is old is as shallow and insincere as the indiscriminate admiration that is lavished by the unmusical on each successive idol of 'ultra-modernity'. All old music was modern once, and much of the music of yesterday already sounds far more old-fashioned than works that were written three centuries ago. All good music, whatever its date, is ageless – as alive and significant to-day as when it was written.[3]

Modernity is commonly associated with a particular sense of the unfolding of time.

This 'time consciousness'[4] is often held to have emerged in the sixteenth century as an understanding of the present as being different from the past, and the future as being different from both the past and the present – a sense that intensified in the cultural sphere in the eighteenth century. At its heart, this conception involved a linear notion of the progression of time and of cause and effect, which differed fundamentally from the cyclic or static-universal structures more commonly associated with pre-modern times. Though it is often construed as monolithic and singular in its effect, conceptions of temporal linearity have proved highly versatile. Linearity is perhaps most commonly understood to underpin narratives of human progress towards enlightenment, and historical reflection predicated on evolutionary, teleological or deterministic assumptions. Alternatively, linearity can also describe the slow winding down of human civilization towards decadence, decline and eventual annihilation. It has been put to the service of progressive calls for radical breaks with tradition, as well as conservative agendas that seek to promote continuity with tradition.

Postmodern critiques have highlighted and sought to correct the tendency of this type of time-consciousness to result in the construction of metanarratives of teleological progress that do violence to minority accounts of the experience of modernity. These critiques are often positioned as a response to the immediate past of early-twentieth-century cultural modernism. So while modernism is often construed as having produced

---

[3] Peter Warlock [Philip Heseltine], 'The Editing of Old English Songs' *The Sackbut* (1926): 183–86, qtd. in Gerald Cockshott, 'Some Notes on the Songs of Peter Warlock' *Music & Letters* 21.3 (1940): 246–258, 252.

[4] See Jürgen Habermas, *The Philosophical Discourse of Modernity: Twelve Lectures*, trans. Frederick Lawrence (Cambridge, MA: MIT Press, 1987), qtd. in Gianmario Borio, 'Musical Communication and the Process of Modernity', in 'Modernism and its Others Roundtable' *Journal of the Royal Musical Association* 139.1 (2014): 178–83, 179.

inflexible and oppressive accounts of history based on ideologically riddled processes of canon-formation and erroneous notions of genius and autonomy, postmodernism sought to re-introduce contingency, plurality, minority and alterity back into our understanding of historical experience. Or in the terms used by Ihab Hassan in his famous list of binaries, modernism was all about 'form', 'purpose', 'art object', 'hierarchy', 'distance', 'narrative/Grande Histoire', 'determinacy' and 'transcendence', while postmodernism championed 'antiform' (or an open conception of form), 'play', 'process/performance', 'anarchy', 'participation', 'anti-narrative/Petite Histoire', 'indeterminacy' and 'immanence'.[5]

In describing the contemporary scepticism towards metanarratives, as well as the judgements of value that attend them, Lyotard likened the advent of musical modernism to the Western grand narrative of human emancipation: 'the history of western music may be thought of globally as the grand narrative of the emancipation of sound'.[6] This view is certainly strengthened by Schoenberg's own strategic historicism in casting his 'emancipation of dissonance' as an 'evolution' rather than revolution – the culmination of an inner necessity – and his twelve-tone composition as a 'discovery', underpinning his agenda to 'ensure the supremacy of German music for the next hundred years'.

The view of Schoenberg's musical innovations and his own theorization thereof as the apotheosis of a gradually unfolding music history aligned with the prominent strain of developmentalism in the music historiography of the period, and the conceptions of linearity and teleological progress that underpinned them.[7] The supposed ubiquity of this approach to historical time in the early twentieth century is matched only by the contemporary

---

[5] Ihab Hassan, 'Toward a Concept of Postmodernism', in *The Postmodern Turn: Essays in Postmodern Theory and Culture* (Columbus: Ohio State University Press, 1987): 84–96.

[6] Jean François Lyotard, 'Music and Postmodernity' *New Formations* 66 (2009): 37–45, 38.

[7] For further discussion of this point see Stephen Downes, *Music and Decadence in European Modernism: The Case of Central and Eastern Europe* (Cambridge: Cambridge University Press, 2010), who notes that 'progressive or revolutionary narratives of secular universal history became definitive of modernity' (175). See also Rachel Mundy, 'Evolutionary Categories and Musical Style from Adler to America' *Journal of the American Musicological Society* 67.3 (2014): 735–67, especially at 748, where she highlights the concerns raised in the 1920s about the implications of applying nineteenth-century evolutionary ideas to the history of musical style, with Paul Bekker writing that 'we have no right to look down on any former times and speak of them as primitive', and 'development in the sense of progress, of higher degree or improvement, I cannot admit; at least not in works of art' (qtd. from Paul Bekker, *The Story of Music: An Historical Sketch of the Changes in Musical Form*, trans. M. D. Herter Norton and Alice Kortschak (New York: Norton, 1927), 22).

ubiquity of calls to 'revise' or 'complicate' the monolithic narratives of modernist historiography.

In a parallel line of investigation, the teleological imperative of modernist narratives in the musical sphere has itself been a topic of contention. In recent years, the primary provocation for reconsidering the nature of modernist historiography in music has come from studies of the musical traditions of groups and regions that were conventionally marginalized by the dominant narrative of musical modernism. In particular, there has been a surge of studies into musical devices designed to subvert a sense of temporal linearity, such as rotational form, unresolved recapitulation, and consciously problematic closures.[8] These devices may be viewed to some extent as responses to a concern about Austro-German musical dominance, particularly in relation to the symphonic tradition. It is not surprising then, that one of the primary sites of contest on this point was the nature of the symphony.

At a particular moment, and likely out of psychological necessity, the compositional devices involved in these processes of temporal subversion in symphonic writing became integrated into a broader epistemology – an epistemology that I am calling here 'the idea of Sibelius'. Posed as a symphonic problem, the 'idea of Sibelius' involved a particular relationship with time, but it also involved a certain view on the processes of the acquisition of knowledge that shaped views on a range of significant aesthetic and historical questions. Significantly, it also implied the cultivation of a particular mode of being which Gray conceived as a racially determined aesthetic disposition, exemplified by the duality of Sibelius's Swedish and Finnish natures – the former 'polished and elegant', and the latter a 'substratum of Finnish granite' characterized by a 'fiercely independent spirit, the sturdy self-reliance, the love of isolation and solitude'.[9] The Sibelian type of being, in these terms, was neither reactionary *nor* revolutionary, but was resolutely individual.

While the type of untimeliness ascribed to Sibelius was certainly a stance of opposition in the same manner as other modernist stances, it was a milder and more pragmatic version, similar to the new 'bleakness' among liberals of the interwar period. As we have seen, the artists who participated

---

[8] See for example J. P. E. Harper-Scott, *Edward Elgar, Modernist* (Cambridge: Cambridge University Press, 2006); Daniel M. Grimley, 'Modernism and Closure: Nielsen's Fifth Symphony' *The Musical Quarterly* 86.1 (2002), 149–73, and *Carl Nielsen and the Idea of Modernism* (Woodbridge: Boydell & Brewer, 2011); and James Hepokoski, *Sibelius: Symphony No. 5* (Cambridge: Cambridge University Press, 1993).

[9] Cecil Gray, *Sibelius* (1931; 2nd ed. London: Oxford University Press, 1945), 56.

in the milieu of late modernism were certainly concerned about the mass market, as the pre-war modernists had been, and regularly voiced rabidly anti-democratic views, but they were also concerned about intellectual elitism. For example, Gray was motivated to throw punches in defence of Jacob Epstein for just these reasons, writing later that the sculptor had been persecuted not only by the general public and popular press, but also by his professional peers, as well as the 'more insidious but even more powerful and malevolent hostility of the high pontiffs of the art world: the Roger Frys and Clive Bells and the whole united pullulating cohort of the willowy aesthetes'. Gray noted that Epstein's fight had been against

an unholy alliance between cretins and *intelligentsia*, between the man in the street and the Bloomsbury chorus of male sopranos and lad tenors, between the mandarin ducks of the Royal Academy and the guttersnipes of Fleet Street – to say nothing of the organized opposition of the Church, the Roman Catholics to Plymouth Brethren – and he has beaten them all.[10]

Here we see Gray distancing himself and his associates from an over-ripened 'high' modernism, whose plurality he consistently derided as being without value, merely transitory and apt to date. Gray's derision of the Bloomsbury ethos echoed not only Lewis, but also that of his close friend the poet Roy Campbell, who had also become acquainted with William Walton at Oxford, and who wrote a poem about Heseltine and contributed to Heseltine and Gray's radical music journal *The Sackbut*.[11] A number of Heseltine and Gray's other literary acquaintances were similarly ill-disposed towards Bloomsbury, including D. H. Lawrence, Katherine Mansfield and John Middleton Murry.[12]

    Although Gray held similar anxieties to those of the pre-war modernists with respect to the homogenizing effect of the mass market, his derision of their ethos was based on what he saw as the uncritical reception of artistic novelty and experimentation, and the absence of critical tools to 'objectively'

[10] Cecil Gray, *Musical Chairs: or Between Two Stools* (London: Home & Van Thal, 1948; reprt. London: Hogarth Press, 1985), 206. Original emphasis.
[11] Campbell recalled that 'during the year I was at Oxford [...] William introduced me to the people who have influenced and helped me most in my subsequent literary career, Edith, Osbert, and Sacheverell Sitwell, Eliot, Wyndham Lewis, Thomas Earp, Philip Heseltine, Cecil Gray and others' (Roy Campbell, *Light on a Dark Horse: An Autobiography, 1901–1935* (Hollis & Carter, 1951), 181, qtd. in Stephen Lloyd, *William Walton: Muse of Fire* (Woodbridge: Boydell & Brewer, 2001)). See also Gray, *Musical Chairs*, 239.
[12] For more on the anti-Bloomsbury position of these figures see Sydney Janet Kaplan, *Circulating Genius: John Middleton Murry, Katherine Mansfield and D. H. Lawrence* (Edinburgh: University of Edinburgh Press, 2010).

evaluate works that radically challenged prevailing conventions. In other words, it was as if Ezra Pound's clarion call to 'make it new' had become a fashionable and uncompromising imperative that had the effect of undermining artistic freedom. With the marketization of 'the new', the avant-garde ethos of experimentation had become a victim of its own success, as it were, and Gray's generation desperately sought an alternative that was grounded in sincerity and would last into perpetuity. Their answer, in a word, was Sibelius.

The historiographical and epistemological implications that attended the support for Sibelius were made particularly clear in the writings of Gray, as well as his younger colleague Constant Lambert. Via Sibelius, Gray sought to construct a static-cyclic view of music history whereby classicism stood outside the quotidian developments of the day. The ahistoricity of classicism made it permanently out of sync with its time – it was forever 'too late' – but yet it was also future-oriented as the impossible ideal always aspired to but never reached. In this sense classicism, as Gray described it in relation to Sibelius, reflected the 'two radically different temporalities' of interwar modernism.[13] This push-me-pull-you effect was alluded to by Lewis in the oft-quoted passage from *Blasting and Bombardiering* that opens this book, about the sense of being the 'last men of an epoch' or the 'first men of a Future that has not materialized'.

In this way, Gray's conception of Sibelius's classicism embodied the 'lateness' of late modernism – its relationship of externality to the ceaseless surge of history. This view saw Gray seeking to revise the revolutionary narrative attached to the music of Schoenberg, Stravinsky and Strauss, preferring to view their music – 'despite its factitious appearance of novelty' – as a mere continuation of Romanticism.[14] He wrote that

While most modern composers still continue desperately seeking for some hitherto unexploited resource, some thrill or sensation not previously experienced, Sibelius, almost alone among them, has gone in the opposite direction. In all his later work one finds a deliberate avoidance of anything in the nature of idiomatic novelty or experiment for its own sake, together with a refinement and intricacy of form which are only paralleled in the art of the great classics.[15]

---

[13] Morag Shiach, 'Periodizing Modernism', in *The Oxford Handbook of Modernisms*, ed. by Peter Brooker, Andrzej Gasiorek, Deborah Longworth and Andrew Thacker (Oxford: Oxford University Press, 2010), 17–30, 18.

[14] Gray, *Sibelius*, 196.

[15] Gray, *Sibelius*, 197.

Gray distinguished Sibelius's classicism from 'the self-conscious neo-classicism of the later Stravinsky, Casella, and many others', describing theirs as 'hopelessly sterile because it is artificial and *voulu* – the outcome of deliberation, calculation, and the desire to set a new fashion', while Sibelius was 'spontaneous, unconscious, classic'.[16] For Gray then, the dual imperatives of restraint and spontaneity defined a classical outlook, as well as the practised effacement of one's individual personality. He wrote, 'in the music of [Sibelius's] later period [...] there are absolutely no individual stylistic features whatsoever, yet no music is more profoundly individual, and this is the essence of classicism'.[17] For Gray, Heseltine and Sorabji, Sibelius's classicism was newer than the music of the modernist mainstream because it was not merely a logical extension of historical precedents – it was new because it was untimely; and its untimeliness meant that it would be forever new.

The Character of 'Modern Classicism'

In an ironic twist of fate, this same type of narrative has been subsequently used to first marginalize and then to revive the music of composers who were sidelined from the mainstream historiography of the period, including Sibelius and Elgar. For example, the claim that pre-World War I progressive music should be characterized as late-Romantic was regularly partnered with the periodization of the beginning of musical modernism 'proper' in the 1920s, with the ebbing of Expressionism (though Gray and Heseltine did not subscribe to this view). This account was famously rejected by Carl Dahlhaus in *Die Musik des 19. Jahrhunderts* (1980), where he described it as a 'polemical barb at the Schoenberg school, consigning its expressionist phase to the nineteenth century'.[18] Dahlhaus's attribution of the term '*musikalische Moderne*' to music from 1889 to 1914 served to designate this earlier period as a watershed moment in Western music history, and thereby to draw an unbroken line of progressive and leading musical developments through the Austro-German tradition, culminating in the music of Schoenberg. As Matthew Riley has pointed out, the teleological

---

[16] Gray, *Sibelius*, 198.

[17] Gray, *Sibelius*, 199–200.

[18] Carl Dahlhaus, *Nineteenth-Century Music*, trans. J. Bradford Robinson (Berkeley: University of California Press, 1989), 334. The book was originally published as *Die Musik des 19. Jahrhunderts* (Laaber: Laaber-Verlag, 1980).

view of the development of musical modernism that Dahlhaus seemed to promote meant that composers who did not embrace the 'Neue Musik' after 1910 were considered

classicists or epigonists, and historians can stop talking about them. This becomes palpable in the next volume in the *Neues Handbuch der Musikwissenschaft*, the one on twentieth-century music by Hermann Danuser, in which the symphonies of Elgar and Vaughan Williams are dismissed out of hand.[19]

Despite the pro-Schoenberg emphasis of Dahlhaus's claim regarding *'musikalische Moderne'*, his revision was based on an approach that has since been adopted in studies designed to recognize the radical nature of the very music that Dahlhaus's claim marginalized. For example, J. P. E. Harper-Scott noted that

We may still need to remind ourselves that Elgar was a 'modern' composer in 1913. The fact that he never emancipated the dissonance is immaterial; as Dahlhaus has said, comparing Brahms's and Wagner's neo-Romanticism, 'The spirit of an age, insofar as there is such a thing, is to be found in questions rather than answers' – the same musical questions that troubled Schoenberg also troubled Elgar.[20]

Harper-Scott also relied on Dahlhaus to support the proposition that untimeliness in music allows it to function as a beacon of an alternative world – a claim that poetically buttresses the argument for reconsidering the work of composers from outside the modernist canon.[21] Similarly, Hepokoski cited Dahlhaus in support of his claim that certain composers faced a 'mid-career decision' about how to respond to 'the musical revolutions of Schoenberg and Stravinsky', in that Dahlhaus similarly noted that 'Strauss's and Reger's [ultimate] rejection of modernism ...[was] obviously influenced if not directly occasioned by the shock of Schoenberg's earliest atonal compositions'.[22]

The use of Dahlhaus's work in revisionist accounts of musical modernism that are designed to undermine the Schoenberg-centred narrative that Dahlhaus sought to promote is undoubtedly paradoxical, as Riley points out. It does highlight, however, that revisionist accounts such as those of

---

[19] Matthew Riley, *'Musikalische Moderne*: Dahlhaus and After', paper given at *Elgar and Musical Modernism*, Gresham College, 2011.

[20] Harper-Scott, *Edward Elgar*, 21, quoting Carl Dahlhaus, *Between Romanticism and Modernism: Four Studies in the Music of the Later Nineteenth Century*, trans. Mary Whittall and Arnold Whittall (Berkeley and London: University of California Press, 1980; orig. ed. 1974), 5.

[21] Harper-Scott, *Edward Elgar*, 25.

[22] Hepokoski, *Sibelius*, 8, quoting Dahlhaus, *Nineteenth-Century Music*, 336.

Hepokoski and Harper-Scott do not centre upon the question of periodization. In other words, the question is not 'when did musical modernism begin?', or 'what types of music should rightly be called modernist?', but rather 'what are the musical markers of a composer struggling to ascertain their relationship with their historical moment?' Similarly, when Heseltine and Gray write about certain composers not being modern, or being late-Romantic, they are making a claim not so much about periodization or style, but rather about temperament and character, akin to T. E. Hulme's parsing of classical and romantic temperaments in both aesthetic and political terms, as we have seen.

Hepokoski has used the term 'modern classicism' to describe Sibelius's resolute untimeliness from his Fourth Symphony onwards. He viewed Sibelius's move towards a 'leaner, condensed classicism' at this time as a reflection of the composer's conscious withdrawal from modernist competition, though not as a rejection of modernism. The term 'modern classicism' might well be used to describe formal attributes, as when Arnold Whittall used the term to refer to compositional practices of composers such as Britten, Bartók and Sibelius who sought to 're-establish synthesis as the main technical and structural factor in music'.[23] Significantly, like Gray, Whittall emphasized the marked distinction between 'modern classicism' and neo-classicism, observing how Sibelius's 'modern classicism' was 'distinct from classicism proper, rooted in diatonic tonality as also from a more genuinely modernistic neo-classicism' and involved a 'tendency to subvert structural fundamentals (both formal and harmonic) as well as the effort to affirm them'.[24]

In addition to these formal implications, Hepokoski used the term 'modern classicism' quite specifically to refer to Sibelius's consolidation of his 'compositional *persona*' during this period. In describing this *persona*, Hepokoski used characterological rhetoric that shared something of the masculinizing tendencies of Sibelius's British supporters between the wars, emphasizing the resolute and committed nature of the withdrawal. For example, Sibelius's choice to compete on different terms was described as 'unflinching'; as a 'refusal to yield to diffuse sentiment'; a 're-dressing of the balances'; as 'hard-edged' and in terms of 'risk'.[25] It also exhibited:

---

[23] Arnold Whittall, *Exploring Twentieth-Century Music: Tradition and Innovation* (Cambridge: Cambridge University Press, 2003), 13.

[24] Arnold Whittall, 'The Later Symphonies', in *The Cambridge Companion to Sibelius*, ed. by Daniel M. Grimley (Cambridge: Cambridge University Press, 2004), 49–65, 64.

[25] Hepokoski, *Sibelius*, 11.

1. a sober 'classicistic' critique of the modernists against whom he was competing;
2. an acknowledgement of the importance of the inner logic of his own best music, which he always (disingenuously?) insisted was not rationally plotted during the compositional process but arose naturally, or even mystically, apart from his own volition;
3. anxiety, often veering into indulgent self-pity, over the galling lack of acceptance of his modern-classical works in the continental marketplace of 'progressive' compositions (a variant of this theme concerns his inability to escape the 'nationalist' label originally affixed to the earlier, more successful works);
4. a resolute declaration to continue pursuing his increasingly unique musical path.[26]

The alignment between this type of compositional persona and the ethos of lateness invites us to re-examine the function of the 'idea of Sibelius' within the discourse of late modernism. Within this milieu, the 'idea of Sibelius' functioned as an assertion of the importance of character or disposition in judging musical innovations. The characterological attributes just outlined echo the 'dogmatic untimeliness' of the literary and musical figures involved in the milieu of late modernism – the self-same impotent passion of Lewis's 'Men of 1914', the visionary yet pragmatic aspects of Anderson's 'bleak liberalism', Hulme's political temper of classicism, and D. H. Lawrence's impossible vividness.

The 'idea of Sibelius', including its characterological implications, began to be forged even before the War. In 1912, Sibelius visited England for the third time to conduct his contentious Fourth Symphony at the Birmingham Festival, less than a month after Henry Wood had directed the premiere of Schoenberg's *Five Pieces for Orchestra* (*Fünf Orchesterstücke*), Op. 16, at The Queen's Hall in London.[27] Sibelius's music had received an encouraging reception by English audiences, assisted by the support of emerging and influential conductors such as Granville Bantock, Henry Wood and Hans Richter; and by sympathetic critics, especially Rosa Newmarch and

---

[26] Hepokoski, *Sibelius*, 12–13.

[27] Schoenberg's work was performed on 3 Sept. 1912, and Sibelius's on 1 Oct. 1912. For more on the reception of this performance of Sibelius's Fourth Symphony see Byron Adams, ' "Thor's Hammer": Sibelius and British Music Critics, 1905–1957', in *Jean Sibelius and His World*, ed. by Daniel M. Grimley (Princeton and Oxford: Princeton University Press, 2011), 125–57; and Philip Ross Bullock, *The Correspondence of Jean Sibelius and Rosa Newmarch, 1906–1939* (Woodbridge: Boydell & Brewer, 2011).

Ernest Newman, and later Gray and Constant Lambert. On the occasion of the performance of Sibelius's Fourth Symphony at Birmingham, Newman's perspective on the work helped fashion the enduring critical narrative that Sibelius's music should be viewed as presenting a viable progressive alternative to Schoenbergian modernism. Indeed, as Peter Franklin has noted, 'Sibelius left England on 30 October 1912 almost as an honorary member of its musical avant-garde', and the next generation of British Sibelians such as Constant Lambert continued this narrative in the interwar context, 'reconfiguring Sibelius as a kind of honorary British anti-atonalist'.[28]

This perception that Sibelius's music presented an alternative modernism, as it were, was bolstered by a range of other discourses in circulation in Britain in the first decades of the twentieth century – on notions of manliness, on the purity and strength of the Northern races, on Wagner and the 'symphonic problem' (particularly the perceived limitations of sonata-form structures), and on Teutonic culture and politics more generally.[29] Gray was pivotal in sustaining what Constant Lambert would later describe as the 'Sibelius Cult' in England, in the 1920s and 30s, though it was not until 1929 that Gray first met Sibelius, visiting him in Finland as a music critic for *The Daily Telegraph*. The collection of intellectual practices I am seeking to describe under the rubric of 'the idea of Sibelius', then, were based on an underlying sympathy in aesthetic perspective across a range of cultural forms, that, in the case of Gray and Sibelius, pre-existed personal acquaintance.

Expanding upon this broader intellectual frame, it may be that we can discern a link between the temporal and historiographical implications of Sibelius's particular form of engagement with the symphonic tradition (and the idea that he presented an alternative modernism thereby); Cecil Gray's views on music history and aesthetics and the cyclic and sinusoidal histories penned by other modernist literary figures who became associated with 'late modernism'; and the notion of the 'turbine' and 'image' in Vorticism and Imagism respectively. These similitudes were strengthened by personal

[28]   Peter Franklin, 'Sibelius in Britain', in *The Cambridge Companion to Sibelius*, ed. by Daniel M. Grimley (Cambridge: Cambridge University Press, 2004), 182–95, 187 and 193.

[29]   For further discussion of the intellectual conditions for Sibelius's reception in Britain in the early twentieth century, see Laura J. Gray, ' "The Symphony in the Mind of God": Sibelius Reception and English Symphonic Theory', in *Proceedings from the Second International Jean Sibelius Conference, Helsinki, 25–29 November 1995*, ed. Veijo Murtomäki, Kari Kilpeläinen, and Risto Väisänen (Helsinki: Sibelius Academy, Department of Composition and Music Theory, 1998); and Adams, ' "Thor's Hammer": Sibelius and British Music Critics, 1905–1957'.

interactions between the musical and literary figures involved, such that they might be said to constitute an attribute of a particular milieu.

Cyclic Histories and Modernism

Alongside the contemporary calls to revise our understanding of the nature of musical modernism, there have been parallel demands from within the literary field to re-describe modernist historiography. Particularly relevant in the present context is the work of Louise Blakeney Williams, who mapped the decline of the idea of linear historical development among the Edwardian generation of writers, and showed how a collection of modernists – primarily W. B. Yeats, Ford Madox Ford, Ezra Pound, D. H. Lawrence and T. E. Hulme – developed cyclic conceptions of history that were designed to better serve the psychological and aesthetic concerns of the time.[30]

In essence, this development was designed to perform a number of functions that enabled late modernists to cope with the overwhelming pace of change. Cyclic histories rationalized a desire to withdraw from modernist competition in order to escape the imperatives of the market, and of the mass sentiment that they felt had come to characterize modern democracy. Most importantly, perhaps, this conception of history and time enabled any extreme changes to be seen as recurrences of what had come before, and as a part of the normal ebb and flow of the cycle. For certain artists, this temporal sensibility was expressed in the view that revolutionary shifts in art were based on a misguided understanding of the possibility of progressive change, while the 'true artist' was one who could comprehend the cycle as a whole, beyond the rhetoric of progress, or of decline and decadence, and especially beyond the market of bourgeois modernism. We can see this idea in T. S. Eliot's influential essay 'Tradition and the Individual Talent' (1919), where he called for a combination of the 'timeless' and the 'temporal', characterizing great poets as those who have a 'feeling that the whole of the literature of Europe from Homer and within it the whole of the literature of his own country has a simultaneous existence and composes a simultaneous order.'[31] Gray proffered a similar notion: 'Past, present, and future,

---

[30] Louise Blakeney Williams, *Modernism and the Ideology of History: Literature, Politics, and the Past* (Cambridge: Cambridge University Press, 2002).

[31] T. S. Eliot, 'Tradition and the Individual Talent' *The Egoist* 6.4 (1919): 54–5. Eliot was himself the literary editor of this journal at the time of the serial publication of this article. Growing

indeed, are in reality one and indissoluble, interpenetrating and impinging upon each other to such an extent that it is impossible to form a clear idea of the one without taking the others into consideration.'[32] This type of view can be seen in terms of a response by artists to perceived threats that modernity posed to art, including by the Victorian tendency towards moral didacticism and social comment; by determinism and reason; and by the consumer-driven imperatives of the market.

Concerns about the impact of the forces of a globalized capitalist market in art were accompanied by political fears about the 'tyranny of the majority', seeing a number of prominent modernist writers adopt radical conservative political positions that with post-war hindsight often seem sympathetic with an emerging fascism. Radical conservatives were unlike conventional conservatives in that they called for radical change and the reinstitution of older forms of order, in this case a class hierarchy that would see the aristocracy as once again the custodians of art, promising an alternative to instrumentality and utility driving forces of production. Aristocrats could see the requisite necessities of culture because, according to Ford, writing in 1907, they could '[analyse] things from a height'.[33] For these modernists, democracy meant opening policy up to the whim of the market, promoting opportunistic political moves performed through an all-pervasive media and consumer culture. Modernist writers such as Hulme, who sympathized with what is described above as 'radical conservatism', sought the reinstatement of the 'Classical' and Hobbesian view of human nature as a type that required external regulation, as opposed to the 'Romantic' view which saw in man limitless potential for enlightened development, as we saw in the previous chapter.

In August 1911, the final bulwark to a democracy unfettered – at least by non-governmental or aristocratic forces – was abolished with the removal

out of the significant journal *The New Freewoman*, *The Egoist* was a 'little magazine' that by that time had come to be a highly influential forum for literary modernism. It published, in series form, the first novel of James Joyce (*A Portrait of the Artist as a Young Man*), as well as Wyndham Lewis's vorticist novel *Tarr*, criticism by Pound and significant essays by Dora Marsden. A similar sentiment to that expressed in the quoted passage above can be seen in the opening of Eliot's later poem 'Burnt Norton' (1936): 'Time present and time past / Are both perhaps present in time future, / And time future contained in time past. / If all time is eternally present / All time is unredeemable. / What might have been is an abstraction / Remaining a perpetual possibility / Only in a world of speculation / What might have been and what has been / Point to one end, which is always present.'

[32] Cecil Gray, *Predicaments, or, Music and the Future: An Essay in Constructive Criticism* (London: Oxford University Press, 1936), 7.

[33] Ford Madox Hueffer, 'Literary Portraits. II – M. Anatole France' *Tribune*, 3 August 1907, 2, qtd. in Blakeney Williams, *Modernism and the Ideology of History*, 81.

of the power of veto of the House of Lords on parliamentary legislation. Governance was now entirely in the hands of the voting masses, and many modernists hankered after a renewed class hierarchy as a cultivated foil to what they imagined to be the blind irrationality and self-interest of the public. Blakeney Williams traces the direct link between this kind of radical conservatism and the modernists who developed cyclic-sinusoidal (rather than spiral) theories of history, based on the notion of Classical and Romantic alternations. She notes that cyclic theories of history achieved a renewed resonance in the early twentieth century because they presented one of the most coherent and viable alternatives to the legacy of eighteenth-century narratives of progress. Narratives of progress reflected the impact of the type of thinking associated with Darwinism and the Whig tradition, together with ideas about decadence and decline, and the scientific revolution (which engendered the notion that spheres of human endeavour were governed by laws, akin to nature). The cyclic alternative, in contrast to these traditions, allowed for the idea that humanity's progressive decline was merely the anterior corollary of progress, with both presenting linear notions of change.

Blakeney Williams also highlighted the resurgence of 'spiral' theories of history in the nineteenth century, which presented a combination of 'linear advance with cyclic regression or repetition'. 'Spiral' theories projected a return to an older tradition after the fall, which, together with the benefit of knowledge gained from the fall, would see a steady advancement over time.[34] The spiral narrative can be characterized then by an alternation of positive and negative principles as part of an overarching upward progression whose apotheosis can be likened to Hegel's *aufheben*. This notion found expression in Arnold's Hebraism and Hellenism, Carlyle's systole and diastole of faith, Pater's centrifugal and centripetal, Ionic and Doric, Asiatic and European, and Nietzsche's Apollonian and Dionysian.[35] For the romantics, these alternate traditions were cyclic in nature, though progress still underpinned their movement throughout history as they spiralled towards perfection.

While modernist theories of history drew from these post-Enlightenment cyclic conceptions, the optimistic faith in progress that had characterized the Romantic and Victorian conceptions was replaced by a pre-modern awareness of organic recurrence. With this variance of cyclic conceptions of history, Blakeney Williams distinguishes the 'cycloid'

---

[34] Blakeney Williams, *Modernism and the Ideology of History*, 7.
[35] Blakeney Williams, *Modernism and the Ideology of History*, 8.

from the 'sinusoidal' – terms she borrows from Frank E. Manuel's *Shapes of Philosophical History*.[36] The former idea, which applies an observation of biological lifestyle to a theory of history, was most aptly characterized in Oswald Spengler's *The Decline of the West* (1918), a book with which Cecil Gray was very familiar and to which he often referred.

Cyclic notions, according to Blakeney Williams, 'posit the growth, maturity, and decay of one civilization or tradition and the repetition of that pattern within that civilization or another'.[37] On the other hand, sinusoidal notions envisaged recurrence, through an alternation between two types of tradition, usually identified as 'Romantic' and 'Classical' (such as in Hulme), or 'Romantic' and 'Modern' (such as in Gray), respectively: 'in other words, rather than theorize about one eternally repeated life cycle, an alternation view postulates the existence of two sets of phenomena, principles, or traditions that cyclically alternate throughout time'.[38]

Historical accounts based on the continual alternation between two traditions necessarily rejected the set of assumptions that underpinned linear conceptions of time and history. They were predicated on wildly divergent assumptions about time, processes of change and questions of value that were so central to cultural modernism. These assumptions generated a particular collection of ideas about history and aesthetics that can be traced across different spheres of cultural expression. They include the idea that:

1. History is made up of the alternation of two distinct traditions and underpinned by the static permanence of the cyclic structure, generating an aspiration towards, and a high value placed on, timelessness, or transcending the governing conditions of your time.

2. Change is not cumulative and there is no endpoint to history, so the future will not be radically different from what has come before, and therefore it can be predicted in general terms. Nothing is new, therefore timelessness is the only goal.

---

[36] Frank E. Manuel, *Shapes of Philosophical History* (Stanford: Stanford University Press, 1965), 125. In an earlier article, Blakeney Williams also pointed to other explorations of cyclic conceptions of history, including Mircea Eliade, *The Myth of Eternal Return: Cosmos and History* (1954; reprt. Princeton: Princeton University Press, 1965); and Romila Thapar, *Time as a Metaphor of History: Early India* (London: Oxford University Press, 1996), cited in Louise Blakeney Williams, 'Overcoming the "Contagion of Mimicry": The Cosmopolitan Nationalism and Modernist History of Rabindranath Tagore and W. B. Yeats' *The American Historical Review* 112.1 (2007): 69–100.

[37] Blakeney Williams, *Modernism and the Ideology of History*, 10.

[38] Blakeney Williams, *Modernism and the Ideology of History*, 10.

3.   Aesthetic values associated with the two alternating traditions are reasonably constant throughout time, so that works from the distant past and the present of the same tradition are accorded the same value and can be drawn from equally, as inspiration for new works, without the charge of anachronism.

The temporal sensibility that governed these ideas found expression in historical terms – such as in modernist cyclic histories – and also musical histories (such as Gray's) that rejected developmental narratives. It also found expression in stylistic terms and aesthetic principles, such as in Sibelius's post-Fourth Symphony works, in some forms of *vers libre* in poetry, and in the idea of non-linearity inherent in poetic Imagism. Cecil Gray served as a pivot point between these disparate spheres, drawing from his personal interactions with imagist and vorticist poets on the one hand, and his dedication to the 'idea of Sibelius' on the other.

Image, Vortex and Turbine: Poetic Cycles

A number of the figures occupied with writing cyclic histories had also been involved with the constellation of ideas associated with Imagism – a movement that marked a substantial reorientation of poetics that was to have a significant impact on the development of modernist poetry. In practical terms, Imagism was essentially an invention of Pound, coined as part of a strategy to get five extraordinary poems of his then-fiancée H. D. published in the journal *Poetry*. H. D. later married Richard Aldington – who was also part of the original imagist trio – and during the War had an intimate relationship with Cecil Gray, while Gray was living in Cornwall near to D. H. Lawrence. Hugh Kenner wrote that the term '*imagisme*'

was a name coined to describe a quality of H. D.'s verse: by one account in the British Museum tearoom, where Pound with a slashing pencil made excisions from her 'Hermes of the Ways' and scrawled 'H. D. Imagiste' at the bottom of the page before sending it off (October 1912) to Harriet Monroe at *Poetry*.[39]

Pound included a covering letter describing imagist poetry as 'objective – no slither – direct – no excess of adjectives. etc. No metaphors that won't permit examination. – It's straight talk – straight as the Greek!'[40] The opening of H. D.'s 'Hermes of the Ways' lends actuality to this description:

---

[39] Hugh Kenner, *The Pound Era* (London: Faber and Faber, 1972), 174.
[40] Qtd. in Kenner, *The Pound Era*, 174.

> The hard sand breaks
> And the grains of it
> Are clear as wine.
>
> Far off over the leagues of it
> The wind,
> Playing on the wide shore,
> Piles little ridges,
> And the great waves
> Break over it.[41]

To the extent that we can view Imagism as involving doctrine, Pound credited its central tenets to T. E. Hulme, whom he met at the Café Tour d'Eiffel in 1909 – a noted artists' haunt that Cecil Gray was to frequent at length immediately after the War. Of particular importance to the development of Imagism was Hulme's 'Lecture on Modern Poetry', which he had read to the Poets' Club in London in November 1908, during a period in which he was heavily influenced by Bergson.[42] These tenets were later further clarified by F. S. Flint and Ezra Pound in their contributions to the March 1913 issue of *Poetry*, titled 'Imagisme' and 'A Few Don'ts by an Imagiste', respectively.[43] The year after Hulme delivered his lecture to the Poets' Club, he left that group and began meeting with F. S. Flint and a number of other like-minded poets at the Café Tour d'Eiffel, initiating a group that T. S. Eliot joined in April 1909, and with which H. D. and Richard Aldington were also involved.

Although Flint and Pound's essays were both cast in largely negative terms – seeking to define Imagism by what it rejected – they did manage to articulate a reasonably coherent idea of poetry as image, as well as indicating a range of stylistic determinants which might flow from this central idea. Flint wrote that the *imagistes* recognized their contemporaneity with

---

[41] H. D., 'Hermes of the Ways', Des Imagistes: An Anthology, *The Glebe* 1.5 (Feb. 1914), 21–3, 21.

[42] The precise date of Hulme's lecture is contested. See T. E. Hulme, *The Collected Writings of T. E. Hulme*, ed. by Karen Csengeri (Oxford: Clarendon, 1994), 49. For a fuller chronology see Ronald Schuchard, *The Last Minstrels: Yeats and the Revival of the Bardic Arts* (Oxford: Oxford University Press, 2008), 258; and Christos Hadjiyiannis, 'T. E. Hulme and the Beginnings of Imagism' Networks and Archives of Modernism. Special Issue of *Global Review* 1.1 (2013): 141–64, n. 3. For more on the influence of Bergson on T. E. Hulme see Matthew Gibson, 'Contradictory Images: the Conflicting Influences of Henri Bergson and William James on T. E. Hulme, and the Consequences for Imagism' *The Review of English Studies* New Series, 62 (2010): 265–95.

[43] F. S. Flint, 'Imagisme' *Poetry* 1.6 (1913): 198–200; and Ezra Pound, 'A Few Don'ts by an Imagiste' *Poetry* 1.6 (1913): 200–206.

the post-impressionists and the futurists, but their mandate was not revolutionary and they did not seek radical rupture from the past:

They had not published a manifesto. They were not a revolutionary school; their only endeavor was to write in accordance with the best tradition, as they found it in the best writers of all time – Sappho, Catullus, Villon. [...]

They had a few rules, drawn up for their own satisfaction only, and they had not published them. They were:

1.   Direct treatment of the 'thing', whether subjective or objective.
2.   To use absolutely no word that did not contribute to the presentation.[44]
3.   As regarding rhythm: to compose in sequence of the musical phrase, not in sequence of a metronome.[45]

The aesthetic implications of these informal guidelines might be productively viewed in terms of a rejection of theory, an extreme economy of expression, and an aversion to pre-fabricated forms (which includes, as the editor notes, *vers libre* 'as a prescribed form').[46] All of these, except perhaps economy of expression, were also features of Sibelius's post-1910 compositional style, and consequently also features that determine Gray's conception of music history.

Pound expanded upon these ideas in his corresponding essay 'A Few Don'ts by an Imagiste', where he adjures the budding poet to 'use no superfluous word, no adjective, which does not reveal something'.[47] The extraordinarily condensed poetic expression that resulted from this position served an explicit epistemological purpose, enabling the 'direct treatment of the "thing"'. Hulme had also focused on the directness of the image as a form of communication, in contrast to the reliance of prose on rhetorical devices, or 'figures of speech', which were indirect or at best, dead images.[48] In this sense, the purpose of the image is not as a window to a higher realm,

---

[44] Note here what Gray said of Sibelius's Fourth Symphony – 'the farthest point to which the principle of the elimination of non-essentials has been used. There is not a superfluous note in the score from beginning to end, and hardly one that is not of thematic origin' (Gray, *Sibelius*, 143). Gray concedes that Sibelius's symphonic writing after his Fourth Symphony does not aspire to economy to the same extent.

[45] Flint, 'Imagisme', 199.

[46] Flint, 'Imagisme', 198.

[47] Pound, 'A Few Don'ts', 201.

[48] 'One might say that images are born in poetry. They are used in prose, and finally die a long lingering death in journalists' English. Now this process is very rapid, so that the poet must continually be creating new images, and his sincerity may be measured by the number of his images' (Hulme, 'A Lecture on Modern Poetry', in *Collected Writings*, 55).

or a distillation of an idea, as in the role of the symbol in symbolist poetry – rather, it aimed at a form of scientific objectivity – it aimed to be an accurate description, pared back to its barest elements.

This purported directness relied on the idea that one can perceive an image instantaneously, without requiring an understanding that is revealed temporally (such as in narrative poetry, prose literature, or indeed music).

An 'image' is that which presents an intellectual and emotional complex in an instant of time […] It is the presentation of such a 'complex' instantaneously which gives that sense of sudden liberation; that sense of freedom from time limits and space limits; that sense of sudden growth, which we experience in the presence of the greatest works of art.[49]

To achieve this 'sudden liberation', the imagists sought to plasticize their poetics, as it were, evoking the static nature of sculpture, as well as its tangibility, and its sensual existence beyond the mind. They sought after an ecstatic moment of revelation, whose potency cut through what they saw as the lumbering intellectualizations of philosophy and criticism, or the descriptiveness of prose literature and romantic poetry.

There are a number of important points to extract from the focus on the instantaneousness of perceiving an image, that help illuminate the intellectual practices which I am claiming here are common features across the literary and musical spheres. The first relates to the matter of rhythm and music. In the quotation above, Flint makes reference to the idea of composing poetry 'in sequence of the musical phrase, not in sequence of a metronome' and Pound similarly associates the imagist mandate with a symbolist-inspired veneration of music's autonomy from conceptual or linguistic reference. Pound wished to focus on the sound values of words, rather than their meaning – he wanted to 'dissociate the vocabulary from the cadence',[50] echoing Walter Pater's famous dictum on the confluence of form and content which characterizes the 'condition of music'.

On the other hand, in Hulme's earlier lecture he seemed to disassociate imagist poetry from the character of music:

this new verse resembles sculpture rather than music; it appeals to the eye rather than to the ear […] It builds up a plastic image which it hands over to the reader,

---

[49] Pound, 'A Few Don'ts', 200–201.
[50] Pound, 'A Few Don'ts', 203. Also see Pound's other music criticism for his developing elucidation of the conception of rhythm (Ezra Pound, *Ezra Pound and Music: the Complete Criticism*, ed. by Murray Schafer (London: Faber, 1977)).

whereas the old art endeavored to influence him physically by the hypnotic effect of rhythm.[51]

Hulme's position on the 'hypnotic effect of rhythm' is consistent with the way he cast his whole view on modern poetry as working against the 'hocus pocus' of poetic criticism that regards poetry as an access point to a higher realm.[52] He viewed idealism in poetic aesthetics as akin to 'selling a patent medicine in the market-place',[53] a sentiment echoed by Pound when he encouraged poets to 'consider the way of the scientists rather than the way of an advertising agent for a new soap'.[54] The new focus on objectivity and instantaneousness as a 'scientific' aspiration of poetry has been associated, by Graham Hough, with a reaction against Victorian realism, whereby 'no natural object can appear without trailing its inglorious little cloud of moralizing behind it'.[55] The underlying principle behind this shift was art's autonomy – from social convention, from the market and from conceptual reference.

Despite this apparent divergence between Hulme, Pound and Flint on the matter of poetry's relationship with music, the liberty with which music is invoked in both positive and negative terms in relation to imagist poetry should not obscure our view of how the concept of music supported the imagist mandate. Flint's reference to music referred specifically to a point that he was trying to make about adopting a particular approach to poetic metre – namely one that was not tied to a pre-determined verse-form, rather whose form originated in poetic material itself. In contrast, when Pound referred to music, he was referring to the non-linguistic character of music, as an ideal for the poetic focus on constructing an 'image' with sufficient directness. And when Hulme referred to music, he referred to the tendency of regular rhythm to result in cognitive laziness and passive acceptance akin to the hypnotic effect of market advertising. He noted that the difference between the image that could be achieved in poetry and the 'figures of speech' in prose was that 'while one arrests your mind all the time with a picture, the other allows the mind to run along with the least possible effort to a conclusion'.[56] So while music informed an aspiration towards

---

[51] Hulme, 'A Lecture on Modern Poetry', in *Collected Writings*, 56.

[52] 'I want to speak of verse in a plain way as I would of pigs: that is the only honest way' (Hulme, 'A Lecture on Modern Poetry', in *Collected Writings*, 49).

[53] Hulme, 'A Lecture on Modern Poetry', in *Collected Writings*, 49.

[54] Pound, 'A Few Don'ts', 203.

[55] Graham Hough, *Image and Experience: Studies in a Literary Revolution* (London: Gerald Duckworth, 1960), 14.

[56] Hulme, 'A Lecture on Modern Poetry', in *Collected Writings*, 55.

freer and more content-based forms, and an emphasis on sound over concept in poetry, it was also a dangerous example of the hypnotic effects of rhythm. Equally, the fact that music is an art whose realization requires the passing of time ran contrary to the emphasis on the instantaneousness of the image – its static existence outside of time, which, for Hulme, also defined its ability to exist beyond market forces.

These conflicting views on music suggest that Imagism was underpinned by a desire to transcend the progressive passage of time, and it may be that the interest in cyclic histories proceeded from a similar impulse. Indeed, there is a relationship between the static and the cyclic in that both subvert linearity and teleology (both formally and historically). Thus the very old and the very new can be conceived as part of the same aesthetic plane. Writing about Pound's poem *The Return*, Kenner noted,

> A shift in tense, a change of rhythm, and a termination that contains no tenses but draws pallor and slowness into sculptured stasis: these are the devices by which the poem encompasses a long historical span, as from Sappho's time to H. D.'s.[57]

Pound's first anthology of imagist poetry, *Des Imagistes*, published in March 1914, included several poems by both Richard Aldington and H. D., and also by Pound himself, as well as works by F. S. Flint, Amy Lowell, Ford Madox Ford, James Joyce and William Carlos Williams.

As a disparate group of poets became attached to the imagist mandate, Pound was already transforming its rhetoric into that of Vorticism, and aligning himself with new manifesto colleagues, notably Wyndham Lewis. The vorticist credo exploded onto the London literary scene in the two extant issues of *BLAST* (1914 and 1915), edited by Lewis, with contributions by Pound, Jacob Epstein (with whom Gray later became friends at the Café Royal), Edward Wadsworth, Spencer Gore, Rebecca West and, in the second issue, T. S. Eliot. Richard Aldington was also a signatory to the 'manifesto' section of the journal, and many of these same figures were contributors to *The Egoist*, for which Aldington was assistant editor at this time, and which ran a special issue on 'Imagism' in May 1915.

Between the hot-pink covers of the first issue of *BLAST* the signatories proclaimed in bold stylized text 'Long Live the Vortex!', with Lewis and his fellow associates giving a declamatory voice to a credo that was the more radical and organized counterpart to H. D.'s Imagism. Like Imagism,

---

[57] Kenner, *The Pound Era*, 190–91.

Vorticism was clear about what it rejected, with the 'blasting' occupying far more space than the 'blessing' in the journal. Indeed the blasting had enormous scope – ranging from 'the Post Office', 'Codliver Oil', 'Captain Cook', 'Croce' and 'The British Academy' to, rather curiously, 'Beecham (Pills, Opera, Thomas)', 'Joseph Holbrooke' and 'Edward Elgar'.[58] The vorticists were agnostic in their scope of rejection – they blasted *the past and the future* ('We stand for the Reality of the Present – not for the sentimental Future, or the sacripant [sic] Past'[59]); *the masses and the elites* ('The Man in the Street and the Gentleman are equally ignored [...] We are against the glorification of "the People", as we are against snobbery' and 'Curse abysmal inexcusable middle-class (also Aristocracy and Proletariat)'[60]; and *folk culture and machinery*.

They were particularly careful to distance themselves from the futurists ('We don't want to go about making a hullo-bulloo about motor cars, anymore than about knives and forks, elephants or gas-pipes. Elephants are VERY BIG. Motor cars go quickly').[61] So just as Pound had attempted to distance Imagism from the French poetic movement Symbolism by using a word that had not appeared on the continent as a poetic ideal ('I made the word – on a Hulme basis – and carefully made a name that was not and never had been used in France'[62]), so too Vorticism distanced itself from the Italian avant-garde, explicitly proclaiming its origins in the culture of England, as a 'Review of the Great English Vortex'.

The vorticists were fundamentally opposed to collective identification of any kind, with the exception of course of their shared contempt for identity itself. They positioned the *individual* at the very centre of their mandate – the timeless, classless individual who was entirely self-created: 'Beyond Action and Reaction we would establish ourselves'[63] and 'there is one Truth, ourselves, and everything is permitted'.[64] According to this mandate, the person who could successfully extricate themselves from a relation to their time – either a reactionary or revolutionary relation – was a true artist: 'The moment a man feels or realizes himself as an artist, he ceases to belong to

---

[58] 'Manifesto – I', *BLAST* 1 (1914): 21.
[59] 'Long Live the Vortex!', *BLAST* 1 (1914): n.p.
[60] 'Manifesto – I', *BLAST* 1 (1914), 13.
[61] 'Long Live the Vortex!', *BLAST* 1 (1914): n.p. Still, in other sections of the first issue, many of the things blasted at the outset receive a more positive treatment later, especially machinery, English temperament, and even the timeliness of the artist.
[62] Qtd. in Kenner, *The Pound Era*, 178.
[63] 'Manifesto – I', *BLAST* 1 (1914): 30.
[64] Wyndham Lewis, 'Our Vortex' *BLAST* 1 (1914): 147–9, 147.

any milieu or time. *Blast* is created for this timeless, fundamental Artist that exists in everybody.'[65]

In this sense, the idea of the vortex was a call for a particular style of being, rather than just a particular style of art – a style of being that had a particular relationship to historical time, whereby the past and the future presented co-existent possibilities.

Pound imagined the vortex as a spinning turbine:

All experience rushes into this vortex. All the energized past, all the past that is living and worthy to live […] All the past that is vital, all the past that is capable of living into the future, is pregnant in the vortex, NOW.[66]

While this approach could accommodate an aspect of timeliness, or rather artists who happened to be 'in sync' with their historical context – and indeed Lewis makes some contradictory remarks on this point – the primary feature of Vorticism's historical time consciousness is a call to be untimely. Or as Edward Wadsworth highlighted in his review of Kandinsky's *Ueber das Geistige in der Kunst*, one of Kandinsky's three 'mystical fundamentals' for 'inner necessity' is that

Every artist, as the servant of art, has to express what is particular to all art. (Element of the pure and eternal qualities of the art of all men, of all peoples and of all times, which are to be seen in the works of art of all artists of every nation and of every epoch and which as the principal elements of art, know neither time nor space).[67]

In this sense the artist must speak in the language of their time in order to communicate, but must draw equally and without discrimination from all times, viewing the cycle of history 'from a great height'.

Gray's Critique of Linear Music History

All great works are equal, because incomparable. Excellence is not relative but absolute. No period is good or bad in itself, there are only good and bad works.[68]

---

[65] 'Long Live the Vortex!', *BLAST* 1 (1914): n.p.

[66] Ezra Pound, 'Vortex' *BLAST* 1 (1914): 153.

[67] Edward Wadsworth, 'Inner Necessity' *BLAST* 1 (1914): 119. A number of the figures associated with Vorticism were painters (including Lewis) who sympathized with Kandinsky and Picasso. Note, though, that the year before, in 1913, Hulme had written disparagingly of the spiritualism of Kandinsky in *The New Age*.

[68] Gray, *Predicaments*, 50.

The assumptions about time and value that underpin the cyclic-static view of history and poetics permeate Gray's thinking on the question of historical change, agency and the relationship between artist and context. This similitude is by no means arbitrary, and it had consequences that reach further than hitherto acknowledged when focusing on the literary sphere.

In the summer of 1917, disillusioned with wartime London, Gray moved to Land's End, into a house at Bosigran Castle, only a few miles from where D. H. Lawrence and his wife Frieda were living. Gray had an immediate concern with the prevailing anti-Continental sentiment, after his confrontation with Edwin Evans at the Café Royal over Evans's derision of Gray and Heseltine's plans to host a concert of the music of Béla Bartók, and Evans's threat to 'bring a contingent of drunken Australian soldiers to wreck the hall'.[69] Gray had become acquainted with Lawrence through Philip Heseltine, who had been living with the Lawrences in their Cornwall house for some time prior to the summer when Gray arrived, as we saw in Chapter 3. It was at this time, however, that exemptions from military service were withdrawn, and Heseltine fled to Ireland in order to thwart his summons to a medical examination. During Gray's stay at Land's End, his relationship with the Lawrences became such that, when in October 1917 the couple was compelled to hurriedly move to London after several local incidents resulting from intimations of their pro-German sympathies, Gray provided them with the funds to relocate, and offered his mother's house in Earl's Court as refuge.

During Gray's period in the house at Land's End, he began a relationship with Hilda Doolittle. In her semi-autobiographical novel *Bid Me to Live* (1960), H. D. described how she became attached to Gray almost by accident, after a sequence of traumatic events including losing a baby; her husband taking a mistress and then leaving for war service; and her thwarted intimacy with D. H. Lawrence. H. D. described how it was Lawrence (represented by the character of Rico) who had initially brought the pair together, but that in following Gray (represented by the character of Vane) back to Cornwall, H. D. (Julia) felt as though she were escaping Lawrence's manipulative tendencies and the psychological bleakness of wartime London. H. D. described Gray/Vane's manner as detached, with an 'air of indifference, the feudal hallmarks. Perfectly, he was there to help her'.[70] Vane was presented as a steadying figure, though not someone about whom the

---

[69] Reported by Gray in his autobiography *Musical Chairs*, 113.

[70] H. D., *Bid Me to Live*, intro. by Helen McNeil, afterword by Perdita Schaffner (London: Virago, 1984), 120. The book was originally published in 1960, a year before H. D.'s death.

narrator felt passionate: there was 'no blur, no fizz or fireworks in her head, not aftermath, not beginning, not end, something running in a straight line, a pattern'.[71] Gray and H. D. had a child together, Perdita Schaffner, though they became estranged very early on and Schaffner only met Gray once, much later, on the island of Capri when Gray came to visit Norman Douglas. In a letter to Gray some years after their relationship had come to an end, H. D. referred warmly to remembering the 'old ghosts' of their time together, commenting that 'Cornwall has always remained a dream, for which I deeply thank you!', and signing off 'I am still: Mrs. H. D. Aldington'.[72]

The extent to which Gray's subsequent thinking may have been influenced by the temporal implications of Imagism described above, and intensified by this period of emotional involvement with H. D. and D. H. Lawrence, is open to speculation. In any case, there are some striking similarities in his ideas about the instantaneousness of conceiving musical styles from across history – which he developed over the following years – and the notions of cycles and turbines from poetic theory and modernist histories that by this time had achieved a prominent (if localized) cultural currency that could hardly have escaped Gray's notice.

Tracing Gray's intellectual development through the 1920s and 1930s, we see him becoming extremely broad in his thinking, well informed, and demonstrating a more-than-passing familiarity with contemporary texts of philosophy, literature and art history in both English and French. His judgements are firm and precocious, though he is careful to support all statements with evidence or examples – in other words, he is reflective about method. Gray repeatedly lamented the dominant impact of the 'doctrine of evolution' on music historians, with historical accounts of musical development being 'habitually represented as a gradual but steady and undeviating process of growth and development from the simplest and most primitive beginnings in early times up to the refinements and complexities of our present Western European practice'.[73] For Gray, this view of music history, while not without merit, tended to be cold and deterministic, viewing musical objects 'like a corpse, a fit subject for scientific analysis or dissection but not for aesthetic appreciation'.[74]

---

[71] H. D., *Bid Me to Live*, 132.

[72] Hilda Doolittle (H. D.), letter to Cecil Gray, 15 Dec. [no year given], *GB-Lbl*, MS 57784.

[73] Gray, *Predicaments*, 26.

[74] Cecil Gray, *The History of Music* (London: Kegan Paul; New York: Alfred A. Knopf, 1928), 2. He described this method as being the result of a 'genealogical malady', and wrote that 'it does not constitute the history of an expressive art such as music any more than a philological study of language could pass for a history of literature' (2–3).

In opposing the scientism of a Spencerian view of music history, Gray's focus in his own history-writing was on examples of untimeliness – of music that could not be explained as a product of its time, or as a culmination of historical development preceding it. Through this lens, he constructs an alternative canon designed to counterbalance the evolutionary narrative that tended to view the work of Palestrina, Bach, Handel, Haydn and Mozart as the apotheosis of cumulative technical development. Instead, he offered an account of music history that sought to illuminate:

> the three great regiments of the Netherlanders under Dufay, Ockeghem and Josquin des Prés, the great Roman school of Palestrina, together with the Venetians under Gabrieli, the Spanish under Victoria, and the English under William Byrd: the second Venetian and Roman schools of the seventeenth century, side by side with the Neapolitan school of Alessandro Scarlatti, and many others – their work as alive now as the day it was composed, if we only care to exercise our sympathy and imagination a little.[75]

Gray's emphasis on the eternal newness of untimely music had the effect of subverting developmental music histories, but it also implied an uncanny absence of genealogy that made his ideal compositions seem almost like miraculous conceptions, rather than representatives of broader trends. For example, in rejecting the prevailing understanding of Gregorian chant as having gradually developed from the music of antiquity, Gray believed that

> a fine example of Gregorian chant, or plain-song, is as perfect and moving a thing now as the day when it was composed. It seems to have *sprung fully grown and completely developed* from the heart of the Christian religion, like Pallas Athene from the brain of her father Zeus. […] It is extremely important that this intrinsicality and independence of Gregorian chant should be insisted on.[76]

Gray's claim adheres to the 'myth of self-creation' (related to Eliot's ideas about individualism) that was so prevalent in his milieu, with both Heseltine and Sorabji buttressing their support for composers such as Delius, Busoni, Van Dieren and Sibelius with assertions about their non-categorical nature, and the fact that they belonged to no school or tradition. Gray articulates the evidence for his claim about the newness of Gregorian chant in musical, historical and cultural terms. He drew from and critiqued the work of French musicologists such as M. Gastoué and M. Pierre Aubry, as well as Tovey, Wooldridge and Riemann – the latter two over their accounts of the

---

75   Gray, *The History of Music*, 3–4.
76   Gray, *The History of Music*, 12. Emphasis added.

evolution of modern harmony, which he believed demonstrated the 'confusion over the early history of harmony'.[77] Gray believed that this humble and self-denigratory tendency to view music on a trajectory towards increasing maturity and complexity was still a common view in the 1930s at the time of making his own speculations on the music of the future, though he notes that it is a view most stridently held, paradoxically, by those who reject the work of the avant-garde.

The anterior corollary of developmental notions of music history was the doctrine of entropy, which Gray associated with the views of the younger generation – with their 'disillusioned, somewhat jaundiced outlook'.[78] While in the evolutionary narrative the golden age of art is yet to come, under the doctrine of entropy, we are in a perpetual devolution from a golden age in the past.[79] This was an equally plausible, and equally unreasonable theory, according to Gray:

It would be easy to make out a plausible case for the contention that Bach, with his introduction of equal temperament in tuning, and in other ways, was the arch-destroyer of music, and the case for Palestrina as against Monteverdi and his fellow innovators is an exceedingly strong one.[80]

A third conception of history that Gray described was a combination of the evolutionary and devolutionary, or:

postulating all developments as parts of a *curve* – a steady ascent up to a point and a subsequent steady fall, constituting three main phases which may be conveniently designated as the primitive or archaic, the mature or classical, and the romantic or decadent.[81]

Under this view, the future of music would either be conceived in terms of decline, or alternatively as part of a new cycle – in a way seeing the 'end of history' as a new kind of 'pre-history' of the next cycle: 'a fresh primitive or archaic period'.[82]

---

[77] Gray, *The History of Music*, 17.
[78] Gray, *Predicaments*, 29.
[79] Gray saw examples of this conception of art history in Robert Byron's *The Birth of Western Painting*, and Bernard Berenson's *Studies in Mediaeval Painting*, and indeed the unconscious perceptions of concert-goers who preferred Beethoven and Schubert to Wagner and Brahms (Gray, *Predicaments*, 30). He also noted that Huysmans in *En Route* reflected this idea of perpetual decline by writing that Gregorian chant was the highest point of musical art.
[80] Gray, *Predicaments*, 31.
[81] Gray, *Predicaments*, 32. Emphasis added.
[82] Gray, *Predicaments*, 33.

Gray examined each of these three conceptions of history in turn, acknowledging their strengths but ultimately settling on a position of critique in each case. He noted that evolution sometimes tended towards simplicity rather than complexity, and questioned the aesthetic merit of complexity as an aesthetic category itself. He did acknowledge, however, that it would be

idle to deny that the art [of music] has developed and grown, in some way or another, for better or for worse, from the simple unison of Gregorian chant up to the complexities of, say, Schoenberg's *Pierrot Lunaire*. It is a childish error, however, to suppose that this development is synonymous with progress in a purely aesthetic sense of the word.[83]

Gray also admitted that the view of history in terms of decline – a view with which he associated Hegel's *Philosophy of Fine Art*, and Spengler's *Decline of the West* – did have an 'uncomfortable ring of truth',[84] yet he suggests that this perception of decline or transition can be applied to all times, and that the artists who last into perpetuity are often momentarily obscured by more transient and sensationalist fashions of their time.

Significantly, Gray believed that narratives of decline in art historiography were informed by an increasing valorization of scientific thought in modernity. He pointed to the fact that Hegel's indictment was followed by an exceptionally creative period artistically, despite his exhortations of immanent decline, and surmised that this perception is founded in philosophy's vested interest in art's demise. Thus, Gray reads into narratives of the death or decline of art an implicit ascent of abstract thought and scientific thought in its place, and counters this opposition by arguing that the intellectual processes and activities involved in science, philosophy and art are all an equal combination of *reason, intuition and emotion*. He describes the *aesthetic side of science*:

To contemplate a great philosophic system, to see it working inevitably, relentlessly towards its appointed goal, branching out into infinite multiplicity of detail yet all the time preserving its basic unity, its ultimate purpose, is to experience as authentic and exquisite a thrill, as genuine and deep an aesthetic emotion, as any that we receive from a work of art [...] To ask whether the proposition involved is 'true' or not would be just about as reasonable as to ask if a Bach fugue is 'true'.[85]

---

[83] Gray, *Predicaments*, 38.
[84] Gray, *Predicaments*, 41.
[85] Gray, *Predicaments*, 46.

And, likewise, the *rational function of art*:

In precisely the same way that a great intellectual achievement gives us this indefinable sense of exaltation and satisfaction, quite apart from what it proves or demonstrates, so the work of art must convince us by virtue of its power of pure reasoning, by its absolute logic and inevitability. [...] The E major Fugue in the second book of Bach's Forty-eight is in its way as logical, as closely reasoned as the proposition in Spinoza's Ethics proving the existence of God by mathematical demonstration.[86]

Gray's view that art and science both employ intellect and intuition in equal measure, both being directed towards expressions and explorations of truth, is therefore contingent with his notion that aspects of evolution and devolution are present in all ages, so that historical change and transition is a permanent condition of all ages, as both work against the tendencies of developmental history.

Of the third, cyclic conception of history, Gray was decidedly more positive. He rated among its advantages a parallel with the course of organic objects and natural events such as the operation of the seasons, and day and night, which makes this look like something approaching an 'unescapable [sic] law'.[87] He attributed this approach to Sir Flinders Petrie (who was influential for Hulme) in *Revolutions of Civilization*, to Oswald Spengler in *The Decline of the West*, and also saw the tendency for this kind of cyclical assumption in Goethe, Hegel, Vico and Nietzsche, as well as in works prior to the modern era. In this way, Gray acknowledged the attraction of considering a close relationship between processes of nature and processes of human history, in a way that saw him reject the agenda of 'purification' usually ascribed to high modernists.

From the cyclic point of view, Gray's interwar standpoint looks decidedly wintery:

does it not seem that there is something in the spiritual atmosphere and temperature of our epoch that renders difficult any further fruitful cultivation of the opulent, mellow art of our immediate predecessors, such as Strauss, Delius, Elgar, or Debussy, and withers and shrivels up any attempt at lyricism and emotional warmth?[88]

Even so, Gray holds to a regulated view of the present – he does not seek sanctity in future potentials, nor lament a past golden age, nor is he nihilistic at accepting present conditions with a view to a cyclic regeneration; rather,

---

[86] Gray, *Predicaments*, 47.
[87] Gray, *Predicaments*, 51.
[88] Gray, *Predicaments*, 54.

he takes the Nietzschean embrace of the present as containing within it all the possibilities of history.

> In the same way that there is a beauty of evening and night as well as of dawn and noontide; a beauty of old age and even of death as well as of youth and maturity; a beauty of autumn and winter as well as of spring and summer; a beauty of waste and desert places as well as of tropical luxuriance – so are there equal possibilities of aesthetic beauty and artistic achievement in any and all of the phases of the Great Year of a culture or a civilization.[89]

In this way, it is Gray's historical sense – his ability to empathize with past times, as if seeing all of music history simultaneously – which shields him from the uncertain winteriness of his present. It became a psychological necessity then, in the same way that cyclic histories became so for the literary modernists discussed earlier.

Spontaneity of Being and Form

In line with Gray's view of music history as non-cumulative and non-linear, as well as his related focus on untimely figures, Sibelius's art appeared to Gray as if from nowhere – entirely spontaneous and unconscious. It was akin to the instantaneousness of Hulme, Pound and H. D.'s poetic 'image' (together with its historical implications), and an embodiment of the ecstatic simultaneity of past, present and future described by Eliot in his essay on 'Tradition and the Individual Talent' (discussed in Chapter 3). As in Eliot's essay, Gray's propagation of the myth of Sibelius's self-creation was aligned with claims about Sibelius's exemplary achievement of impersonality, with his late works exhibiting 'absolutely no individual stylistic features whatsoever, yet no music is more profoundly individual, and this is the essence of classicism'.[90] Indeed, so complete was Sibelius's impersonality, according to Gray, that it had resulted in a level of anonymity that had relegated the composer to relative obscurity in his own time.

For Gray, Sibelius had nothing in common with either his contemporaries or his 'immediate predecessors':

> He seems, in fact, to bear no relation to any other composer, past or present, and in consequence the ordinary historical-comparative methods of musical criticism are utterly useless in attempting to deal with him. [...]

---

[89] Gray, *Predicaments*, 55.
[90] Gray, *Sibelius*, 199–200.

It is perhaps hardly to be expected that a generation whose aural palate has been vitiated and debauched by excessive indulgence in sonorous alcohol should take kindly to such an art as this.[91]

For Gray then, Sibelius stands outside of history, and is equal to – or rather synonymous with – all other great masters who stand outside of history. There is, in this sense, what Eliot described as a 'conformity between the old and the new' because the 'existing order [was] complete before the new work arrives'.[92] The difficulty in rationalizing Sibelius's musical style within a narrative of evolutionary development makes him untimely, and this feature had reached its culmination in his late works, which Gray related directly to a similar achievement in Beethoven's late works – works which Adorno claimed were emblematic of 'late style' *tout court*.

Gray sought to cast the imagists' rejection of abstraction and pre-conceived form – and therefore, the 'modern spirit' as discussed by Hulme in his 'Lecture on Modern Poetry' – as a particularly English trait. Calling the 'Anglican indifference to form' a 'positive trait in the hands of a master – it is perhaps the supremest manifestation of genius, this capacity to dispense with form, and simply to move as the spirit moves one, without precon-ceived destination or *arrière pensée*'.[93] Given what Gray saw as the English indifference to form, it was no wonder that Sibelius was received so warmly in England. Gray believed that the English interest in Sibelius was due to the lack of national tradition, which he believed had hampered the reception of Sibelius in other nations: 'In England, on the other hand, we have been musically as well as economically free-traders; not being self-supporting, we have opened our doors to works of every nationality without favour or prejudice.'[94] Gray conceded that while 'our policy of free imports has acted as a powerful deterrent to the cultivation of a national art' it still allowed for 'a more enlightened, eclectic, and impartial body of critical opinion than is possible elsewhere'.[95]

Gray contrasted the spontaneity of the English indifference to form with the French obsession with form, mirroring Pound's wish to distance his Imagism from the French poetic tradition, and also Hulme's admonishment of Rousseauian ideals and the revolutionary mandate that they precipitated. As part of a significant tradition of English scepticism towards the French

---

[91] Gray, *Sibelius*, 9 and 11.
[92] Eliot, 'Tradition and the Individual Talent', 6.4 (1919): 55.
[93] Gray, *Musical Chairs*, 22.
[94] Gray, *Sibelius*, 12.
[95] Gray, *Sibelius*, 12.

ideals of equality and liberty (emblemized in Edmund Burke's anti-Jacobinism), Gray viewed content-based, intuitive form and spontaneity as deeply ingrained in the English psyche. He even compared the greatness of the city of London – because it is 'utterly shapeless and amorphous, lacking in even the most elementary factors of design – a vital organic growth and nothing more' with the 'pre-ordained' and 'logically planned' layout of his home town of Edinburgh, which he noted was an 'outcome of the Old Alliance between Scotland and France'.[96]

These types of tropes held an ongoing currency in discussions of music and the idea of English 'national character' for many decades to come.[97] For example, in his 1950 study of Vaughan Williams, Hubert Foss included a lengthy aesthetic characterization of the English temperament that lighted upon precisely the kinds of elements that have been discussed in this chapter as features of late modernism and modern classicism.[98] Characteristics such as the 'power of distillation' or 'pregnant simplicity';[99] the absence of planning or predetermined systems;[100] and suspicion of over-intellectualization were all made to appear by Foss as natural outgrowths of an 'English way of life', which comprised 'the English character of mind, the English language, the English landscape, English folk-song, an earlier English music, and the English Church'.[101]

The Future's Past

As a consequence of Gray's insistence upon the uncanny spontaneity of the master artist, and his staunch rejection of the evolutionary view of music history, he ascribed a special responsibility to the individual composer. Gray was highly critical of what he termed the 'mechanistic and material-istic doctrine of the Marxian school of historians and the Hegelian school from which they derive', which he viewed as objectifying individuals as

---

[96] Gray, *Musical Chairs*, 23.

[97] For more on the history of these notions see Sarah Collins, 'Anti-intellectualism and the Rhetoric of English "National Character" in Music: the Vulgarity of Over-refinement', in *British Musical Criticism and Intellectual Thought, 1850–1950*, ed. by Jeremy Dibble and Julian Horton (Woodbridge: Boydell & Brewer, 2018), 199–234.

[98] Hubert Foss, *Ralph Vaughan Williams: A Study* (Oxford: Oxford University Press, 1950).

[99] Foss, *Ralph Vaughan Williams*, 59.

[100] 'We may talk of "planning," but we are in fact men of action first and consideration after. Of intellectual and artistic planning we are particularly suspicious' (Foss, *Ralph Vaughan Williams*, 57).

[101] Foss, *Ralph Vaughan Williams*, 50.

instruments of an 'anonymous directing power'.[102] He similarly criticized the doctrines of critics such as Taine, 'for whom the great artist is nothing more than the outcome of the combination and interaction of such impersonal forces as race, environment, and tradition, and therefore readily calculable'.[103] According to Gray, the process of objectification underpinning the Hegelian view of history and 'Marxian' view of culture had the effect of abstracting the stylistic development of music from the creative individuals responsible for it. Further, musical development was made to look like a collective phenomenon that was shorn of particular expressive identity, articulating the classic problem of cultural criticism of how to construe the relationship between forms of expression and the structuring conditions of the historical moment. The oppressive dissolution of the individual into the collective and anonymous abstraction was compounded by the unavoidable forwardness of history, so that, overall, Gray viewed the dominant perception of the development of musical style as *abstracted, collective, anonymous* and *inevitable*, and much of his own view was directed against these features – features which seemed to run counter to the romantic nature of music as an art of rebellion.[104] As we have seen, and in line with the literary modernists with whom he associated, Gray developed an alternative view of the history of style as individualistic, untimely, and non-developmental.

Despite Gray's views on the importance of untimeliness, his desire to speculate on the future of music and his heightened awareness of processes of canon-formation led him nonetheless to recognize a 'certain element of necessity, logic, and inevitability in the workings of history'.[105]

In other words, while it may be true that the achievement of many great artists is largely individual and independent of extraneous circumstances, others, on the contrary, seem to arise as if in response to a definite need, and accomplish tasks which were ready waiting for them, so to speak. Between these two extremes of the purely individual genius, owing practically nothing to any one or anything outside himself, and the artist who simply exemplifies a tendency or performs an historically necessary role, there are others – and they probably comprise the majority of great artists – in whom there is an intermingling in varying degrees of the personal

---

[102] Cecil Gray, *A Survey of Contemporary Music* (Oxford: Oxford University Press, 1924, 2nd ed., 1928), 2.

[103] Gray, *Predicaments*, 3.

[104] For example, he wrote: 'Indeed, the whole history of the art is generally conceived as a collective and almost anonymous activity, in which individual genius is merely a secondary consideration in comparison with the formal and idiomatic development of musical language' (Gray, *History of Music*, 2).

[105] Gray, *Predicaments*, 2.

and impersonal elements, a synchronization of individual genius and historical necessity.[106]

This moderating view enabled Gray to undertake the task of making predictions about the future of music, which he likened to the meteorologist's task – acknowledging that both were speculative, though were based on evidence and observation of 'present conditions, past analogies, and all the complex phenomena which together make up the *Zeitgeist*, or spirit of the age, and the *genius loci*, or spirit of the place', in this sense suggesting a level of determinism.[107]

A concern for the future was, according to Gray, a part of the human condition, in as much as our understanding of the present and our daily lives are ordered in relation to expectations of future events. On a historical level too, he discussed the impact of future expectations on musical developments, such as the suspension of creative vitality in the lead up to the first Millennium in the Middle Ages and the subsequent surge after the non-event of Final Judgement; and the greatness of art and literature around the time of the French Revolution and the apparently boundless opportunity of the future, and then the disillusionment with failed revolutionary ideals, which he saw as being reflected in the art of the time.[108]

He saw his own period in similar terms – namely, that after the exuberant optimism of Darwinian theory and the pre-war era, the 1920s and 30s were characterized once again by disillusionment with future possibilities. Gray noted how the ominousness of the future had conditioned the prevailing feeling of being in a mode of transition and of decay, and he speculated that the present's expectations of imminent future collapse might have a constitutive effect on the future, bringing about the collapse that it predicts. He observed pragmatically that a sense of transition and decadence was common to all periods, citing from the English tradition Bertrand Russell, Matthew Arnold, Ruskin and Carlyle, as well as Burke, Cowper, Edmund Spenser and earlier to Roger Bacon; and from the French tradition Musset and Montaigne.[109]

The 'time consciousness' of modernity, then, was not merely what Gray described as the 'historical sense' – namely, being in sympathy with past ages – and not merely about looking to the future, as embodied in the manifestos of Futurism or the utopianism of Edwardian social alternatives.

[106] Gray, *Predicaments*, 3–4.
[107] Gray, *Predicaments*, 4–5.
[108] Gray, *Predicaments*, 9.
[109] Gray, *Predicaments*, 17.

More than this, the awareness of the past and interest in the future shaped a deep self-consciousness with how the future would view the present – indicating a concern about codification. In this sense, the interest in the future was not only about present expectations, but rather a concern for how the legacy of the present would be interpreted in future times, and how to ensure that the best work would not be buried by history.

Musicians and writers of Gray's milieu lived in a present that was constituted essentially as the future's past. In a desperate bid to survive into history, they cultivated a vision of static-cyclic time that suggested that it was possible to be truly untimely. And while the historical sense gave them self-awareness about the contingency of critical reflection, they sought to escape its clutches by seeking after eternals. There is something of our current struggles in this 'predicament' – in our difficulty in coming to terms with the permanent contingency or situatedness of our viewpoint as scholars. In response to this crippling awareness, Gray called on critics to be boldly untimely in their judgements, in a way that is neither reactionary nor revolutionary:

My critics and opponents, in fact, try to represent me as *laudator temporis acti*, one out of touch with the present; it is true, in so far as I am always a few steps ahead of them, and look for my sense of values and guidance to the great masters of former days. I am always simultaneously ahead of and behind my time; I live more in the past and the future than in the present – in the eternal, in fact. Hence, in part, my isolation. I am not grumbling; as I say, I would not have it otherwise – except at moments when the spirit falters, and the flesh is weak. (But they do not last long, these moments!).[110]

---

[110] Gray, *Musical Chairs*, 179.

Select Bibliography

Adams, Byron. ' "Thor's Hammer": Sibelius and British Music Critics, 1905-1957'. *Jean Sibelius and His World*. Ed. by Daniel M. Grimley. Princeton and Oxford: Princeton University Press, 2011, 125-57.

Albright, Daniel. *Personality and Impersonality: Lawrence, Woolf and Mann*. Chicago: University of Chicago Press, 1978.

Anderson, Amanda. 'Character and Ideology: the Case of Cold War Liberalism' *New Literary History* 42.2 (2011): 209-29.

The Powers of Distance: Cosmopolitanism and the Cultivation of Detachment. Princeton: Princeton University Press, 2001.

Ardis, Ann L. 'The Dialogics of Modernism(s) in the *New Age*' *Modernism/Modernity* 14.3 (2007): 407-34.

Asmussen, Kirstie. 'Hubert Foss and the Politics of Musical Progress: Modernism and British Music Publishing'. PhD diss., University of Queensland, 2016.

Baldick, Chris. *Criticism and Literary Theory 1890 to the Present*. London: Longman, 1996.

Beer, John. 'Lawrence's Counter-Romanticism'. *The Spirit of D. H. Lawrence*. Ed. by Gāmini Salgādo and G. K. Das. Hampshire and London: Macmillan, 1988, 46-74.

Bekker, Paul. *The Story of Music: An Historical Sketch of the Changes in Musical Form*. Trans. M. D. Herter Norton and Alice Kortschak. New York: Norton, 1927.

Bell, Daniel. 'Modernism Mummified' *American Quarterly* 39.1 (1987): 122-32.

Bell, Michael. *D. H. Lawrence: Language and Being*. Cambridge: Cambridge University Press, 1992.

'Lawrence and Modernism'. *The Cambridge Companion to D. H. Lawrence*. Ed. by Anne Fernihough. Cambridge: Cambridge University Press, 2001, 179-96.

'Perceptions of Lateness: Goethe, Nietzsche, Thomas Mann, and D. H. Lawrence'. *Late Style and its Discontents: Essays in Art, Literature, and Music*. Ed. by Gordon McMullan and Sam Smiles. Oxford and New York: Oxford University Press, 2016, 131-46.

Belloc, Hilaire. *The Servile State*. London: Foulis, 1912; 3rd ed. London: Constable, 1927.

Bernstein, J. M. *Against Voluptuous Bodies: Late Modernism and the Meaning of Painting*. Stanford: Stanford University Press, 2006.

Bhimani, Nazlin. 'Sorabji's Music Criticism'. *Sorabji: A Critical Celebration*. Ed. by Paul Rapoport. Aldershot: Scolar Press, 1992, 256-84.

Blakeney Williams, Louise. *Modernism and the Ideology of History: Literature, Politics, and the Past.* Cambridge: Cambridge University Press, 2002.

'Overcoming the "Contagion of Mimicry": The Cosmopolitan Nationalism and Modernist History of Rabindranath Tagore and W. B. Yeats' *The American Historical Review* 112.1 (2007): 69–100.

Bodley, Lorraine Byrne and Julian Horton, eds. *Schubert's Late Music.* Cambridge: Cambridge University Press, 2016.

Borio, Gianmario. 'Musical Communication and the Process of Modernity'. Modernism and its Others Roundtable. *Journal of the Royal Musical Association* 139.1 (2014): 178–83.

Bridgwater, Patrick. *Nietzsche in Anglosaxony: A Study of Nietzsche's Impact on English and American Literature.* Leicester: Leicester University Press, 1972.

Brinkmann, Reinhold. *Late Idyll: The Second Symphony of Johannes Brahms.* Trans. Peter Palmer. Cambridge, MA: Harvard University Press, 1995.

Brooker, Peter and Andrew Thacker, eds. *The Oxford Critical and Cultural History of Modernist Magazines: Vol I: Britain and Ireland, 1880-1955.* Oxford and New York: Oxford University Press, 2009.

Busoni, Ferruccio. 'The Oneness of Music and the Possibilities of Opera' (1921). *The Essence of Music and Other Papers.* Trans. Rosamond Ley. New York: Dover, 1957.

Cockshott, Gerald. 'Some Notes on the Songs of Peter Warlock' *Music & Letters* 21.3 (1940): 246–58.

Collini, Stefan. 'British Exceptionalism Reconsidered: Annan, Anderson and other Accounts'. *Anglo-French Attitudes: Comparisons and Transfers between English and French Intellectuals since the Eighteenth Century.* Ed. by Christophe Charle, Julien Vincent and Jay Winter. Manchester: Manchester University Press, 2007, 45–60.

Public Moralists: Intellectual Life in Britain, 1850-1930. Oxford: Clarendon Press, 1993.

Collins, Sarah. 'A Critical Succession: Aesthetic Democracy and Radical Music Criticism between the Wars' *Music & Letters* 95.3 (2014): 404–28.

'Anti-intellectualism and the Rhetoric of English "National Character" in Music: the Vulgarity of Over-refinement'. *British Musical Criticism and Intellectual Thought, 1850-1950.* Ed. by Jeremy Dibble and Julian Horton. Woodbridge: Boydell & Brewer, 2018, 199–234.

'Review of *Late Style and its Discontents: Essays in Art, Literature, and Music,* ed. by Gordon McMullan and Sam Smiles (New York and Oxford: Oxford University Press, 2016)' *Music & Letters* 98.3 (2017): 489–92.

'What is Cosmopolitan?: Busoni and Other Germans' *Musical Quarterly* 99.2 (2017): 201–29.

Comentale, Edward P. and Andrzej Gasiorek. 'On the Significance of a Hulmean Modernism'. *T. E. Hulme and the Question of Modernism.* Ed. by Edward P. Comentale and Andrzej Gasiorek. Aldershot: Ashgate, 2006, 1–22.

Copley, Ian A. *A Turbulent Friendship: A Study of the Relationship between D. H. Lawrence and Philip Heseltine (Peter Warlock)*. London: Thames, 1983.

Dahlhaus, Carl. *Between Romanticism and Modernism: Four Studies in the Music of the Later Nineteenth Century*. Trans. Mary Whittall and Arnold Whittall. Berkeley and London: University of California Press, 1980; orig. ed. 1974.

—— *Nineteenth-Century Music*. Trans. J. Bradford Robinson. Berkeley: University of California Press, 1989.

Davis, Mary E. *Classic Chic: Music, Fashion and Modernism*. Berkeley: University of California Press, 2006.

Davis, Thomas S. *The Extinct Scene: Late Modernism and Everyday Life*. New York: Columbia University Press, 2016.

Deghy, Guy and Keith Waterhouse. *Café Royal: Ninety Years of Bohemia*. London: Hutchinson, 1955.

Delany, Paul. *D. H. Lawrence's Nightmare: The Writer and His Circle in the Years of the Great War*. Hassocks, Sussex: Harvester, 1979.

—— 'Halliday's Progress: Letters of Philip Heseltine' *D. H. Lawrence Review* 13 (1980): 119–33.

Delavenay, Emile. *D. H. Lawrence: the Man and his Work: the Formative Years, 1885–1919*. Trans. Katharine M. Delavenay. London: Heinemann, 1972.

—— 'Lawrence, Otto Weininger and "Rather Raw Philosophy"'. *D. H. Lawrence: New Studies*. Ed. by Christopher Heywood. London: Macmillan, 1987, 137–57.

Derus, Kenneth. 'Sorabji's Letters to Heseltine'. *Sorabji: A Critical Celebration*. Ed. by Paul Rapoport. Aldershot: Scolar Press, 1992, 195–255.

Doolittle, Hilda [H. D.]. *Bid Me to Live* (1960). Intro. by Helen McNeil. Afterword by Perdita Schaffner. London: Virago, 1984.

—— 'Hermes of the Ways'. Des Imagistes: An Anthology. *The Glebe* 1.5 (Feb. 1914): 21–3.

Downes, Stephen. *Music and Decadence in European Modernism: The Case of Central and Eastern Europe*. Cambridge: Cambridge University Press, 2010.

Eagleton, Terry. *Literary Theory: an Introduction*. Oxford: Basil Blackwell, 1983.

—— 'The Novels of D. H. Lawrence'. *The Eagleton Reader*. Ed. by Stephen Regan. Oxford: Blackwell, 1998.

Earle, Ben. 'Modernism and Reification in the Music of Frank Bridge' *Journal of the Royal Musical Association* 141.2 (2016): 335–402.

Eliot, T. S. 'The Function of Criticism' (1923). *The Complete Prose of T. S. Eliot: The Critical Edition: The Perfect Critic, 1919-1926*. Ed. by Anthony Cuda and Ronald Schuchard. Baltimore: Johns Hopkins University Press and Faber & Faber, 2014, 458–68.

—— 'Tradition and the Individual Talent' *The Egoist* 6.4 (1919): 54–5 and 6.5 (1919): 72–3.

Esty, Jed. *A Shrinking Island: Modernism and National Culture in England*. Princeton: Princeton University Press, 2004.

Fernihough, Anne. *D. H. Lawrence: Aesthetics and Ideology*. Oxford and New York: Oxford University Press, 1993.

' "Go in Fear of Abstractions": Modernism and the Spectre of Democracy' *Textual Practice* 14.3 (2000): 479–97.

Ferrall, Charles. *Modernist Writing and Reactionary Politics*. Cambridge: Cambridge University Press, 2001.

'The *New Age* and the Emergence of Reactionary Modernism Before the Great War' *Modern Fiction Studies* 38.3 (1992): 653–67.

Flint, F. S. 'Imagisme' *Poetry* 1.6 (1913): 198–200.

Foss, Hubert. 'Cecil Gray, 1895–1951' *The Musical Times* 92 (1951): 496–8.

'Introduction'. *Frederick Delius*. By Peter Warlock. London: Bodley Head, 1923; rev. ed. 1952, 9–26.

Ralph Vaughan Williams: A Study. Oxford: Oxford University Press, 1950.

Foster, John Burt. *Heirs to Dionysus: A Nietzschean Current in Literary Modernism*. Princeton: Princeton University Press, 1981.

Franklin, Peter. 'Sibelius in Britain'. *The Cambridge Companion to Sibelius*. Ed. by Daniel M. Grimley. Cambridge: Cambridge University Press, 2004, 182–95.

Garver, Lee. 'Neither Progressive nor Reactionary: Reassessing the Cultural Politics of *The New Age*' *The Journal of Modern Periodical Studies* 2.1 (2011): 86–115.

Gasiorek, Andrzej. 'Towards a "Right Theory of Society"?: Politics, Machine Aesthetics, and Religion'. *T. E. Hulme and the Question of Modernism*. Ed. by Edward P. Comentale and Andrzej Gasiorek. Aldershot: Ashgate, 2006, 149–68.

Ghuman, Nalini. *Resonances of the Raj: India in the English Musical Imagination, 1897–1947*. Oxford and New York: Oxford University Press, 2014.

Gibson, Matthew. 'Contradictory Images: the Conflicting Influences of Henri Bergson and William James on T. E. Hulme, and the Consequences for Imagism' *The Review of English Studies* New Series, 62 (2010): 265–95.

Gilbert, Sandra M. 'Apocalypse Now (and then), or, D. H. Lawrence and the Swan in the Electron'. *The Cambridge Companion to D. H. Lawrence*. Ed. by Anne Fernihough. Cambridge: Cambridge University Press, 2001, 235–52.

Goldie, David. *A Critical Difference: T. S. Eliot and John Middleton Murry in English Literary Criticism, 1919–1928*. Oxford: Clarendon, 1998.

Goldstone, Andrew. *Fictions of Autonomy: Modernism from Wilde to de Man*. Oxford and New York: Oxford University Press, 2013.

Gray, Cecil. 'Bernard van Dieren: a Reply to Critics' *The New Age* 20.22 (29 March 1917), 516–17.

The History of Music. London: Kegan Paul; New York: Alfred A. Knopf, 1928.

'Modern Tendencies Again' *The Sackbut* 1.5 (1920): 214–20.

Musical Chairs: or Between Two Stools. London: Home & Van Thal, 1948; reprt. London: Hogarth Press, 1985.

Peter Warlock: A Memoir of Philip Heseltine. London: Jonathan Cape, 1934.

Predicaments, or Music and the Future: An Essay in Constructive Criticism. London: Oxford University Press, 1936.

Sibelius. London: Oxford University Press, 1931; 2nd ed. 1945.

A Survey of Contemporary Music. Oxford: Oxford University Press, 1924, 2nd ed., 1928.

Gray, Laura J. ' "The Symphony in the Mind of God": Sibelius Reception and English Symphonic Theory'. *Proceedings from the Second International Jean Sibelius Conference, Helsinki, 25–29 November 1995*. Ed. by Veijo Murtomäki, Kari Kilpeläinen, and Risto Väisänen. Helsinki: Sibelius Academy, Department of Composition and Music Theory, 1998.

Grimley, Daniel M. *Carl Nielsen and the Idea of Modernism*. Woodbridge: Boydell & Brewer, 2011.

'Modernism and Closure: Nielsen's Fifth Symphony' *The Musical Quarterly* 86.1 (2002), 149–73.

'Storms, Symphonies, Silence: Sibelius's *Tempest* Music and the Invention of Late Style'. *Jean Sibelius and His World*. Ed. by Daniel M. Grimley. Princeton and Oxford: Princeton University Press, 2011, 186–226.

Guest, Barbara. *Herself Defined: the Poet H. D. and her World*. New York: Doubleday, 1984.

Hadjiyiannis, Christos. 'T. E. Hulme and the Beginnings of Imagism'. Networks and Archives of Modernism. Special Issue of *Global Review* 1.1 (2013): 141–64.

Harington, John. *The Metamorphosis of Aiax: a New Discourse of a Stale Subject by Sir John Harrington and the Anatomie of the Metamorpho-sed Aiax*. Ed. by Peter Warlock and Jack Lindsay. London: Fanfrolico, 1927.

Harper-Scott, J. P. E. *Edward Elgar, Modernist*. Cambridge: Cambridge University Press, 2006.

' "Our True North": Walton's First Symphony, Sibelianism, and the Nationalization of Modernism in England' *Music & Letters* 89.4 (2008): 562–89.

Harris, Alexandra. *Romantic Moderns: English Writers, Artists and the Imagination from Virginia Woolf to John Piper*. London: Thames & Hudson, 2010.

Harris, Jose. 'Political Thought and the Welfare State 1870–1940: An Intellectual Framework for British Social Policy' *Past & Present* 135 (1992): 116–41.

Harrison, John R. *The Reactionaries*. London: Victor Gollancz, 1966.

Hassan, Ihab. *The Postmodern Turn: Essays in Postmodern Theory and Culture*. Columbus: Ohio State University Press, 1987.

Hastings, Beatrice. *The 'Old New Age': Orage – and Others*. London: Blue Moon Press, 1936.

Hepokoski, James. *Sibelius: Symphony No. 5*. Cambridge: Cambridge University Press, 1993.

Heseltine, Nigel. *Capriol for Mother: a Memoir of Philip Heseltine*. London: Thames, 1992.

Heseltine, Philip. 'Delius: Composer and Interpreter of Nature' *Radio Times* 25 (4 Oct. 1929): 7–18.

Frederick Delius. London: John Lane, 1923.

'Predicaments Concerning Music' *The New Age* 21.2 (10 May 1917): 46.

'Review of *The English School of Lutenist Song Writers* and *English Madrigal Verse*' *The Sackbut* 1.9 (March 1921): 424–6.

'Some Reflections on Modern Musical Criticism' *Musical Times* 54 (1 Oct. 1913): 652–4.

Heseltine, Philip and Cecil Gray. *Carlo Gesualdo: Prince of Venosa: Musician and Murderer*. London: Kegan Paul, 1926.

Hinnells, Duncan. *An Extraordinary Performance: Hubert Foss, Music Publishing, and the Oxford University Press*. Oxford: Oxford University Press, 1998.

Hough, Graham. *Image and Experience: Studies in a Literary Revolution*. London: Gerald Duckworth, 1960.

Hulme, T. E. *The Collected Writings of T. E. Hulme*. Ed. by Karen Csengeri. Oxford: Clarendon, 1994.

'Romanticism and Classicism' (1911). *Speculations: Essays on Humanism and the Philosophy of Art*. Ed. by Herbert Read. London: Routledge & Kegan Paul, 1960.

'Translator's Preface to Sorel's *Reflections on Violence*' *The New Age* 17.24 (14 Oct. 1915): 569–70.

Hutchinson, Ben. *Lateness and Modern European Literature*. New York and Oxford: Oxford University Press, 2016.

Jameson, Fredric. *A Singular Modernity: Essay on the Ontology of the Present*. London: Verso, 2002.

Jencks, Charles. 'Postmodern and Late Modern: The Essential Definitions' *Chicago Review* 35.4 (1987): 31–58.

John, Augustus. 'Foreword'. *Peter Warlock: A Memoir of Philip Heseltine*. By Cecil Gray. London: Jonathan Cape, 1934; second impression, 1935.

Johnson, Julian. *Out of Time: Music and the Making of Modernity*. New York and Oxford: Oxford University Press, 2015.

Kaplan, Sydney Janet. *Circulating Genius: John Middleton Murry, Katherine Mansfield and D. H. Lawrence*. Edinburgh: Edinburgh University Press, 2010.

Kelly, Barbara L. *Music and Ultra-Modernism*. Woodbridge: Boydell & Brewer, 2013.

'Ravel's Timeliness and his Many Late Styles'. *Late Style and its Discontents: Essays in Art, Literature, and Music*. Ed. by Gordon McMullan and Sam Smiles. Oxford and New York: Oxford University Press, 2016, 158–73.

Kenner, Hugh. *The Pound Era*. London: Faber and Faber, 1972.

Kermode, Frank. *The Sense of an Ending: Studies in the Theory of Fiction with a New Epilogue*. Oxford: Oxford University Press, 2000/1966.

Kinkead-Weekes, Mark. *D. H. Lawrence: Triumph to Exile, 1912–1922. Vol. II of The Cambridge Biography of D. H. Lawrence, 1885–1930*. By David Ellis, Mark Kinkead-Weekes and John Worthen. Cambridge: Cambridge University Press, 1996.

Kuhn, Elizabeth. 'Toward an Anti-Humanism of Life: The Modernism of Nietzsche, Hulme and Yeats' *Journal of Modern Literature* 34.4 (2011): 1–20.

Lambert, Constant. *Music Ho!: A Study of Music in Decline*. 1934; 3rd ed. London: Penguin, 1948.

Lawrence, D. H. *Apocalypse and the Writings on Revelation*. Ed. by Mara Kalnins. Cambridge: Cambridge University Press, 2002.

    Phoenix: The Posthumous Papers of D. H. Lawrence. Ed. by Edward D. McDonald. London: Heinemann, 1936.

    The Rainbow. 1915; Harmondsworth: Penguin, 1958.

    'The Reality of Peace (III)' *English Review* 25.1 (July 1917): 24–9.

    'The Reality of Peace (IV)' *English Review* 25.2 (Aug. 1917): 125–32.

    Reflections on the Death of a Porcupine and Other Essays. Bloomington: Indiana University Press, 1963.

    'Reflections on the Death of a Porcupine'. *Reflections on the Death of a Porcupine and Other Essays*. Ed. by Michael Herbert. Cambridge: Cambridge University Press, 1988, 347–64.

    Study of Thomas Hardy and Other Essays. Ed. by Bruce Steele. Cambridge: Cambridge University Press, 1985.

    Women in Love. Ed. by David Farmer, John Worthen and Lindeth Vasey. Cambridge: Cambridge University Press, 1987.

Levenson, Michael H. *A Genealogy of Modernism: A Study of English Literary Doctrine, 1908–1922*. Cambridge: Cambridge University Press, 1984.

Lewis, Wyndham. *Blasting and Bombardiering*. London: Eyre & Spottiswoode, 1937; London: John Calder, 1982.

    'Our Vortex' *BLAST* 1 (1914): 147–9.

Lindsay, Jack, Robert Graves and Peter Warlock, eds. *Loving Mad Tom: Bedlamite Verses of the XVI and XVII Centuries*. London: Fanfrolico, 1927.

Litz, A. Walton. 'Lawrence, Pound, and Early Modernism'. *D. H. Lawrence: A Centenary Consideration*. Ed. by Peter Balbert and Phillip L. Marcus. Ithaca, NY: Cornell University Press, 1985, 15–28.

Lloyd, Stephen. *Constant Lambert: Beyond the Rio Grande*. Woodbridge: Boydell & Brewer, 2014.

    William Walton: Muse of Fire. Woodbridge: Boydell & Brewer, 2001.

'Long Live the Vortex', *BLAST* 1 (1914): n.p.

Lyotard, Jean François. 'Music and Postmodernity' *New Formations* 66 (2009): 37–45.

Mäkelä, Tomi. 'The Wings of a Butterfly: Sibelius and the Problems of Musical Modernity in 1957'. *Jean Sibelius and His World*. Ed. by Daniel M. Grimley. Princeton and Oxford: Princeton University Press, 2011, 89–124.

'Manifesto – I', *BLAST* 1 (1914): 21.

Mann, Thomas. *Reflections of a Nonpolitical Man*. Trans. Walter D. Morris. New York: Frederick Ungar, 1983.

Manuel, Frank E. *Shapes of Philosophical History*. Stanford: Stanford University Press, 1965.

Martin, Wallace. *The New Age Under Orage: A Chapter in English Cultural History*. Manchester: Manchester University Press, 1967.

McHale, Brian. *Postmodernist Fiction.* New York: Methuen, 1987.

McPhail, Edward. 'Does the Road to Serfdom Lead to the Servile State?' *European Journal of Political Economy* 21 (2005): 1000–1011.

Metzer, David. *Musical Modernism at the Turn of the Twenty-First Century.* Cambridge: Cambridge University Press, 2009.

Miko, Stephen J. *Toward Women in Love: the Emergence of a Lawrentian Aesthetic.* New Haven and London: Yale University Press, 1971.

Miller, Tyrus. *Late Modernism: Politics, Fiction, and the Arts Between the Wars.* Berkeley: University of California Press, 1999.

Milton, Colin. *Lawrence and Nietzsche: a Study in Influence.* Aberdeen: University of Aberdeen Press, 1987.

Mundy, Rachel. 'Evolutionary Categories and Musical Style from Adler to America' *Journal of the American Musicological Society* 67.3 (2014): 735–67.

Munton, Alan. 'Abstraction, Archaism and the Future: T. E. Hulme, Jacob Epstein and Wyndham Lewis'. *T. E. Hulme and the Question of Modernism.* Ed. by Edward P. Comentale and Andrzej Gasiorek. Aldershot: Ashgate, 2006, 73–91.

Noolas, Rab [Philip Heseltine]. *Merry-go-down: a Gallery of Gorgeous Drunkards through the Ages: Collected for the Use Interest Illumination and Delectation of Serious Topers.* London: Mandrake, 1929.

North, Michael. *The Political Aesthetic of Yeats, Eliot, and Pound.* Cambridge, Cambridge University Press, 1991.

Notley, Margaret. *Lateness and Brahms: Music and Culture in the Twilight of Viennese Liberalism.* New York and Oxford: Oxford University Press, 2007.

Orwell, George. 'Some Recent Novels' *New English Weekly* (14 Nov. 1935): 96–7.

Pater, Walter. *The Renaissance: Studies in Art and Poetry.* 1873; Berkeley: University of California Press, 1980.

Peters Corbett, David and Andrew Thacker, 'Raymond Williams and Cultural Formations: Movements and Magazines' *Prose Studies* 16.2 (1993): 84–106.

Potter, Rachel. *Modernism and Democracy: Literary Culture 1900–1930.* Oxford and New York: Oxford University Press, 2006.

Pound, Ezra. *Ezra Pound and Music: the Complete Criticism.* Ed. by Murray Schafer. London: Faber, 1977.

'A Few Don'ts by an Imagiste' *Poetry* 1.6 (1913): 200–206.

'Vortex' *BLAST* 1 (1914): 153.

Rapoport, Paul. 'Sorabji: A Continuation'. *Sorabji: A Critical Celebration.* Ed. by Paul Rapoport. Aldershot: Scolar Press, 1992, 58–87.

Riley, Matthew (ed.). *British Music and Modernism.* Farnham: Ashgate, 2010.

Robinson, Emily. *The Language of Progressive Politics in Modern Britain.* London: Palgrave Macmillan, 2017.

Rosenquist, Rod. *Modernism, the Market, and the Institution of the New.* Cambridge: Cambridge University Press, 2009.

Ross, Charles L. and George J. Zytaruk. 'Goats and Compasses and/or Women in Love: An Exchange' *D. H. Lawrence Review* 6 (1973): 33–46.

Ross Bullock, Philip. *The Correspondence of Jean Sibelius and Rosa Newmarch, 1906–1939*. Woodbridge: Boydell & Brewer, 2011.

Said, Edward. *Humanism and Democratic Criticism*. New York: Columbia University Press, 2004.

    On Late Style: Music and Literature Against the Grain. London: Bloomsbury, 2006.

    'Thoughts on Late Style' *London Review of Books* 26.15 (2004): 3–7.

Schoenbach, Lisi. *Pragmatic Modernism*. New York: Oxford University Press, 2011.

Schuchard, Ronald. *The Last Minstrels: Yeats and the Revival of the Bardic Arts*. Oxford: Oxford University Press, 2008.

Selver, Paul. *Orage and the New Age Circle: Reminiscences and Reflections*. London: Allen & Unwin, 1959.

Shiach, Morag. 'Periodizing Modernism'. *The Oxford Handbook of Modernisms*. Ed. by Peter Brooker, Andrzej Gasiorek, Deborah Longworth and Andrew Thacker. Oxford: Oxford University Press, 2010, 17–30.

Smiles, Sam. 'From Titian to Impressionism: the Genealogy of Late Style'. *Late Style and its Discontents: Essays in Art, Literature, and Music*. Ed. by Gordon McMullan and Sam Smiles. Oxford and New York: Oxford University Press, 2016, 15–30.

Smith, Barry (ed.). *The Occasional Writings of Philip Heseltine (Peter Warlock)*. 4 Vols. London: Thames, 1997–99.

    Peter Warlock: the Life of Philip Heseltine. Oxford: Oxford University Press, 1996.

Sorabji, Kaikhosru Shapurji. *Around Music*. London: Unicorn, 1932.

    Mi Contra Fa: The Immoralisings of a Machiavellian Musician. London: Porcupine Press, 1947.

    'The Validity of the Aristocratic Principle'. *Art and Thought: Issued in Honour of Dr. Ananda K. Coomaraswamy on the Occasion of his 70th Birthday*. Ed. by K. Bharatha Iyer. London: Luzac, 1947, 214–18.

Spencer, Robert. 'Lateness and Modernity in Theodor Adorno'. *Late Style and its Discontents: Essays in Art, Literature, and Music*. Ed. by Gordon McMullan and Sam Smiles. Oxford and New York: Oxford University Press, 2016, 22–34.

Stewart, Garrett. 'Lawrence, "Being", and the Allotropic Style' *Novel* 9.3 (1976): 217–42.

Thatcher, David. *Nietzsche in England 1890–1914: the Growth of a Reputation*. Toronto and Buffalo: University of Toronto Press, 1970.

Trilling, Lionel. *The Liberal Imagination: Essays on Literature and Society* (1950). New York: New York Review Books, 2012.

Tunbridge Laura. 'Saving Schubert: The Evasions of Late Style'. *Late Style and its Discontents*. Ed. by Gordon McMullan and Sam Smiles. Oxford and New York: Oxford University Press, 2016, 120–30.

    Schumann's Late Style. Cambridge: Cambridge University Press, 2007.

Van Dieren, Bernard. 'Epstein' *The New Age* 20.19 (8 March 1917): 451–3.

Villis, Tom. 'Elitism and the Revolt of the Masses: Reactions to the "Great Labour Unrest" in the *New Age* and *New Witness* Circles' *History of European Ideas* 31 (2005): 85–102.

Reaction and the Avant-Garde: the Revolt Against Liberal Democracy in Early Twentieth-Century Britain. London: Tauris, 2006.

Wadsworth, Edward. 'Inner Necessity' *BLAST* 1 (1914): 119.

Walkowitz, Rebecca L. *Cosmopolitan Style: Modernism Beyond the Nation.* New York: Columbia University Press, 2006.

Warlock, Peter [Philip Heseltine]. 'The Editing of Old English Songs' *The Sackbut* 6 (1926): 183–6 and 8 (1926): 215–20.

The English Ayre. London: Oxford University Press, 1926.

English Ayres: Elizabethan and Jacobean: a Discourse by Peter Warlock. London: Oxford University Press, 1932.

Frederick Delius. London: John Lane, The Bodley Head; rev. ed. with annotations by Hubert Foss, Oxford and New York: Oxford University Press, 1952.

Thomas Whythorne: an Unknown Elizabethan Composer. London: Oxford University Press, 1925.

Wheeldon, Marianne. *Debussy's Late Style.* Indianapolis: Indiana University Press, 2009.

Whittall, Arnold. '1909 and After: High Modernism and "New Music"' *Musical Times* 150 (2009): 5–18.

Exploring Twentieth-Century Music: Tradition and Innovation. Cambridge: Cambridge University Press, 2003.

'The Isolationists' *Music Review* 27 (1966): 122–9.

'The Later Symphonies'. *The Cambridge Companion to Sibelius.* Ed. by Daniel M. Grimley. Cambridge: Cambridge University Press, 2004, 49–65.

Wilde, Alan. *Horizons of Assent: Modernism, Postmodernism, and the Ironic Imagination.* Baltimore: Johns Hopkins University Press, 1981.

Williams, Raymond. 'The Social Thinking of D. H. Lawrence'. *A D. H. Lawrence Miscellany.* Ed. by Harry T. Moore. Carbondale: Southern Illinois University Press, 1959, 295–311.

'When Was Modernism?' *New Left Review* 175 (1989): 48–52.

Youens, Susan. *Schubert's Late Lieder: Beyond the Song Cycles.* Cambridge: Cambridge University Press, 2002.

Zytaruk, George J. 'Rananim: D. H. Lawrence's Failed Utopia'. *The Spirit of D. H. Lawrence.* Ed. by Gāmini Salgādo and G. K. Das. London: Macmillan, 1988, 266–94.

'What Happened to D. H. Lawrence's Goats and Compasses?' *D. H. Lawrence Review* 4 (1971): 280–86.

Index

David Beard *Harrison Birtwistle's Operas and Music Theatre*

Heather Wiebe *Britten's Unquiet Pasts: Sound and Memory in Postwar Reconstruction*

Beate Kutschke and Barley Norton *Music and Protest in 1968*

Graham Griffiths *Stravinsky's Piano: Genesis of a Musical Language*

Martin Iddon *John Cage and David Tudor: Correspondence on Interpretation and Performance*

Martin Iddon *New Music at Darmstadt: Nono, Stockhausen, Cage, and Boulez*

Alastair Williams *Music in Germany Since 1968*

Ben Earle *Luigi Dallapiccola and Musical Modernism in Fascist Italy*

Thomas Schuttenhelm *The Orchestral Music of Michael Tippett: Creative Development and the Compositional Process*

Marilyn Nonken *The Spectral Piano: From Liszt, Scriabin, and Debussy to the Digital Age*

Jack Boss *Schoenberg's Twelve-Tone Music: Symmetry and the Musical Idea*

Deborah Mawer *French Music and Jazz in Conversation: From Debussy to Brubeck*

Philip Rupprecht *British Musical Modernism: The Manchester Group and their Contemporaries*

Amy Lynn Wlodarski *Musical Witness and Holocaust Representation*

Carola Nielinger-Vakil *Luigi Nono: A Composer in Context*

Erling E. Guldbrandsen and Julian Johnson *Transformations of Musical Modernism*

David Cline *The Graph Music of Morton Feldman*

Russell Hartenberger *Performance and Practice in the Music of Steve Reich*

Joanna Bullivant *Modern Music, Alan Bush, and the Cold War: The Cultural Left in Britain and the Communist Bloc*

Nicholas Jones *Peter Maxwell Davies, Selected Writings*

J. P. E. Harper-Scott *Ideology in Britten's Operas*

Jack Boss *Schoenberg's Atonal Music: Musical Idea, Basic Image and Specters of Tonal Function*

Nathan Seinen *Prokofiev's Soviet Operas*

Sarah Collins *Lateness and Modernism: Untimely Ideas about Music, Literature and Politics in Interwar Britain*

Printed in Great Britain
by Amazon

37766852R00110